Looking Up at Love

Looking Up at Love

Sermons for the Lectionary, Year B,
Advent through Eastertide

Bruce L. Taylor

WIPF & STOCK · Eugene, Oregon

LOOKING UP AT LOVE
Sermons for the Lectionary, Year B, Advent through Eastertide

Copyright © 2020 Bruce L. Taylor. All rights reserved. Except for brief quotations in critical publications or reviews, no part of this book may be reproduced in any manner without prior written permission from the publisher. Write: Permissions, Wipf and Stock Publishers, 199 W. 8th Ave., Suite 3, Eugene, OR 97401.

Wipf & Stock
An Imprint of Wipf and Stock Publishers
199 W. 8th Ave., Suite 3
Eugene, OR 97401

www.wipfandstock.com

PAPERBACK ISBN: 978-1-7252-6153-2
HARDCOVER ISBN: 978-1-7252-6152-5
EBOOK ISBN: 978-1-7252-6154-9

Manufactured in the U.S.A.   05/27/20

Scripture quotations are from Common Bible: New Revised Standard Version Bible, copyright © 1989 National Council of the Churches of Christ in the United States of America. Used by permission. All rights reserved worldwide. The italics are the author's.

PHILO, VOL. IV, translated by F. H. Colson and G. H. Whitaker, Loeb Classical Library Volume 261, Cambridge, MA: Harvard University Press, first published 1932. Loeb Classical Library ® is a registered trademark of the President and Fellows of Harvard College. Used by permission.

ARISTOTLE, VOL. XIX, translated by H. Rackham, Loeb Classical Library Volume 73, Cambridge, MA: Harvard University Press, first published 1926. Loeb Classical Library ® is a registered trademark of the President and Fellows of Harvard College. Used by permission.

THE INTERPRETER'S BIBLE ©1952 Abingdon Press. Used by Permission. All rights reserved.

95 words from Early Christian Writings edited and introduced by Andrew Louth and translated by Maxwell Staniforth (Penguin Books Ltd, 1968, 1987) Copyright © Maxwell Staniforth, 1968. Revised translation, Introductions and new editorial material copyright © Andrew Louth, 1987.

In memory of my parents

Contents

Introduction — xi

First Sunday of Advent: "A Matter of Perspective" — 1
  Isaiah 64:1-9; 1 Corinthians 1:3-9; Mark 13:24-31

Second Sunday of Advent: "Accepting Salvation" — 6
  Isaiah 40:1-11; 2 Peter 3:8-15a; Mark 1:1-8

Third Sunday of Advent: "The Remedy for Fear" — 13
  Isaiah 61:1-4, 8-11; 1 Thessalonians 5:16-24; John 1:6-8, 19-28

Fourth Sunday of Advent: "Picture of Mary, Portrait of God" — 18
  2 Samuel 7:1-11, 16; Romans 16:25-27; Luke 1:26-38

Christmas Eve (early evening): "A Letter from Bethlehem" — 23
  Isaiah 9:2-7; Titus 2:11-14; Luke 2:1-20

Christmas Eve (late evening): "Joy to Our World" — 28
  Isaiah 9:2-7; Titus 2:11-14; Luke 2:1-20

Christmas Day: "First, Last, and Always" — 33
  Isaiah 52:7-10; Hebrews 1:1-4; John 1:1-14

First Sunday after Christmas: "To Be a Child" — 39
  Isaiah 61:10—62:3; Galatians 4:4-7; Luke 2:22-40

Second Sunday after Christmas: "Sainthood" — 44
  Jeremiah 31:7-14; Ephesians 1:1-14; John 1:1-18

Epiphany of the Lord: "To Make Everyone See" — 50
  Isaiah 60:1-6; Ephesians 3:1-12; Matthew 2:1-12

Baptism of the Lord: "Unwrapping the Gift" — 55
  Genesis 1:1-5; Acts 19:1-7; Mark 1:4-11

Second Sunday in Ordinary Time: "Come and See" — 60
  1 Samuel 3:1-20; 1 Corinthians 6:12-20; John 1:43-51

Third Sunday in Ordinary Time: "Leopard's Spots" *Jonah 3:1–5; 1 Corinthians 7:29–31; Mark 1:14–20*	66
Fourth Sunday in Ordinary Time: "Yield to the Right" *Deuteronomy 18:15–20; 1 Corinthians 8:1–13; Mark 1:21–28*	72
Fifth Sunday in Ordinary Time: "The 'Whole' Gospel" *Isaiah 40:21–31; 1 Corinthians 9:16–23; Mark 1:29–39*	78
Sixth Sunday in Ordinary Time: "To Be Made Clean" *2 Kings 5:1–14; 1 Corinthians 9:24–27; Mark 1:40–45*	83
Seventh Sunday in Ordinary Time: "A New Thing" *Isaiah 43:18–25; 2 Corinthians 1:18–22; Mark 2:1–12*	88
Eighth Sunday in Ordinary Time: "A Passion for Salvation" *Hosea 2:14–20; 2 Corinthians 3:1–6; Mark 2:13–22*	94
Transfiguration of the Lord: "Make Way for the Cross" *2 Kings 2:1–12; 2 Corinthians 4:3–6; Mark 9:2–9*	99
Ash Wednesday: "Trying it Again" *Joel 2:1–2, 12–17; 2 Corinthians 5:20b—6:10; Matthew 6:1–6, 16–21*	104
First Sunday in Lent: "Never Again" *Genesis 9:8–17; 1 Peter 3:18–22; Mark 1:9–15*	108
Second Sunday in Lent: "Radical Faith" *Genesis 17:1–7, 15–16; Romans 4:13–25; Mark 8:31–38*	113
Third Sunday in Lent: "Only the Cross" *Exodus 20:1–17; 1 Corinthians 1:18–25; John 2:13–22*	118
Fourth Sunday in Lent: "Looking Up at Love" *Numbers 21:4–9; Ephesians 2:1–10; John 3:14–21*	123
Fifth Sunday in Lent: "This Side of the Covenant" *Jeremiah 31:31–34; Hebrews 5:5–10; John 12:20–33*	128
Palm/Passion Sunday: "Putting the Pieces Together" *Isaiah 50:4–9a; Philippians 2:5–11; Mark 11:1–11*	134
Maundy Thursday: "Remembering the Future" *Exodus 12:1–14; 1 Corinthians 11:23–26; John 13:1–17, 31b–35*	140

Contents

Good Friday *Isaiah 52:13—53:12; Hebrews 10:16-25; Mark 15:1-47*	145
Resurrection of the Lord (Sunrise): "Where We Know the Resurrection" *Isaiah 25:5-9; Acts 10:34-43; Mark 16:1-8*	150
Resurrection of the Lord: "The World Turned Upside Down" *Acts 10:34-43; 1 Corinthians 15:1-11; John 20:1-18*	154
Second Sunday of Easter: "Beyond Charity" *Acts 4:32-35; 1 John 1:1—2:2; John 20:19-31*	159
Third Sunday of Easter: "The Resurrection Body" *Acts 3:12-19; 1 John 3:1-7; Luke 24:36b-48*	164
Fourth Sunday of Easter: "We Know Love by This" *Acts 4:5-12; 1 John 3:16-24; John 10:11-18*	169
Fifth Sunday of Easter: "From Believers to Disciples" *Acts 8:26-40; 1 John 4:7-12; John 15:1-8*	174
Sixth Sunday of Easter: "From Servants to Friends" *Acts 10:44-48; 1 John 5:1-6; John 15:9-17*	179
Ascension of the Lord: "'Up, Up, Up,' Not 'Away'" *Acts 1:1-11; Ephesians 1:15-23; Luke 24:44-53*	184
Seventh Sunday of Easter: "Lord, Make Us Apostles" *Acts 1:15-17, 21-26; 1 John 5:9-13; John 17:6-19*	189
Appendix: Week of Prayer for Christian Unity: "Bound Together" *Ezekiel 37:15-19, 22-24a; Romans 8:18-25; John 17:8-11*	195
List of Sources Cited	201

Introduction

I once heard a minister state matter-of-factly that the Gospel of Mark is the "least theological" of the canonical Gospels. While we might agree that this Gospel, considered by most biblical scholars to be the earliest of the four books recounting the words and deeds of Jesus to have been included in the Bible, is the least *elaborated* of the genre, I think it is incorrect to regard it as in any sense wanting in theological perspective or insight. Shorter than the other three, its author perhaps did not have access to the material from the hypothesized "Q" source of Jesus' sayings upon which Matthew and Luke later drew for their compositions. Lacking any pre-natal or birth narrative, in contrast to those two Gospels, or even the cosmological implications of Jesus' birth laid out in the Fourth Gospel, Mark frankly disappoints people whose interest in the New Testament falls squarely on images of shepherds and wise men and the winsome charm of God's Word made flesh in infant innocence. So the lectionary during Advent must depart from Mark altogether after a grim portrait of the future and a focus on the first player in the Gospel's saga—not Jesus, but John, the forerunner who even himself did not fully perceive the answer to the question that permeates the book with sometimes haunting urgency. Who is Jesus?

Beyond its jump past any description or pondering of Jesus' birth directly to God's claim upon Jesus in his baptism, the popularity of Mark suffers from its lack of liturgical familiarity. The book has no version of the Lord's Prayer, for instance, and contains no canticles or hymns that we recognize from years of repeated recitation in the patterns and practices of worship. And therefore, perhaps, Mark reads more journalistically than lyrically. Nor does it offer much in the way of parables, and those that it does include lack the imaginative attraction that has endeared to generations of readers the stories Jesus tells in Luke and Matthew. Whether Christian worship was structured by the New Testament or vice versa, it is the other three Gospels that have generally scripted believers' weekly offering of thanks for and expression of allegiance to Christ.

But it is the Gospel of Mark that poses most insistently the stark existential theological demand of Jesus' dismayed appeal from the cross, "My God, my God, why have you forsaken me?" unbuffered by the additional last words recorded in Luke and John and leaving the phenomenon of the empty tomb an open question. In its original ending, Mark's Gospel presents no confirming evidence of the resurrection in congenial scenes of abiding fellowship between the risen Christ and his disciples. Whereas the Gospels of Matthew and Luke are simply set aside in Eastertide to make room for readings from John, those who have designed the lectionary had no alternative in Year B if they were to honor the themes of the paschal season; Mark offered no lections for the days and weeks following the women's sad and bewildering sabbath morning discovery.

The sermons contained herein, of course, also treat the Old Testament, Acts, and epistolary lections for the Sundays and feast days from Advent through Eastertide, in response to the Reformed injunction of providing God's people with access to the fullness of Scripture. (Also included, in an appendix, is a sermon delivered on the occasion of the Week of Prayer for Christian Unity.) But I have found that the nature of Mark presents some unique challenges in the preparation of sermons based on the Gospel reading. Particularly imposing for someone in the rationalist tradition characteristic of the Reformed heritage has been the lectionary's triennial quartet of healing and restoration stories on the fourth, fifth, sixth, and seventh Sundays in Ordinary Time, for which the lection for the eighth Sunday in Ordinary Time includes something of a summary. It is tempting for the preacher to dismiss the Bible's reports of miracles with concocted appeals to the known laws of nature and, in the case of physical or mental illness, theories about psychosomatic disturbances. And venturing into the realm of spiritual ailments seems fraught with ethical hazards. Observance of the lectionary has disciplined me to honest reflection on a subject whose excessive attention in some other Christian traditions has left me, first, intellectually uncomfortable, and then, when asked by a parishioner, "Why did my loved one not get well?," feeling pastorally inadequate. The response that Jesus worked a miracle of healing or exorcism to advance the faith of a few witnesses way back when is not particularly satisfying to a faithful believer who is grieving and perplexed and doubting today. I suspect I am not the first minister whose sincere intention to preach honestly has landed her or him in some intense soul-searching and commenced a prayerful quest for understanding. Perhaps this subject, most of all, invites the pastor into a humble partnership with his or her parishioners of growing and maturing in faith and trust.

Once again, I wish to express my conviction about the wisdom and usefulness of following a lectionary in the normal course of preaching, and of sharing the task and privilege of proclaiming and hearing texts in common with Christians worldwide on any given Sunday or feast day. When that finds us worshiping together, even though in congregations widely scattered, with a scriptural focus on Mark and the associated Old Testament and epistolary texts, it quickly becomes apparent that faithful worship gathering is never theologically void, but itself constitutes what has been called "primary theology." Moreover, the penetrating question that Mark repeatedly places before us in every word and deed of Jesus recorded in his Gospel makes the book fundamentally theological throughout, beginning with the insight that it was in baptism that Jesus' (and our) true identity was pronounced, and it is the trusting surrender of Jesus (and us) to the mysterious but sure and purposeful love of God, even at the price of a cross, that completes what baptism began.

First Sunday of Advent
Spanish Springs Presbyterian Church, Sparks, Nevada
November 30, 2008

Isaiah 64:1–9
1 Corinthians 1:3–9
Mark 13:24–31

"A Matter of Perspective"

A German soldier trying to warm himself by a campfire hears rumors that the Allies are advancing toward Berlin. While American soldiers move across France, Canadian forces are pouring into the Netherlands, reclaiming cities and villages that the German army has occupied, pushing the forces of the Third Reich eastward, putting in jeopardy the vision that motivated the soldier all these long months, raising doubts about the inevitability of the promise voiced by the Führer and his lieutenants about the domination of Europe by the Aryan race and the German nation and the new world order it would bring. The possibility that *God* might have a *different* future in store had never before crossed his mind. He had never been troubled by questions about the destiny he and millions of others had determined to force upon humankind. But the rumors have become more numerous in recent days, and there is no question but that his company is retreating, not advancing or even holding its position. His commanders are not as boastful as they were a few weeks ago. The meals are being rationed more severely than they were a few days ago. The planes in the skies overhead are more regularly Allied aircraft than Luftwaffe. The soldier is nervous and afraid.

A Dutch family huddles around the radio listening to the news on the BBC that the Allies are advancing toward Berlin. While American soldiers move across France, Canadian forces are pouring into the Netherlands, reclaiming cities and villages that the German army has occupied, pushing the forces of the Third Reich eastward, bringing optimism that the long nightmare is coming to an end, raising the likelihood that

Holland will soon be liberated and that the Dutch and the other peoples of western Europe will once again be free of the terrors of Nazism and the venom flowing from Hitler and his lieutenants about the domination of Europe by people of the Aryan race and the German nation and the new world order it will bring.

It has seemed like this day would never come, so complete has been Germany's grip on western Europe. The Dutch people's doubts about whether anyone will be able to help them, even about whether there is still a God who cares enough to save them, are finally weakening in light of the news of Allied victories, of towns being liberated one by one. Even the fact that German soldiers still patrol the streets outside their door is not enough to suppress their growing hope now that *tomorrow* or the *next* day or the *next*, no matter *how* long it takes, the war will end and peace will come and respect and dignity and mercy will once again be not only *possible* but the way of *life*. They had all but resigned themselves to the prospect of a future of hatred and cruelty and terror. But the rumors have become more numerous in recent days, and there is no question but that the Allies are advancing. And the people of the town are not as despondent as they were a few weeks ago. They talk about the day that is surely coming when their pantries will again be full and their tables will again be places of joy. The planes in the skies overhead are now more regularly Allied aircraft than Luftwaffe. The family is hopeful and expectant.

It is a time of disappointment and distress. Yes, the exile is over. Many of the people taken to Babylon have returned to Palestine and even come to worship in the temple that has at long last been rebuilt. But things have not gone as expected. The religious leaders are corrupt and the people's worship is false; their rituals are insincere and their prayers are selfish and their treatment of the poor is abusive. But a prophet has arisen, calling upon God to make himself known among the people as in the stories told about God's miracles in the past, when God did unexpected and awesome deeds and the neighboring nations all around Israel trembled at the power of God and even the forces of nature were disrupted. God must be angry at the people to absent himself when there is so much that is wrong and needs correcting. But the prophet remembers and proclaims that God is faithful, that God is still the fashioner of Israel's destiny, that God's purpose established in the mists of prehistory will be worked out *in* and *through* and *in spite of* the very discouragements of the present day. And so the despair that the people have endured is but a sure and certain prelude to God's salvation. The grief and the dismay that the righteous have felt is the very precondition to God's revelation. And, thus, it is a time pregnant with possibility and every reason for hope.

Dark clouds are once again rolling over Israel's horizon. The rhetoric of nationalistic and religious zealots is provoking the Roman occupiers to tighten their control over Jerusalem and the outlying areas. The situation is tense. *Some* counsel *appeasement. Others* call for *revolt*. The future of God's chosen people hangs in the balance as a young teacher and healer who has gathered a following speaks and acts in a way that seems to challenge authority on all sides, referring to himself in echoes of the ancient scriptures, predicting a cosmic reordering that signals the end of the age and all of its entrenched power structures and customary assumptions. The *religious* and now even some of the *civic* authorities are increasingly alarmed at his preaching and the growing popularity of his movement, and they begin to plot how to have him arrested and killed. They are frightened of the changes he is advocating. But the people who are attracted to him—the poor, the sick, the outcast, and the despised—love him and pray his words and deeds are true; indeed, *hear* in his *sermons* the very *promises* of *God*, *see* in his *miracles* the very *power* of *God*, and they have *hope* again.

"I give thanks to my God always for you," the apostle Paul, himself a victim of persecutions and suffering, wrote to the little band of Christians at Corinth,

> because of the grace of God that has been given you in Christ Jesus, for in every way you have been enriched in him, in speech and knowledge of every kind—just as the testimony of Christ has been strengthened among you—so that you are not lacking in any spiritual gift as you wait for the revealing of our Lord Jesus Christ. He will also strengthen you to the end, so that you may be blameless on the day of our Lord Jesus Christ. *God is faithful*; by him you were called into the fellowship of his Son, Jesus Christ our Lord. (1 Cor 1:4–9 NRSV)

Is the day of Christ's revealing a day to be *feared*? Or will it be a day of *rejoicing*? Will the day of judgment be a *catastrophe*? Or will it be the climax of *salvation*? Most biblical scholars think that the Gospel of Mark, including Jesus' speech to his disciples in our Gospel reading this morning, was written about the time the Roman army put down a major revolt by the Jews and destroyed the temple in Jerusalem and brought an end to Israel's nationhood. For *Rome*, it was just another regional uprising suppressed—nothing like the end of the world, very much business as usual.

But the *Jews* would have interpreted it as an unmitigated *disaster*—very *much* the end of the world, or virtually so, history's denial that they were God's chosen people, dear to God, favored by God, remembered by God. Jesus said his followers should regard it as the beginning of a series of events in nature and in human affairs that would result finally in "'the Son of Man coming in clouds' with great power and glory. Then he will send out the angels, and gather his elect from the four winds, from the ends of the earth to the ends of heaven" (Mark 13:26–27 NRSV). The appearance of the Son of Man would be as inevitable, Jesus said, as the coming of summer after leaves start appearing on the fig tree. "So also, when you see these things taking place, you know that he is near, at the very gate" (Mark 13:29 NRSV).

For anyone who *loves* Christ, who *yearns* for Christ, and who *thirsts* for the *justice* that he will execute and the *peace* he will bring, that prospect is a joyful one. For anyone who *opposes* Christ, who wants to *delay* his rule, and who *benefits* from *injustice* and *profits* from *discord*, that prospect is a *threatening* one. It's a matter of perspective.

Advent is the season of preparation for Christ's return. For the *Christian*, it is a season of yearning and expectancy and hope. And if that is true for the *Christian*, so it should ultimately be true for *all creation*. Mark does not here describe a judgment of the wicked. Jesus was not encouraging us to speculate about the fate of our enemies, not even the fate of *Jesus'* enemies. All the attention here is on anticipating the eternal rule of the Son, and the participation of every one of Jesus' followers in the new order that he will inaugurate: "Then he will send out the angels, and gather his elect from the four winds, from the ends of the earth to the ends of heaven" (Mark 13:27 NRSV). As Christians begin to witness events that conform to the things of which Jesus spoke, we are not to be fearful or apprehensive, nor are we to anticipate the punishment of non-Christians, but we are to be assured that the day of our *salvation* is approaching, the day when all of creation will be made whole, the day when all of creation will be conformed to the eternal purpose of God.

The issue then becomes whether we *welcome* a world in which all of humankind and all of nature is at peace, a world in which God's purpose of justice and righteousness and generosity and mercy is observed and followed by all, a world which has been saved from the ways of hatred and greed and suspicion and destruction. Those in Jesus' time who abused power and grasped at privilege, who oppressed the weak and imposed their own prerogatives, would have been alarmed at any suggestion that the status quo might be disrupted. For *them*, if justice and righteousness and generosity and mercy were to reign, the stars might as well fall from the sky, so overturned would be the rules by which they thought the universe should operate, *did* operate. If equity and virtue and hospitality and forgiveness were to be shown to *everybody*, then the God they had thought was on their side and blessed their prejudices and confirmed their claims of superiority actually *opposed* their behavior and *condemned* their worldview and regarded *them* as no better than anyone *else*. Desperately, they tried to cling to the established order and to guarantee that what Jesus forecasted would never come about. But their very resistance to Christ was a sign of the inevitability of what he preached.

The revealing of the Son of Man, the return of Christ, the day of judgment—for *some* it will be the *end* of everything that they *treasure*, for *others* it will be the *beginning* of everything for which they *hope*. How people interpret it is a matter of perspective. But the fact it is approaching, Mark wants us to know, is beyond question. "From the fig tree," said Jesus, "learn its lesson: as soon as its branch becomes tender and puts forth its leaves, you know that summer is near. So also, when you see these things taking place, you know that *he* is near, at the very gates" (Mark 13:28–29 NRSV). Whether that's good news is a matter of perspective. Is it good news for *you*?

Second Sunday of Advent
Spanish Springs Presbyterian Church, Sparks, Nevada
December 4, 2005

Isaiah 40:1–11
2 Peter 3:8–15a
Mark 1:1–8

"Accepting Salvation"[1]

Paul Sandoval leaned back in his chair and scratched his scalp of thick, black hair after hanging up the receiver of his office telephone, and glanced out the window at the few flakes of an early December snowsquall. The call had come directly from Santa Fe within an hour of the governor's signing the clemency order. A letter would be arriving via facsimile transmission within a few minutes; he should wait for that before walking through the security station and opening the iron gate that would give access to the cell block and eventually the eight foot-square cubicle where Billie Yellowhorse had been jailed for nearly two years. Billie would have been transferred to the state penitentiary on Thursday, but he had already been an inmate of the McKinley County Jail for longer than any other prisoner in recent history—ever since the night of the accident that had taken the lives of Joseph Sam and his little daughter Martha. The trial had been postponed three times—once, due to the resignation of the public defender assigned to the case, who had departed Gallup for greener pastures, then the prolonged illness of the second public defender who had been assigned to the case, then the illness of the judge. Finally, trial was made to a jury, which had found Billie Yellowhorse guilty on all counts.

Deputy Sandoval had been on duty on the night of the accident, back in the days when he was on patrol, and he had been the first sheriff's deputy to respond to the grisly scene on State Highway 197 eight and a half miles east of the junction with Highway 371. Joseph Sam and his

---

1. The story was suggested by an incident in Hillerman, *Coyote Waits*.

daughter had been turning right out of a dirt road onto Highway 197 when Billie Yellowhorse's pickup truck jerked out of the west-bound lane, at a high rate of speed, to pass another vehicle headed west on the highway. The pickup had struck Joseph Sam's blue Ford sedan essentially head-on. It was a miracle that Billie wasn't killed, in fact, wasn't even injured. But the road-side breathalyzer test had been confirmed by a blood alcohol reading that Billie was well beyond the legal limit of intoxication.

Tragic as the accident was, it seemed even worse because of the fact, as reported in *The Gallup Times*, that Joseph Sam and his daughter were on their way home from a revival meeting, one of many held frequently on and around the edges of the vast Navajo reservation. The circumstances of the accident resulted in multiple charges against Billie, a man then seventy-two years old, with a face wrinkled by sun and wind and whiskey, his hair long and gray. His family had complained to him of his drinking, had even called the Navajo Tribal Police one night when he had driven off from his home near Standing Rock to ask them to intercept him on the highway before he hurt himself or someone else. His New Mexico driver's license had been suspended, and then eventually revoked, but then he started driving again, frequently into Gallup where, inevitably, he would find a bottle.

"Jim Nakai," Paul Sandoval had finally written down on his notepad that night. It took some time to untangle the slurred utterance that Billie Yellowhorse had kept repeating as he swayed back and forth in the patrol car's headlights.

"What *about* Jim Nakai?" Sandoval had asked. "What *about* him?"

"Jim Nakai," Billie had repeated, and then he had passed out and collapsed on the narrow shoulder of the highway.

After a brief examination at the clinic in Crownpoint, Billie had been driven to the jail, and had been there ever since, except for the arraignment and the trial. The name "Jim Nakai" meant nothing to Billie's family, they told the sheriff's investigator, and Billie had never again said anything about a Jim Nakai, whether to Deputy Sandoval, either of his public defenders—who both seemed rather uninterested in the comment—or the jury. When asked directly by Deputy Sandoval the day after the accident who Jim Nakai was, Billie had just returned a blank stare. Without some help from Billie or his family, it would have been an impossible job, anyway—there were probably hundreds of "Jim Nakais" on and off the reservation, common as the name was among the Navajos.

But about two weeks ago, on the second day after the trial had ended, and a day after the news of Billie's conviction had been disseminated through both *The Gallup Times* and *The Navajo Times* as well as *The Albuquerque Journal*, one Alice Nez had called the sheriff's office inquiring if the police had ever questioned the man who ran away from the accident. Her husband, it seems, had been the driver of the car that Billie's pickup was passing when it collided with Joseph Sam's car, and Hosteen Nez had immediately pulled off of the pavement and started on foot back toward the accident. While jogging eastward on the highway, he had seen the figure of a man running off down the dirt road that led to the church and, beyond, to a little cluster of hogans. It was pointless asking Alice Nez why she or her husband had not come forward with the information at the time, and it was two days before a deputy was sent out to inquire of the residents and church attenders whether they had seen anyone running down their road that night.

It turned out that the hogans belonged to various members of one branch of the Nakai family, and while, predictably, no one acknowledged seeing anyone running down the road toward them that night, they did admit to having a Jim Nakai among the relatives; he was now sitting in the San Juan County Jail awaiting trial on charges of petty theft and assault and battery in the purloining of a CD player from a store in Farmington. In an altercation over the theft, the store owner had received a blow from Jim Nakai's right fist. In exchange for dropping the petty theft charge, which would have been Nakai's "third strike" under a new state statute, Nakai had admitted to the district attorney in Aztec that *he* had been the driver of the Yellowhorse pick-up the night of the accident. Billie had picked him up, a hitchhiking stranger, and Nakai, becoming nervous about Billie's intoxicated state, had persuaded the older man to let *him* drive. That disclosure led to a quick review of the case, and the decision to release Billie Yellowhorse and expunge his conviction.

At length, a young woman in a sheriff's department uniform entered Paul Sandoval's small office with a piece of paper in her hand. "This just came by fax," she explained, and laid it on his desk. Deputy Sandoval, who already knew what the letter said, read the instructions in cursory fashion, and rose from his chair, document in hand, and started his walk to cell number six. When he reached the cell, he unlocked the frame of iron bars that was its door. Billie, sitting on his bunk, looked up as the deputy announced, "You're a free man, Billie. The governor has issued a pardon on the basis of new evidence in your case, and has directed me to apologize to you on behalf of the people of the State of New Mexico."

Billie looked more *bewildered* than *grateful*. In fact, he did not look *happy* at *all*. Paul Sandoval wondered whether he had heard him correctly. The man *did* speak English, he knew, but he looked so pathetic, sitting there in his jail-issued blue denim shirt and jeans and much older than his seventy-four years, that Sandoval wondered whether he comprehended what he had just been told.

"Jim Nakai confessed to being the driver. You're free to leave. Do you want me to call someone to come get you?"

The man in the jail cell lowered his head and looked at his hands.

"Did you hear me, Billie? You're free."

After a few seconds, still looking at his hands, Billie Yellowhorse said slowly, "I belong in jail."

"Jim Nakai—the man you picked up that night. He says you weren't driving. *He* was. Are you telling me that isn't *so*?"

"I don't know," Billie said, still looking at his hands. "I don't remember. I don't remember any of it." He paused, but Paul Sandoval did not break the silence. Eventually, Billie added, "I was too drunk." After another pause, he said, "I am ashamed. I belong in jail. I am a sinner."

"Well, sinner or not, the people of McKinley County aren't going to pay for me to feed you any longer. You're going to have to leave."

"I'm a sinner," Billie repeated, shaking his head slowly, his long gray hair, loose and disheveled when Paul Sandoval first saw him at the accident scene, now neatly pulled back in a ponytail. "I belong in jail."

"Now, listen," Paul tried to reason with him. "Your family has been without you helping them for two years now. You may think you belong in here, but there are people somewhere who are depending upon you," though, in truth, he didn't know who that would be. The man had family, yes, but none of them had ever come to visit him in jail, so far as he knew. "Don't you have sheep?" the deputy asked, and immediately thought that that was a rather stupid thing to say, as if sheep were more important than a wife and children and grandchildren and perhaps great-grandchildren.

"Had to sell them all," the man said slowly. "Too much liquor." Then, after a few seconds, he said, "That preacher told me, whiskey is the devil's drink. He was right. And now two people are dead. I belong in jail."

In his eighteen months of being assigned to supervise the county jail, Deputy Sandoval had never been faced with a prisoner who didn't want to leave. But the reference to a preacher and the devil gave him the idea that Billie Yellowhorse needed to talk to a minister. He went back to his office, leaving the door to Billie's cell open, and pulled out a list of telephone numbers from his desk drawer. He studied the names under the title "Chaplain," and put his left forefinger under the one opposite the name "Rev. Mark Johnson," then reached for the telephone and dialed. A few seconds later, he said into the receiver, "Reverend Johnson? This is Deputy Sandoval down at the jail. We've got a situation here . . ."

"Hello, Billie," Reverend Johnson said to the old Navajo who was still sitting on his bunk, looking at his hands folded in his lap. "Yah-teh."

Billie looked up at him with mournful eyes. "Yah-teh." He returned the greeting without any enthusiasm in his voice. "Hello, Rev'ren," he added.

"May I come in?" the minister asked, sounding unsure of himself.

"Yeah."

"May I sit down?"

The Navajo looked up again, and scooted a couple of inches toward the far end of the bunk to accommodate the minister.

"Well, Billie, I understand that you're free to leave and go home. I regret very much that you've been kept here unjustly." Billie Yellowhorse was silent, still looking at his hands. Eventually, the minister ventured, "But I understand from Deputy Sandoval that you don't think you should leave."

"I'm a sinner," Billie said, without moving his head. "I got drunk. I killed two people."

"No, Billie, *you* didn't kill them. You weren't *driving*. That's what they've found out. That *other* man, Jim Nakai, the one you picked up—*he* was driving. And then he ran away from the accident, but they found him."

"Why was he driving my truck?"

Reverend Johnson didn't know whether Billie had forgotten the circumstances, or was trying to drive home a point. The minister began slowly. "Well, according to Deputy Sandoval, the man said he had offered to drive. He, um, he thought you shouldn't be driving."

Billie turned his head to look at the minister sitting beside him. "You know that man, Brother Wilson, up there at Tohatchi? He told me, 'Liquor is the devil's drink.' Up there, at that revival he had up there one night. 'The devil's drink,' he said. 'You wanna be a friend of the *devil*, drinking what *he* drinks?'" Billie turned his gaze back at his hands, still folded in his lap. "I've been drinkin' with the devil. I'm a sinner. And so that man, that Jim Nakai, he started driving, because I was drunk, and two people are dead. I belong in jail."

Reverend Johnson cleared his throat with a little cough. "When I've been here before," he started tentatively, "we've talked about how God forgives sinners. We've talked about how everyone needs to repent—change their ways, change their habits, change their way of thinking—and that when we do that, and have faith in God's forgiveness, then God does what he promises—forgives us—and lets us start over again."

"I believe in God. I believe in Jesus," Billie said, matter-of-factly. "And I know there's a devil," he added, and then said, conclusively, "and I know there's a hell."

"Billie," the minister said, more earnestly now, with urgent conviction in his voice, "then you must believe God has forgiven you. You must believe that God does not want you to sit in this jail cell the rest of your life. For two years, you haven't had any alcohol. You know now that you can live without it, even when things look the most discouraging."

"I don't want to drink anymore," said Billie. "I don't want anybody else to die."

The minister refrained from putting his hand on Billie's shoulder, aware that such personal contact was considered impudent by many older Navajos. "Billie, God has *heard* you. Now, *you* need to hear *God*. He sent his own Son to take on the punishment for our sins, so we could be free. Do you believe that? Are you grateful for that?"

"Yes," the man nodded, still looking at his hands, but the minister could see a tear trickling down his face.

"Are you grateful enough to quit drinking?"

"Yes," Billie nodded again. "I don't want anyone ever to be hurt again."

"Are you grateful enough to leave this jail?"

Billie was silent.

"You believe in God," the minister said. "You believe in Jesus. Then you need to believe that you are forgiven, and you can go home."

Reverend Johnson's gray Toyota bumped to a halt at the end of the long, rutted dirt road a few miles southwest of Standing Rock. The old Navajo man's eyes had taken in every piece of the landscape on the drive from Gallup, and now were misty with tears welling up but not quite spilling down his cheeks. The two men sat in the car in front of the tiny frame house surrounded by little skiffs of snow, giving time, in the traditional way, for whoever might be inside the house to come into harmony with the idea of receiving visitors. But, of course, Billie Yellowhorse wasn't a visitor. This was his home. Or was it still? It was the *house* he had lived in. But how would his wife and whatever relatives might be there that day receive him?—he who had disgraced them, he who had abandoned them, he who had surrendered his will and his freedom to a bottle of whiskey one night two years ago and had been an exile in the white man's world of laws and courts and jails ever since?

"I think it's time to get out," Reverend Johnson said. He opened the driver's side door as, with a shaky hand, his companion opened the passenger door, got out, and closed it. The minister moved around the front of the car to stand alongside the gray-haired Navajo, and they both looked at the door of the house with uncertainty. It took only a few seconds for the door to be opened, and Agnes Yellowhorse to emerge.

At first, the husband and wife stood where they were, looking at each other. Then, slowly, because of age, not because of dampened affection, they walked toward each other and met halfway between the car and the house. They looked deeply into each other's eyes. At length, Billie said, "No more whiskey. I'm home."

Agnes Yellowhorse put her hand around her husband's arm, and they walked together toward the open door. Reverend Johnson thought to himself, "Just in time for Kishmus"—the Navajo name for "Christmas."

Third Sunday of Advent
Spanish Springs Presbyterian Church, Sparks, Nevada
December 14, 2008

Isaiah 61:1–4, 8–11
1 Thessalonians 5:16–24
John 1:6–8, 19–28

"The Remedy for Fear"

"If you're not *terrified*," the bumper sticker reads, "you haven't been paying attention." Well, some pretty terrifying headlines have been getting the attention of all of us: General Motors, the flagship of American manufacturing, teetering on the edge of bankruptcy; the stock market down by nearly 50 percent from its high; the biggest names in banking and brokerage and insurance begging for bailouts or forced into shotgun weddings; job losses at half a million in a single month; home values plummeting and foreclosures skyrocketing. Whose job is next? Whose house? Whose pension? And *those* headlines merely forced to the back pages *other* headlines that would be terrifying *enough*: the threat posed by rogue states and terrorist groups that have the capacity to build or steal nuclear bombs and biological weapons; climate change that is altering geography and will change life as we have known it; the risk of disease from the foods we eat and the toys our children play with. Fear and uncertainty pile upon fear and uncertainty until it seems no place is immune from anxiety, not even the church. We are being conditioned to live in a perpetual crisis mode, sometimes at the *instigation* of our leaders, sometimes despite the *assurances* of our leaders, and it is affecting our politics, it is affecting our relationships, it is affecting our health, it is even affecting our genetic make-up. It is making us something less than human, all this anxiety. It is making us, in the observation of the Alban Institute's Peter Steinke, *reptilian*—reactive, unreasoning, ready to strike out, feeling at home in the world's rocks and crevices.[1]

---

1. See, generally, Steinke.

In the face of all this, scripture's command to "rejoice always" can sound very Pollyannaish in our ears, less a word from the *Lord* than a word from a *fairy tale*. Yet Paul was no Pollyanna. And his life was *anything* but a fairy tale. Paul was not only aware of the hardships of the people to whom he was *writing*—distress and persecution—*he* was living the *same* hardships and would eventually *die* for standing firm in the Lord against all of the reptilian thinkers who tried to silence his witness and discredit his testimony. It is really rather surprising that the church was able to survive its infancy, given the enemies arrayed against it and given the fears that such opposition would naturally raise. But it wasn't simply a matter of *deciding* to be joyful. There's *more* to Paul's sentence: "pray without ceasing, give thanks in all circumstances; for this is the will of God in Christ Jesus for *you*" (1 Thess 5:17–18 NRSV).

Paul was not oblivious to the real dangers that the Christians at Thessalonica faced—dangers from the government authorities, from the leaders of the synagogue, from the idolatries of the pagan culture that surrounded them. Nor was he oblivious to the dangers that *he* faced. But rather than being *fearful*, and rather than *counseling* fear, Paul was *joyful* and *encouraged* joy. How could that be? Rather than being cautious, and rather than *retreating* from the gospel, Paul was *confident* and preached the good news more *boldly*. How was that possible? The answer is simply this: faith. Paul was convinced that God had not destined the saints for *wrath*, but for *salvation*. Paul was certain that God had not brought the new creation of the church into being for *death*, but for *life*. Paul was sure that the long witness of the scriptures anticipated *fulfillment* of God's *promises*, not God's *abandonment* of God's *people*. And in Jesus Christ, God had made the greatest possible commitment to all of creation by becoming personally involved in its tragedies and its conflicts. The very glory of God, as the Gospel of John would later testify, was visible in the Word become flesh which lived among us, "and we have seen his glory, the glory as of a father's only son, full of grace and truth" (John 1:14b NRSV)—glory manifested in and through and because of the very sort of suffering the Thessalonian Christians and Paul himself faced. Not *incidental* to salvation or *isolated* from holiness, but the very circumstance by which salvation was *worked* and the very experience through which holiness was *confirmed*.

Faith is not the same thing as a silver lining, not even the same thing as positive thinking. Faith is more than expecting the present circumstances to get better. Faith involves trusting that God is faithfully at work even *in* and *through* the present circumstances to bring about a salvation that is more complete than just the hope that things will turn out alright. "Heaven and earth will pass away," we heard Jesus say in the Gospel reading a couple of weeks ago, hardly an event that most people would covet. "[B]ut my words will not pass away" (Mark 13:31b NRSV). That is a promise to put faith in. *Other* words will pass away—the words of hatred, the words of greed, the words of anger, the words of vengeance, even the words of fear, and all the silly words of false hope and false assurance and false expectation. The Bible does *not* say that the stock market will turn around, Christ does *not* pledge an increase in your 401(k), God does *not* assure us that we will wake up tomorrow to full employment or a throng of buyers for our house. The gospel does not even promise peace in the church. There are very good reasons out there to be fearful. But there is an even *better* reason *not* to be fearful—the promise of God that *beyond* and *through* and even in the *midst of* the world's crises, God's salvation is sure for those who have faith, because God is unshakably faithful.

But the very certainty of God's faithfulness unto a salvation beyond the stubborn reality of today's headlines, and *in spite of* them, compels us to reflect the image of God's promised salvation onto the episodes of suffering that people are experiencing even now, to roll up our sleeves and open our treasuries and risk our reputations in the cause of justice and freedom and reconciliation. Everything should have been fine when the people of God, long exiled in Babylon, were allowed to return to the promised land. But life was still hard. The ruined temple did not rebuild itself. And hearts grown cold did not soften to the needs of the poor and the sick *after* the exile any more than they had *before* the exile. Many individuals still could count off reasons to be fearful. But the prophet of God called upon the people to have faith, and to *act* in faith *in* and *through* and *because of* the suffering that surrounded them.

> The spirit of the Lord GOD is upon me,
>   because the LORD has anointed me;
> he has sent me to bring good news to the oppressed,
>   to bind up the brokenhearted,
> to proclaim liberty to the captives,
>   and release to the prisoners;
> to proclaim the year of the LORD's favor,
>   and the day of vengeance of our God;
> to comfort all who mourn;
> to provide for those who mourn in Zion—

notice the reasons that people have been in mourning are not magically eliminated—

> to give them a garland instead of ashes,
> the oil of gladness instead of mourning,
> the mantle of praise instead of a faint spirit. . . .
> They shall build up the ancient ruins,
> they shall raise up the former devastations;
> they shall repair the ruined cities,
> the devastations of many generations. (Isa 61:1–3a, 4 NRSV)

Indeed, only people who had faith in a God who is steadfast *through* and *beyond* such devastations could take on such a task—the God who hates robbery and wrongdoing. "I will greatly rejoice"—and here is the key, the object of the same rejoicing of which Paul spoke—"I will greatly rejoice in the Lord, my whole being shall exult in my God; for he has clothed me with the garments of salvation, he has covered me with the robe of righteousness, as a bridegroom decks himself with a garland, and as a bride adorns herself with her jewels" (Isa 61:10 NRSV).

"You've got to be kidding," some of the people must have said, standing in the rubble of their civilization and the debris of their dreams. "*These* are the garments of *salvation*? *This* is the robe of *righteousness*?" Not even Norman Vincent Peale could positively think his way out of the devastation they were experiencing. To put it in terms of a later generation, the overwhelming bleakness of the cross stood in the way of their faith in the empty tomb. And they were fearful that the collapse of *their* stock market, the plunge in *their* housing sector, the dismal prospects for *their* employment, signaled the *end* of God's promise. If only the people might be faithful enough to work an end to the country's oppressive habits, to suture the hurts of those whose needs were perennially disregarded, to liberate the poor and powerless from the social structures that sapped hope and penalized misfortune, to clear away the reasons for fear and point through them to the object of faith—the true and living God who is not *oblivious* to our suffering but who *sympathizes* with it, to the extent even of mourning the death of his own Son on the cross for our salvation. *This* is the God who is glorified when mourners are comforted, when captives are set free, when the poor have good news told to them, and when ruins become habitable again. *This* is the God who has promised that Christ is coming again in glory, which must mean that, in the day of his coming again beyond history and headline, beyond objection and obstinacy, there will be no mourning, there will be no captivity, there will be no poverty, there will be no homelessness. To the degree that we are trustful of God, and act not in *fear* but in *faith*, those conditions will now and then, here and now, become an *historical* reality. But *despite* whether now and then, here and now, they become an historical reality, faith sees *beyond* the prisons and soup kitchens a salvation of dignity and peace and plenty and acceptance, *not* because it is the way of *history* but because it is the promise of *God*, already made sure in Jesus Christ. And therefore, despite the circumstances reflected in today's headlines and tomorrow's statistics, faith allows us, even *compels* us, to rejoice always as we pray without ceasing for Christ's return and give thanks in *all* circumstances that God is faithful to work salvation. This is the God who is glorified in the cross—and therefore glorified not in all the praise choruses that have ever been written so much as in our humblest act of feeding the hungry, healing the sick, championing the oppressed, counteracting fear with faith.

None of us can know what tomorrow's headline will be—fresh crisis, no doubt. Were the economy suddenly to return to normal, it would only make room on the *front* page for the fearful situations that have been relegated recently to the *back*. And that's not *pessimism*. It's simply the way of a sinful world. We could very easily succumb to fear. All of our enemies depend upon that. Some advertisers count on it. A few politicians have made a career of it. But *that* should *not* be the way for people who have faith that God has worked our salvation in Jesus Christ. So "[r]ejoice always, pray without ceasing, give thanks in all circumstances; for this is the will of God in Christ Jesus for *you*" (1 Thess 5:16–18 NRSV).

Fourth Sunday of Advent

Spanish Springs Presbyterian Church, Sparks, Nevada
December 19, 1999

2 Samuel 7:1–11, 16
Romans 16:25–27
Luke 1:26–38

"Picture of Mary, Portrait of God"

Throughout the centuries, artists have been fascinated by the figure of Mary the mother of Jesus. At an early stage of Christianity, Mary came to have a special place in the religious affections and practices of believers. We who are in the Protestant tradition reject many of the claims that are made for Mary, but nevertheless, especially as Christmas nears, Catholics and Protestants alike are attracted in sentiment and faith to the peasant girl who was chosen to be the mother of Jesus. Tapping the simple piety that has made Mary chief among the saints, it seems that virtually every well-known classical painter has left us a number of renditions of the Madonna. Almost all of us are familiar with some of these great works of art. Several artists, their imaginations sparked by her devotion, have ventured to paint not only the mother and child, but other scriptural and legendary scenes of Mary as well.

Leafing through an art book recently, I came across paintings inspired by our Gospel reading for this morning, the Annunciation, in which the angel Gabriel appeared to Mary with news that she was to bear a son and call his name Jesus. "Greetings, favored one! The Lord is with you" (Luke 1:28 NRSV), Gabriel said. The paintings of this event picture a woman who is not so much surprised and afraid as she is serene and demure. Doubtless, popular piety had as much to do with the artist's conception as scripture did. But I think that Franco Zeffirelli's production *Jesus of Nazareth*, in which Mary is portrayed as startled and frightened at the appearance of the angel and anxious and agitated at his announcement, is much more plausible than the works of Botticelli and Da Vinci, and certainly truer to the sense of scripture.

Mary's first reaction must have been much as yours or mine would have been—fear and astonishment. "Do not be afraid, Mary," Gabriel quickly assured her, "for you have found favor with God. And now, you will conceive in your womb and bear a son, and you will name him Jesus" (Luke 1:30-31 NRSV). And I think that Mary's response to that news was not merely a polite request for clarification. Her question, "How can this be, since I am a virgin?" (Luke 1:34 NRSV) must have been said with a great deal of feeling. What has won the devotion of many generations of Christians, of course, were Mary's *final* words to the angel, spoken in faith and courage: "Here am I, the servant of the Lord; let it be with me according to your word" (Luke 1:38a-b NRSV). Her statement of humble acquiescence to God's will, standing at the service of the creative word of God, is a model for every Christian.

One commentator has noted that Mary's quiet awaiting of God's act makes her the *very figure* of Advent. Certainly, her quiet and faithful assent is in striking contrast to the frantic activity of our modern society in the last several days before the annual Christmas holiday. Clearly, there is a lot we can learn from Mary about patience and obedience and submission to the will of God.

The great twelfth-century monk St. Bernard wrote of the tremendous anxiety that the whole human race would have felt had they known that an angel of the Lord was bringing Mary such tidings. "Why do you delay?" he wrote, as if addressing a *picture* of Mary as she heard the words of the angel.

> What are you afraid of? Believe, confess, accept. Humility must take on confidence, modesty must take on trust. This is no time for virginal simplicity to forget wisdom. In this matter, surely, do not fear to be presumptuous . . . . For this, tearful Adam implores you, along with his sad progeny exiled from paradise. For this, Abraham, and for this, David, and for this, the other holy Fathers beg you, that is, your very own ancestors, and all those who live in the realm of the shadow of death. The whole world waits undeservedly, down on its knees, since on a word from your mouth depends the consolation of the wretched, the release of the imprisoned, the liberation of the condemned, the salvation, at last, of all the children of Adam, your entire race.[1]

---

1. Bernard of Clairvaux, *Homily IV*, Secs. 7, 8 (author's translation).

From that perspective, it is no wonder that the Annunciation has been such a focus of simple piety.

But while Mary has captured the imagination of painters and sculptors and poets and composers and saints, the annunciation story does not tell us so much about the character of *Mary* as about the nature of *God*. Unlike Luke's statement that the parents of *John the Baptizer* were "righteous before God, living blamelessly according to all the commandments and regulations of the Lord" (Luke 1:6 NRSV), nothing at all is said in scripture about *Mary's* special qualifications for being chosen to bear the Christ child—certainly no description of an immaculate conception or precocious childhood or sinless adolescence. In this morning's Gospel reading, and in the Magnificat, which Mary sang when she visited Elizabeth, her aged kinswoman *also* pregnant with child, Luke gives us an intriguing picture of Mary as one who is sensitive to matters of the spirit—a model of humility and patience before God. But more important than this *picture* of *Mary*, in all these stories leading up to the birth of Christ, Luke provides us with a *portrait* of *God*.

It was a dark time for the people of Israel. Ever since the exile in Babylon, their nation had been passed back and forth between a succession of empires as they rose and fell. There had been some brief attempts at restoring Israel's former glory and honored place as God's special race, but these had not lasted. Most *recently*, *Rome* had conquered the nation—a political disgrace and a religious abomination as imperial soldiers trampled the fields and defiled the holy places. In some circles, the expectation of the Messiah was at fever pitch, but among most people, it must have seemed that they would *never* have reason to hope *again*. Everywhere Israel's *politicians* looked, they saw the emperor's image and the threat of his legions. Everywhere Israel's *priests* looked, they saw the seductions of idolatry and the evidence of irreligion. Everywhere Israel's *poor* looked, they saw the privileges of the wealthy and disregard for the downtrodden. More of the same, it must have seemed, always more of the same! Oh, there were healers and miracle-workers around, and some who claimed to be prophets and even the Messiah, but what fundamental improvement could there be in their lives as long as the world responded more to the *greedy* than to the *needy*, more to the power*ful* than to the power*less*, more to the *shouts* of self-*interest* than to the *whispers* of self-*sacrifice*? To the average person, burdened by high rents and high taxes, it must have seemed like nothing ever changes. What *could* change? Experience taught that human selfishness was as relentless as the desert sun, and that human hearts were as unyielding as rock, and that if there *was* a God, he seemed very, very far away from the back alleys and the country hamlets. There were certain givens in life that could not be changed, any more than a woman could bear a son in her old age, or that a virgin could conceive, or that a child born of a peasant woman could inherit the throne of David!

But God was preparing to do a new thing in the world—something creative beyond all imagination, something that would confound human wisdom and defy human experience. The angel Gabriel said to Mary:

> "The Holy Spirit will come upon you, and the power of the Most High will overshadow you; therefore the child to be born will be holy; he will be called Son of God. And now, your relative Elizabeth in her old age has *also* conceived a son; and this is the sixth month for her who was said to be *barren*. For *nothing* will be impossible with God." (Luke 1:35–37 NRSV)

Mary it was who received the promise of the power of God, Mary it was who sang in thanksgiving and praise that God had chosen *her* for this blessed task, but the emphasis throughout is upon *God*—the God who can bring forth life from a barren, even a virgin, womb; the same God who created the world and everything that is in it out of nothing, and who brought together dry bones and covered them with flesh and breathed upon them and caused them to stand.

Even these first few words of Luke are *gospel*—good news. The most hopeless situation, the most unpromising scene, is capable of being transformed in God's hands to become a locus of God's presence and a sign of God's grace. First, God chose a scruffy band of desert nomads to demonstrate faithfulness to God and so bless all the families of the earth; then God emancipated a nation of slaves to show the world the meaning of freedom; then God catapulted a lowly shepherd boy from tending his flocks to ruling a mighty nation and founding an everlasting dynasty. God promised his people in exile that their captivity was at an end and that they would be a light to all peoples; then an old woman with a barren womb gave birth to a son who grew to adulthood and called upon Israel to return to obedience and prepare for the coming of the Messiah; a young peasant woman gave birth in a cattle stall to a tiny baby who was called the Son of the Most High; a young preacher and teacher and healer was put to death by torture and then rose from the dead as judge and

Savior and Lord of all. The unexpected becomes routine! The improbable becomes commonplace! Even the impossible becomes fact!

This is the nature of God! God is the God of good news, whose infinite love for us stretches from before we were conceived to after we are in the grave. God is the God of surprise, who selects for *his* advent not the halls of the *mighty*, but a *manger*, and who selects for *his* seat of power not a *throne*, but a *cross*. God is the God of promise, whose divine purpose writes its *own* end to our human stories. God is the God of hope, whose unfailing word not only overcomes laws of nature, but even dispels gloomy despair and penetrates closed hearts and changes stubborn minds. God is the God of our Lord Jesus Christ, whose declaration of forgiveness and testimony of salvation threw off the yoke of sin and burst the bonds of death. "He will be great, and will be called the Son of the Most High," proclaimed the angel, "and the Lord God will give to him the throne of his ancestor David. He will reign over the house of Jacob forever, and of his kingdom there will be no end" (Luke 1:32–33 NRSV).

See how Luke's picture of *Mary* reveals a grand portrait of *God*. Do you believe that God has such power? Do you believe that God is faithful? Do you believe that God's will of *salvation* and *peace* is *true, in spite of* the headlines of *oppression* and *war*? Do you believe that God's promise of *joy* and *mercy* is true, *in spite of* the *sorrows* and *disappointments* that may be weighing on your heart as we approach this Christmas? Can you trust in God's redemptive purpose in spite of all that is happening in the world and in your life? Can you recognize God's love for you in spite of the hardness evident in so many human hearts, and perhaps even in your own? Can you wait in patient submission for God to work his miraculous will? "Greetings, favored one! The Lord is with you" (Luke 1:28 NRSV), proclaimed Gabriel. Not in ease and comfort and wealth and prestige did God show his presence with Mary, but in the shame of being unwed, in the pain of childbirth, in the agony of ridicule and threats against her son, in the sight of him dying on a cross. And *also* in the unbounded *joy* of the empty *tomb*.

"Here am I, the servant of the Lord," said Mary; "let it be with me according to your word" (Luke 1:38a–b NRSV). And so it was—the birth of the savior of the world, and of you, and of me. Do not be afraid, for we have found favor with God. God bids us to have patience and confidence, to look for the unexpected miracle and to listen for the unanticipated blessing. And God promises *us good news*—the Lord is coming!

Christmas Eve (early evening)
Spanish Springs Presbyterian Church, Sparks, Nevada
December 24, 2005

Isaiah 9:2–7
Titus 2:11–14
Luke 2:1–20

"A Letter from Bethlehem"

My Dear Cousin Elizabeth,

I am writing to tell you about the wonderful gift that God has given us here in Bethlehem—the birth of a child, a son, to Joseph and me. First, let me assure you he is healthy and beautiful and good and charming and beautiful and strong and adorable and so beautiful, as I am certain his cousin John is. I trust that both you and the baby are well. We rejoice that Zechariah's voice has come back after so strangely disappearing like that.

No doubt you are wondering about my writing you from Bethlehem, of all places. But perhaps you recall that Joseph's family is from here originally, and so, when the emperor's command came to us about the census, Joseph had no choice but to come all this way. He did not want to leave me, as my time was nearing, and I certainly did not want to be parted from him. It seemed that we had little choice but to travel here together, quite a long way, of course, and I was not in traveling condition. But Joseph arranged to get a donkey for me, and we stopped frequently for rest, although we had to travel as far as we could each day, because we could not afford many nights' lodging on the road. Then, too, many inns were full, so many people are having to journey from where they live to where they are required to register. It was uncomfortable, of course, but we passed so many people who were in even *greater* discomfort—many elderly people, many infants and children, many lame people and sick. I, at least, had no fever, no broken bones, nothing of that sort. I *did* worry for the baby's sake, of course, and so did *Joseph*, but our dear little one had the most comfortable journey of all, I suspect, and the donkey was gentle. Poor Joseph had to walk the entire way.

I remember, dear cousin, the day I came to see you and your little John leapt within you!—do you remember that? What a marvelous thing it is to feel another life quickening inside you. What a joyous thing. I did not fully understand at the time what a blessing that is—I suppose that no woman does, before she feels it for herself, and you begin to wonder whether it is a boy or a girl, what the baby will look like, what the child will like to do and eat and play as he or she grows up, what your child will think of you, what will make him or her happy, what will sadden his or her heart—may those days be few in number! You begin to pray more fervently for your child's health and happiness and long life.

I must confide to you now that I did not know exactly how Joseph would react to being a father, the way things—well, you know. It was hard on him. It must have been very hard, when I first told him about the baby. How kind he has been. How very understanding. I do love him so. And I am sure he loves me very much, too. Really, his kindness to me all through these nine months, and especially during our journey here, has been so great. He thought nothing for himself, only my comfort and well-being.

Jesus—yes, that's his name, as we knew it must be—was born shortly after we arrived here, the very night! How God was watching over us that we were not still out on the road somewhere! We had arrived late in the day, and the few inns here—Bethlehem is not a very large town, we discovered—were all full, or so Joseph was told when he went from door to door. He was imagining that the innkeepers did not want a woman moaning and screaming in childbirth under their roof, and was becoming angry as well as frustrated, but it is true there are many visitors here because of the census. Finally, *one* innkeeper *did* say we could use his stable. Joseph was again a little indignant, not thinking *that* a very suitable place for a child to be born or for a mother to give birth. Would they have suggested that if we had been other than poor common folk? he asked me. They surely would have made room for a wealthy woman in need, he said. I don't know—it *is* crowded here in this little town. But by that time, I just wanted to lie down somewhere—anywhere—and at least there was clean straw, and the innkeeper's wife to help. And with the animals in the stable, including our faithful little donkey, it was as warm as the inn would have been, I am sure. For the night, you know, was chilly.

I can't really say how long my labor was. Dear Joseph was so worried—I could see it in his face. Poor man, I'm sure he'd never before been in a place where a baby was being born, nor had even *seen* a newborn, much less *held* one. These things are such mysteries to men, even in the normal course of things. I almost think they're afraid of the entire subject. But I could not want a finer man for a husband, and I am sure Jesus could have no better model for growing into manhood. You should have seen the smile on Joseph's face, and the tears of joy in his eyes. There is a tender side to this man I have married. I hope they will always have a close bond, the two of them. I want Jesus to learn the dignity of work and honesty in dealing and kindness toward people in need that Joseph can teach him.

Here is something that will make you laugh to think of it. Of course, we had no *bed* for Jesus. But we *had* to put him *someplace*. *I* could be on the ground, but we weren't going to place such a precious gift in the dirt and the straw. Joseph was really quite anxious about this, when the innkeeper's wife suggested laying Jesus in the manger. Yes, the manger!—where the animals feed. A place for food became the place for our little boy. At one point, a cow came near, to munch as usual on the hay, I suppose, and looked bewildered and then turned away. Joseph and I just laughed. What must that cow have thought! A squirming and gurgling little bundle in her dinner trough, as if Jesus were food to eat! Joseph took some of the hay from the manger and fed it to the cow, and we just laughed until we cried.

He is such a beautiful boy, as I am sure your John is. You know the great joy that I am feeling. And also the weariness, just two days afterward. We will remain here until he is circumcised as our father Abraham taught us, and then we will go to Jerusalem to offer the sacrifice—turtledoves, if they are available; if not, pigeons. And then the purification. I *do* dislike the thought of being separated from Joseph all that time! Then, too, I think it will be expensive to remain in Jerusalem for so long. But, finally, we will go back home to Nazareth.

Oh, but let me tell you. I almost forgot this in my excitement about the birth itself. Later that night, a most unusual thing happened. I say "unusual," and yet you know that there has been so much about all of this that has been unusual, and blessed in a special way that only you and I understand (if indeed even *we* understand it that well). It was after we had settled Jesus in the manger, and the innkeeper's wife had helped clean me up, and Joseph was just standing there looking at Jesus, too nervous from excitement to lie down himself, poor man, tired though he was, that we had some visitors—shepherds, who had come in from the fields nearby. They just sort of appeared at the door of the stable—*I* saw them first, just standing there, and didn't know who they were or why they had come. Joseph did not want me to be bothered, thinking their coming an intrusion on a new mother's privacy. But they looked so excited, and said that they had come to see the baby—in fact, had been *instructed* to come see the baby. Now, that seemed to us to be very strange. We just looked at each other. Who could have known? Who would have even cared that a baby had been born to a strange pair of travelers that night? And how had they found us in that stable, of all places? And here is the strangest part: They said an *angel* had appeared to them, out there, in the fields, while they were watching over their sheep as usual, and had told them not to be afraid, because the angel was bringing them good news. So much like that night when I was told I would have a baby! Everybody would *rejoice* because of what was happening—that a *Savior* was being born to *them* that night in Bethlehem—the *Messiah*, the *Lord*. And then there were *more* angels filling the skies above them and singing. And so, dear cousin, you see, it is not just to *us* that this blessing has come, and it is not just *we* who know the importance of Jesus. He is for *all* people. And he is a *special* blessing for people who have little *else* in life.

I have been thinking much about what the shepherds said. Is this not a further sign that everything has happened just the way God has intended? And for a purpose much greater than just our own family, or our own generation, even? And to think it has all happened to people such as we—ordinary village folk. To think of God's ancient promise coming true now, and through us, and to us. How are we at all worthy to be the instruments of the Lord? Oh, Elizabeth—what a blessing. Not even *kings* could hope for such a thing, and yet it has happened to *us*! So God looks after and cares for and—dare we say it?—*esteems* even poor folk like us! And God listens to the yearnings of our hearts and the whispers of our souls! What would King Herod think if he knew?

The shepherds—just boys, you understand—said the sign of the truth of all they were being told was that they would find a child wrapped in bands of cloth and lying in a manger. A *manger*, Elizabeth!—just where we had laid him, by *chance* as it seemed to *us*! And so the shepherds naturally thought to look for a stable. And surely, not many stables had a lamp burning well after midnight. And so they had found us. Of course, we invited them to come in closer to the manger. You should have heard them squealing and laughing with each little move that Jesus made. You know, boys like to have people think they are rough and tough, but I believe they are really quite sensitive inside. I might even have let them *hold* Jesus if they had asked—I'm sure they would have been gentle with him—but they didn't, and I suppose Jesus may well have fallen asleep by then. Finally, the innkeeper's wife said it was time for them to leave and let *us* sleep, and *she* went off to sleep as well. But the moment the boys got outside of the stable, we could hear them laughing and singing and chattering excitedly to one another, so that I wouldn't be surprised if they didn't wake up everyone in the street.

And so, dear cousin, I have been praising God for all this miracle—yes, "miracle" is what I must call it, for so it surely is. How I long to see you again and tell you these things face to face, and to hold your little John, and have you hold our little Jesus. Perhaps one day, when they are older, they will meet and get to know each other and find strength in each other and share much in common. I hope so. In the meantime, we have been so blessed. May all the *world* know such a *marvelous* blessing.

Peace be with you, dear cousin, and may God watch over you and your dear little son. For you know, I think that somehow God must know what it is like to rejoice at the birth of a child.

Love, Mary

Christmas Eve (late evening)
First Presbyterian Church, Dodge City, Kansas
December 24, 1996

Isaiah 9:2–7
Titus 2:11–14
Luke 2:1–20

"Joy to Our World"

One of the biggest challenges in leading a Bible study is helping twentieth-century readers to identify with the circumstances in which the ancient biblical writers made their witness—the setting of the story, the culture and customs of the time. So many of the events the Bible deals with, so many of the modes of expression it uses, seem alien to life as you and I know it. In church school and in adult classes, our teachers try to overcome that. Like many of you, I remember as a child in Sunday school taking a shoebox and painting sand dunes in the bottom of it and hunting for weeds which sort of resembled palm trees and propping them up in the corners, and gluing in some rocks, and dressing little figures up in scraps of cloth to look like robes and tying them around the waist with a piece of string or twine, like a belt or a sash. And so David and Goliath would do battle in my little Philistine oasis, or Moses would talk to God on my miniature Sinai, or Jacob would fall asleep and dream at my shoebox Bethel. As children, that sort of activity helped us visualize the original story, perhaps, but it tended to leave the Bible at a distance, culturally and historically, and in the process, tended to make it rather tame and hypothetical. In the very process of learning the old, old stories about the Holy Land, they seemed to remain old, and to remain distant, and to remain stories about someone *else's* experience long ago and far away.

Unfortunately, the stories of the Bible are *still* alien to a lot of people who have grown from childhood to adulthood. Especially if we have not had help relating the experiences of God's people of *old* to the experiences of God's people *today*, the Bible may as well never have been translated from Hebrew and Greek, so far as some people are concerned. What does it have to do with the pressures of *our* times of maximizing profits and minimizing anxiety, of life according to Madison Avenue and life according to Wall Street, of putting faith in plastic cards and plastic surgery? What does it have to do with family crises and career choices and the environment and health, this book whose heroes and heroines and scoundrels and scalawags we remember as pint-sized mannequins in a shoebox? What did the ancient storytellers know of *our* problems? What does the God who revealed himself *long ago* know of our world *today*?

Once a year, we pause to listen again to the most beloved of all the old, old stories. Some of us can probably recite it from memory, or at least parts of it. There is a charming innocence about it, a winsome simplicity, that appeals to us—a young couple on the road, she pregnant and about to deliver, he just doing what the government regulations said to do, taking shelter for the night in the most rustic of places, laying their newborn son in a feeding trough; an angel appearing to shepherds camping out in the pasture with their sheep, directing them to go into town and see the baby; and then the voices of a heavenly choir—can we just imagine the fluttering of wings?—praising God and declaring salvation. And then the shepherds going and doing as they had been instructed, and returning afterward to their fields praising God for having seen a baby lying in a manger.

How are *we* to identify with something like *that*? When did *we* last see an angel, at least one we recognized as such? When did *we* last see shepherds spending the night with their flocks? When did *we* last hear a promise of salvation and believe it was really good news? And yet, perhaps we *do* remember times when *we* felt pushed around by an uncaring, impersonal bureaucracy or faceless rules and senseless orders, no exceptions for inconvenience or unreasonableness or special circumstances. Perhaps we *can* understand the fear and bewilderment of a young mother, unmarried or just married, the eyes of all turned on her in judgment. Perhaps we wonder whether a twenty-four-hour hospital stay for a delivery is much advancement over giving birth in a stable. Perhaps we sometimes feel as lowly and despised by society around us as the shepherds did. Perhaps we would marvel just like *they* did, should an angel of God make history's most astounding announcement to us, even to *us*, of all people. Perhaps sometime in our lives, we have been moved at the sight of a newborn child to praise God for yet another commonplace miracle of life.

Scholars have long noticed that Luke was specially interested to testify that the enfleshment of God occurred at a real place in a real time among real people with real problems. Caesar Augustus. Enrollment for taxes. During the governorship of Quirinius. Suspicious pregnancy. No vacancy. Smelly sheep. Scruffy shepherds. Bethlehem. The people of Israel had long talked about the coming of a Messiah, a new king, righteous and mighty and victorious, not unlike Caesar Augustus, actually, at least in regard to his power. But, as the expectations remained unmet generation after generation, the fulfillment of such a dream had come to seem to *them* as far in the *future* as the birth of Jesus seems to *us* far in the *past*. The people had become so far-sighted that most of them couldn't recognize the astonishing truth of what was happening right under their noses—down in little Bethlehem, a village of no particular distinction, among people rather low on the social ladder, rather poor even by Palestinian standards, rather less seemly than polite society would find respectable, God was struggling forth from a young woman's womb, helpless, innocent, fragile, unknowing. Surely no one like a Caesar Augustus would be born into such humble circumstances as that—no emperor, no king, no general, no one such as the Messiah that the Jews were expecting. And yet, the very powerful Caesar Augustus had unknowingly declared a law that brought all this very unremarkable but very important cast together to fulfill God's even *more* powerful drama of salvation.

Tonight, we will join the ancient angel choir and the shepherds of old in singing their joyful praises of God, "Joy to the world! The Lord is come: Let earth receive her King!" Most of us have sung Isaac Watts's carol many times before, at Christmas, and then quickly afterward tucked it away with the ornaments and stockings until about this time next year. "Why are the Christmas decorations still up in the sanctuary?" one woman wrote on a slip of paper and put it in the offering plate the Sunday after Christmas at one church with which I was familiar. It was still Christmastide, of course. I fear that she was saying, "Let's get back to normal. Put the story away, so that it remains a story. Let it not interfere with our world too much, for it really has not much to *do* with our world."

Does the story of the birth of Christ, the arrival of God's own Son, the coming of God long ago to be born and grow up and walk the streets and know the smell and taste of bread and wine and the sound of laughter and crying and the pleasure of celebration and the satisfaction of work and the dismay of rejection and the pain of crucifixion, and then being raised from the dead, have much to do with our world? Does the news of a Savior prompt us to sing for joy *today*? By the birth of Jesus among the *least* of us, God shows the *value* of *all* of us. By the ministry of Jesus among the sick and the mournful and the hungry and the outcast, God declares that he understands and blesses *our* tragedies, great and small, and shows that success comes not by chasing wealth or privilege, but in being obedient to God's purpose and trustful of God's promises. By the crucifixion of Jesus for his faithful servanthood, God has declared that we experience what life is all about in the degree that we pour ourselves out for others. By the resurrection of Christ, God has promised that, for those who have faith in his Son, sin is not our demise and death is not our defeat.

But none of that is anything that took place *outside* of history. It did not happen *alongside* or *in addition to* what was happening in the real world, but in the *midst* of life's real events and real headlines and real triumphs and real disasters, through the agency of real people in a real place, by the real working of the Holy Spirit. God's love for the world, God's care for each individual, was no different two thousand years ago than it is now, and the earth gave no more heed to the great gift of God *then* than it does *now*—the earth did not stop spinning the night Jesus was born; the movers and shakers didn't even know it was happening, and if they *had* known about it, they might not even have cared. The next morning, soldiers were still marching. Commerce was still flowing. Families were still struggling to make ends meet. And yet a few poor, uneducated shepherds knew the birth of Jesus was good news of a great joy for all the world.

So, too, the coming of God in Jesus Christ is good news of great joy for *our* world, in which refugees still feel pushed about by governments, some people still must live on the road, teenage pregnancy is still a scandal, there are still a lot of "No Vacancy" signs, especially if your skin is the wrong color or you speak with the wrong accent or your name betrays the wrong pedigree, and some lawful and necessary occupations are still dishonored, like shepherds were looked down upon long ago. The coming of God in Jesus Christ is still good news of great joy for *our* world, in which families are still dysfunctional, employees are still laid off work, drought and pestilence still ruin crops, disease still strikes without warning, and death still comes to the young and the good. The coming of God in Jesus Christ is good news for *you*, if your life is not perfect, if your family causes you worry, if you are not as generous or as kind or as loving as you could be, if you feel tempted to yield to unworthy desires and unwanted habits, if the headlines of war and hunger and hatred disturb you, if friends sometimes prove fickle, if you fear that time is running out. Jesus Christ is the risen and living Savior. We do not have to have lived in Palestine two thousand years ago for the message of the angels to be good news for our world. For to us, too, "is born this day in the city of David a Savior, who is the Messiah, the Lord" (Luke 2:11 NRSV). "Joy to *our* world! the Lord is come: Let earth receive her King."

Christmas Day
Spanish Springs Presbyterian Church, Sparks, Nevada
December 25, 2011

Isaiah 52:7–10
Hebrews 1:1–4
John 1:1–14

"First, Last, and Always"

"One religion is just as good as another," we hear some people say. "They all get us where we're going. All of them ultimately are about the same God."

Most of you are aware, as I have tried to give witness among you during my pastorate here, that I am a strong supporter of ecumenical involvement and interfaith cooperation. I think there is no room in the Christian experience for religious hatred or intolerance, certainly not for imposing one's own beliefs upon anyone else.

My impression is that all of you who are here this morning agree. You are respectful of the beliefs and convictions of others, you are insistent that every person has the right to practice his or her own religion without either government opposition or government sponsorship, you would never treat a person of different beliefs with indignity or ridicule or insult. Still, it is not some *general* belief in God that you have come here to express, not some *generic* deity you have come to worship this morning, but, on *this* day of *all* days, you have gathered to acknowledge, with wonder and thanksgiving, the God whom scripture proclaims chose to reveal the divine identity and will to humankind in the most personal way, in the flesh and blood of Jesus of Nazareth. And, for you, Christmas is therefore not simply a traditional holiday of warm fuzzy sentiment, but a high celebration of the most important event of all history. And so, for you, behind and perhaps in spite of all of the decorations and music and gift-giving and feasting, there is this most fundamental truth, both profoundly sober and supremely joyful: "In the beginning was the Word, and the Word was with God, and the Word was God. . . . And the Word became flesh and lived among us, and we have seen his glory, the glory as of a father's only son, full of grace and truth" (John 1:1, 14 NRSV).

And so, because of what you believe about the event commemorated by this holiday, religion can never be for you simply a matter of taste or wish, can never be for you a dilettantish hobby or a clubby pursuit, can never be for you a matter of invention or popularity or convenience or ambivalence. Nor can Jesus Christ be for you simply a good example or a wise teacher or a nice thought, can never remain for you a gentle baby lying in a manger and wrapped in memories of pleasant times passed around the Christmas tree or the dinner table. The truth about the coming of Jesus Christ is of crucial and ultimate importance for the world's present and future, and for the manner and hope in which you live each and every moment of your life.

Maybe it is a professional habit, but I can't help noticing that a majority of my neighbors on the street where I have lived for the thirteen years I have been the pastor of Spanish Springs Presbyterian Church display some kind of decoration this time of year, but that a lot of them don't seem to attend worship anywhere, at least not with any regularity. It's not that they're Buddhist or Hindu or Muslim or followers of any other religion. They've got the tree, they've got the lights, they exchange gifts all on the basis of December 25th being the Christian holiday with which those things have become associated. Arbitrary as it was for the church, just a few decades into its existence, to designate December 25th as the annual Feast of the Nativity, even *non*-Christians and *lukewarm* Christians and people who *sort* of regard themselves as Christians but don't otherwise do much *about* it acknowledge Christmas Day as somehow a special occasion. But for people who truly believe, our worship, our acknowledgment of this day, witnesses to our conviction that in *Jesus*, the world experienced *more* than another good example or wise teacher or nice thought, and that his birth is the pivot around which all of history turns.

"Long ago," the preacher of Hebrews began, "God spoke to our ancestors in many and various ways by the prophets" (Heb 1:1 NRSV). A recent commentary by biblical scholar Tom Long points out that God, by the testimony of the Bible, is a *communicating* God.[1] God is not silent and distant, impassively regulating the universe, checking now and then to make sure that the planets are still spinning and gravity is still working.

---

1. See Long, 7–10.

God is much more interactive than that, much more personally engaged. Throughout the Bible, the testimony is that God speaks, argues, pleads, woos, cajoles, promises—which is also to say that God is interested in revealing himself, his character, his purpose, his concern, and his love.

In large measure, nature itself suggests that God, its creator and sustainer, is majestic and beautiful and wise and purposeful. But there is an ambiguity to nature, or at least our view of it, limited as our perception is by time and space. We can't see the whole, just a small part, and so we also see what appears to be a randomness in nature, sometimes even a viciousness, suggesting a cold detachment. Based on nature alone, our conclusions about God can be only tentative, impressionistic. More eloquent of God's character is the whole movement and tending of history, though even over a period of many centuries it may seem that evil is at least as common as goodness, oppression as prevalent as freedom. How do we know which of these is God's will, or God's working? And if *we* are *victims* of evil or oppression, who can *fault* us for thinking that, if there *is* a God, he is either uninterested or powerless? The giving of the *law* provided greater insight into who God is, but the law can be misinterpreted, can be made by some to be a god in itself, as proved to be the case with the Pharisees two thousand years ago, and which is still the case with Pharisees today. The next step in God's revelation was the prophets, speaking on God's behalf about particular situations and specific issues, sometimes underscoring their words with the testimony of their own behavior. But the revelation that came through the prophets was always fragmentary—a word here, a word there, now and then, with long stretches of what seemed like silence in between. God's spirit visited people like Elijah and Isaiah and Jeremiah and Zechariah for a time, in order to proclaim God's will at a point in history, but in delivering God's words, none of the prophets claimed to be, nor was ever thought of, as him- or herself the *embodiment* of God's Word.

But then, something happened in the chain of God's revelation that was very different from everything that had preceded it. The Gospels tell of the birth of a child one night long ago in Bethlehem that was an event of cosmic importance.

On the face of it, and to most people who might have bothered to notice, there was nothing much unusual about it. But looking back at Christmas from Easter, reflecting on his healing the sick and his forgiving the sin-burdened and his feeding the hungry and his teaching whoever would listen, the miracle of raising Jesus, who had been crucified and buried, from the tomb to eternal life and a place of glory and honor and authority, John was moved to articulate a startling and profound truth: in Jesus, everything that God *is* came into the world and lived much like you and I do, subject to the same hunger and thirst and pain and weariness, vulnerable to the same insults and hatred and punishment and mortality, even. He pitched his tent among us, as the scriptures literally express it, and experienced everything you and I experience, and so blessed our sufferings as well as our hopes, but with this difference: in faithful dependence upon God in heaven and sustained by God the Holy Spirit, active in the world and in his own life, Christ on earth, grown from infant to adult, persisted in obedience to the divine purpose and in love for all humankind.

What you and I celebrate at Christmas is the truth by which we must live all year long: in Jesus we see and experience the fullness of God, who created everything that is and who is guiding it purposefully and inevitably toward its destiny of full and complete redemption in the kingdom of peace, forgiveness, love, and hope—the kingdom that Jesus proclaimed and demonstrated, and in which everyone participates even now who believes, truly believes, that he is the Christ, the Son of God, the perfect revelation of all that God is and all that God desires. There has never been a time that Christ the Son was not in full and complete identity with God the Father, and even now he lies not in a grave, but sits at God's side, reigning in full power and glory, heir to all things of God because, as God's agent of creation, all things belong to him. And that means that you and I, first, last, and always, belong to Jesus Christ. Everything we say and do, first, last, and always, must give witness to who our Lord is. And that Lord of our lives, first, last, and always, is a mirror image of the God of the universe whose Word is our truth, our authority, our comfort, our blessing—the Word that was at the beginning, the Word that will be at the end: Jesus Christ himself. Through him all things came into being, without him nothing came into being. He is the very definition of life, the world's only Light to illumine, to guide, to reveal. And in the eternal contest between light and darkness, between truth and untruth, between life and death, God's Word, Jesus Christ, will be and already is victorious despite every ambivalence of nature, every disappointment and regression of history, every misuse and misinterpretation of the law, every disregard and rejection of prophetic warning and prophetic encouragement. Christmas is the believers' loud affirmation that Jesus Christ is the Son of God, God's mirror image, our intimate look into God's face that until that night in Bethlehem was obscure and forbidden, our intimate exposure to God's heart and mind, even God's voice and touch. And Christmas is the believers' joyful celebration that through this same Jesus, *we* are empowered to become God's genuine children, too, conceived by the Spirit and birthed from the waters of the font into a life of faithful dedication and obedient service in the name of Christ our brother who sits on heaven's throne.

Today is my final Sunday with you as your pastor. I have hoped for much for you. Not all of it has come to pass, yet. But the Bible teaches that, as ministers, we must be content to plant the seed and water it, and then move on, which is itself a sign of trust in God and dependence upon God, in worship centered firmly in God as God is known in Jesus Christ and witnessed to in the scriptures, beyond time and unfettered by culture—an activity profoundly important and expressing the character of God and shaping *our* character as followers of Christ, living and rejoicing in the power of the Holy Spirit; in study of the Bible and the faith by which the church lives and gives witness, which ought to be a commitment of young and old alike; in mission that reaches out to the poor and the outcast and the infirm and the dispossessed in the name and manner of Jesus Christ, and that is not content simply to bind the wounds of those who have been mistreated and forgotten by the world but seeks to *transform* the world to match the priorities of God; in fellowship that celebrates the family into which God has enfolded us as sisters and brothers of Jesus Christ his Son—it has been my goal, first, last, and always, for all of us together to give glory and honor to the one who was, who is, and who is to come.

Isn't that what Christmas is about? Celebrating and declaring to the world that,

> [i]n the beginning was the Word, and the Word was with God, and the Word was God. He was in the beginning with God. All things came into being through him, and without him not one thing came into being. What has come into being in him was life, and the life was the light of all people. The light shines in the darkness, and the darkness did not overcome it. . . .
>
> He was in the world, and the world came into being through him; yet the world did not know him. He came to what was his own, and his own people did not accept him. But to all who received him, who believed in his name, he gave power to become children of God, who were born, not of blood or of the will of the flesh or of the will of man, but of God.

And the Word became flesh and lived among us, and we have seen his glory, the glory as of a father's only son, full of grace and truth." (John 1:1–5, 10–14 NRSV)

May our lives, and may your life together, be a continuous, clear, and unequivocal testimony and proclamation to the world that Jesus Christ is the Word of God, first, last, and always.

First Sunday after Christmas
Spanish Springs Presbyterian Church, Sparks, Nevada
January 1, 2006

Isaiah 61:10—62:3
Galatians 4:4-7
Luke 2:22-40

"To Be a Child"

One of the best things about this time of year is children. Who can begrudge them their excitement, or be annoyed by their chatter, or resent their eagerness, or be embarrassed by their candor? Out of school for two weeks (if they're old enough to *be* in school), delighted to play in the snow (if it happens to snow during Christmas break), fueled by sugar cookies and all of the other sweet delights just there for the taking this time of year, anticipating the visit of relatives, and of course the thought of presents under the tree—that's a normal and important part of childhood, as we have come to understand it. And even the zeal of receiving and opening presents is *appropriate*—who *doesn't* like to receive a gift?—at least until it crosses over from engendering a sense of *gratitude* to fostering a sense of *entitlement*.

Most of us can remember what it was like to experience Christmas as a child, and can still manage, if we try, to see Christmas through a child's eyes, now and then, and rediscover and reclaim some of the *wonder* that adult sophistication and financial concerns and the stress of schedules can squeeze out of the holiday as we grow up. And of course at Christmas, we remember that God came to us, after all, as a *child*—Jesus, the Christ—blessing *each* stage of human growth and development by his own experience of it. We are tempted, each year, to try to keep Jesus in the manger, to try to enshrine the image of the beautiful infant, but to do so would keep us from fully understanding and appreciating and giving thanks for his compassionate ministry and his sympathetic teaching as an adult, and, of course, the crucifixion and the empty tomb. It is not Jesus' *birth* that saves us, but his *death* and *resurrection*, prompting a mature faith that cherishes his instruction and emulates his example. Knowing that, we can join with Simeon in taking the Christ child into our arms and rejoicing that we have seen God's salvation face to face.

We need not regret having to let go of the manger days of Jesus; although he outgrew his swaddling clothes, he remained the child of God—the Son of God—whose birth was heralded by angels, even as he grew through adolescence into adulthood. We are *always* our parents' child, no matter how old we get. In our church in Dodge City, we had three generations of "Bens"—the chairman of the board of the bank, the president of the bank, and the schoolboy who was the son of the president and the grandson of the chairman. During my first few months in Dodge, I was repeatedly confused by everyone's referring to the *oldest* of the three as Ben Jr. He was already in his seventies when we arrived there, and crossed over into his eighties by the time we left. There had not been a Ben Sr. for a number of years. But the fact is that *this* man was Ben Zimmerman II, hence Ben Jr., always referred to that way by people in the bank and in the community, even though his own father had died many years previously. Ben Zimmerman III was spoken of by friends and acquaintances as "Ben Three," and little Ben IV will one day, I am sure, feel an exceeding degree of pressure to name his own son Ben V. No matter how old we get, we are always someone's child, long after we have outgrown the cradle, even when we are well advanced in years.

Last Sunday's Gospel reading from the first chapter of John, the reading for Christmas Day, declared that to all who *received* the Word of God, that is, Jesus the Christ, and *believed* in him, "he gave power to become children of God, who were born, not of blood or of the will of the flesh or of the will of man, but of God" (John 1:12b-13 NRSV). The childhood of which John speaks can happen when we are quite young or when we are quite old or anywhere in between. In one sense, of course, we are *all* children of God; it is by a miracle of God that we have life, that we came into this world, and that there is air and water and soil and sun for everyone, Christian or not. God wants *all* to prosper, *deserving* or not, simply because we are God's creation. But there is a *special* sense in which we *become* God's children in all the *fullness* of that word—not by simply being born into the world, but by being adopted by God as *heirs*, those who are entitled to an inheritance, and receiving it through the gift of the Holy Spirit into our hearts and dwelling there. And this is the sense in which John, and later Paul, speak of being God's children, no matter our age. "[W]hen the fullness of time had come," Paul explained in his letter to the Galatians, "God sent his Son, born of a woman, born under the law, in order to *redeem* those who were under the law, so that we might receive adoption as *children*" (Gal 4:4–5 NRSV). The Jews reckoned that they were the heirs of God's promise because they were the descendants of Abraham, with whom God had made covenant to bless his people, to whom also God gave the law. They were children not only by being Abraham's *biological offspring*, but because they acknowledged their responsibility under the covenant. Being born "under the law," being children "under the law," has two senses here—they were born in fulfillment of the promise made to Abraham and into the nation to whom God had given the Ten Commandments and all of the law of Moses, but they also were reckoned to be children, heirs, by the customs of descent and distribution—they were heirs of God's promise because they were the flesh-and-blood progeny of Abraham to whom the promise was first given. But John the disciple and Paul the apostle proclaim that through *adoption*, even *Gentiles*, *non*-Jews, are brought into God's family circle and given the right of inheritance. Receiving Jesus Christ as the Son of God in faith, we become his sisters and brothers, and therefore *children* of *God* with the *same* privileges and entitlements as *Jesus*—to eternal life, for instance, and to a place in heaven. "And because you are children," Paul goes on, "God has sent the Spirit of his Son into our hearts, crying 'Abba! Father!' So you are no longer a *slave* but a *child*, and if a *child* then also an *heir*, through God" (Gal 4:6–7 NRSV).

To be a child of God means recognizing and calling upon God as our Father, not just in the formal sense of biological relationship, but in the familiar sentimental and affectionate way—"Abba," the very word *Jesus* used, the closest English terminology being "Daddy." That is amazing in *itself*, is it not? That, having received Christ by faith, we are not just in some *official* relationship with God, but can presume such *innocence* as to call the Creator of the universe *Daddy*. But Paul makes another point, and it's regrettable that the lectionary committee followed the subject divisions of the Bible translators, ending the reading just when Paul is really getting into it. Verse 7 reads, "So you are no longer a *slave* but a *child*, and if a *child* then also an *heir*, through God" (Gal 4:7 NRSV). You have to read on into the next verses to understand what Paul's real point is when he draws a distinction between being a child of God and being a slave: "Formerly, when you did not know God, you were enslaved to beings that by nature are not gods. Now, however, that you have come to *know*

God, or rather be known *by* God, how can you turn back again to the weak and beggarly elemental spirits" (Gal 4:8–9b NRSV)? (Compare "the weak and beggarly elemental spirits" with the Spirit of Christ that Paul says God has sent into our hearts.) "How can you want to be enslaved to them again?" (Gal 4:9c NRSV) Paul asks in exasperation. For, as Paul went on to describe, the Galatians had "enslaved" themselves to various pagan observances and beliefs, and the apostle wondered whether all his ministry among them had in fact been wasted.

At this point, we need to make another shift in scenes. Imagine a grand household back in those days. In the Roman world, slavery was a social and economic given. Large households would have had many slaves serving in various capacities, some highly skilled, some well-educated, many of them indispensable, but none of them *free*, none of them entitled to a share of their master's wealth during his *life* or a share of their master's estate after his *death*. In fact, they would have been a *part* of his wealth and his estate, *property*, with no legal rights and no claims on their master's treasure or affection. Before the birth, death, and resurrection of Christ, that is how we non-Jews stood in relationship to God. But even the Jews, the children of Abraham, though they could claim they were entitled to a *place* in the *household*, had only a stiff, formal relationship to God, and that depended upon their following laws, rules, and regulations. The relationship under the law of Moses between child and parent was never so intimate as to permit calling God "Father," much less "Daddy." God was the one whose name was too holy to be spoken, and so the term "Lord" was substituted—hardly a term of endearment or familiarity. But with the Spirit of Christ within us, which comes not as an achievement or a commodity but as a gift offered graciously to be received gratefully, we are adopted into the same ties of tender affection that entwine Jesus and God, and everything that belongs to *Christ*, everything to which *Christ* is entitled, *we* have a *share* in.

A young child, not yet accomplished at music or art, not yet distinguished in academics or athletics, not yet adept at any of the things that earn reward and renown for adults, is yet loved and valued simply for being a child. And *adopted* children, no less than one's children by *birth*, are doted on by their parents, are cherished, are entitled not only to a place at the table but to a share of the estate. To be a *child* is to be an *heir*. To be a child of *God* is to have a place at the dining table *now*, and a place at the heavenly banquet that is *yet to be*, and a full measure of the eternal promise both in *this* life and in the life to *come*. Marvelously, our inheritance is undiminished by the number of brothers and sisters we have in Christ—there is no reason for rivalry among *these* heirs, and there is no place for it; *I* wouldn't get *more* by trying to make sure that someone *else* got *less* (in fact, trying to do something like that would very likely *disqualify* me as an *heir* of my heavenly Father *at all*). And, wonderfully, God is just as eager to adopt us when we are wrinkled by age as when we are wrinkled by childbirth, and delights in us just as much. In fact, even when we are advanced in years, it is appropriate for children of God to have the same wonder and eagerness and excitement at Christmas—to be enchanted by the story of the birth in the stable at Bethlehem, to be charmed by the angels and the shepherds, to be delighted by the expressions of good will and cheerful generosity that *infect* people at this time of year and give rise once again to the hope that such good will and generosity might come to characterize humanity all *through* the year. And, even when we have grown into full adulthood, God is just as willing for us to call him Father, in fact, *Abba*—Daddy.

If, as some have said, Christmas is for *children*, it is for children of *every* age, a celebration for *all* of those who have dwelling inside them the Spirit of Christ that signifies and makes possible their adoption as children of God. And, if *children*, then unsophisticated, uncalculating, uninhibited in the expression of joy and gratitude and love and wonder that marks *us, too,* as being free of enslavement to fear and greed and lust and pride; free of the fear and greed and lust and pride that inevitably accompany reverence for the elemental spirits; free of the fear and greed and lust and pride that too often mark the *end* of childhood and too easily accompany the accumulation of responsibilities and anxieties; free of the fear and greed and lust and pride that clearly confirm our adoption by the *world* to its *own* agenda for our grown-up lives.

It is Christmas. It is time to be a child again. And not just in the eagerness to see what was left for us under the tree, not just in the visions of sugarplums dancing in our heads, not just in the romance of gentle snowfall and a fire in the fireplace, but in welcoming the Spirit of Christ in our hearts to dwell there throughout the year, which makes us true children of God, no matter how young or how old we are.

Second Sunday after Christmas
Spanish Springs Presbyterian Church, Sparks, Nevada
January 5, 2003

Jeremiah 31:7–14
Ephesians 1:1–14
John 1:1–18

"Sainthood"

A long time ago, in the foothills of the Apennine Mountains in central Italy, a young man began rebuilding a small, ruined church. Dressed in rags, working through the cold and snow of winter, he slowly restored the walls and repaired the roof and made over the place that had once housed a congregation of the faithful but, for whatever reason, had been abandoned to the elements. Others, admiring his dedication, even if they did not quite understand it, joined him in the task as the weeks and months wore on. And, when the building was complete, they brought their offerings of produce and flowers and whatever they had to give, and worshiped God there, a joyous company of the poor and the lame and the sick and the humble. It wasn't that there wasn't *already* a church in the neighborhood—a magnificent one. But *it* was where the well-fed and well-bred of the town worshiped, and many of the common townspeople and country folk did not regard themselves as holy enough to be in the company of such, nor even to be looked down upon by the statues that adorned the building. They didn't feel that they belonged with the *good* folks of the town, and the good folks of the town didn't feel that they belonged with them, either.

Sometime before he had started rebuilding the church of San Damiano, the young man had been to Rome on a pilgrimage, and had noticed the many beggars asking for money on the steps of St. Peter's Basilica. Moved by compassion, he asked to exchange his clothes with one of the beggars, and spent a day himself asking for alms. He was the son of a wealthy cloth merchant back in his hometown, and had perhaps never before seen such an abundance of wretchedness as he witnessed in St. Peter's Square. He spent the whole day living as the beggars did, holding his hand out to the people who were coming and going, receiving the scorn of some, enduring the curses of a few, simply being ignored by many, as if he weren't even there. Profoundly affected by what he had experienced, he returned home and began ministering to lepers and rebuilding the little ruined church. His father, in disgust, disowned him. And when, sometime later, he heard the words of Jesus in Matthew 10:7–19—the passage in which Jesus commissions his twelve disciples to go out to cure the sick and raise the dead and cleanse the lepers and cast out demons, taking with them no money and no extra clothing,—he discarded his own staff and sandals, put on a simple robe girded with a cord, and set out to live among the poor and the outcast, "pitching his tent," so to speak, with the ones whom polite society regarded as not only unwashed, but unworthy, lodging on sidewalks, feasting on table scraps, rubbing shoulders with those whom no one else would even touch. Hardly an heroic picture. But it identified Francis as a saint long before any pope awarded him the title.

Think of how extraordinary was Francis's willingness to exchange privilege for poverty, a life of ease for a life of not knowing where his next meal was coming from, friends in circles of influence for wretches considered untouchable by the mores and the medics of the time. It was actually a Calvinist pastor at Strasbourg, Paul Sabatier, whose scholarship a century ago brought Francis to modern attention. Ever since, Francis has been just as revered among Protestants as among Catholics. And clearly it is because all of us see in Francis perhaps the most Christ-like life since Christ himself—someone whose dedication to the self-sacrificing care of others reminds us so much of Jesus' own willingness to embrace lepers, befriend the outcast, and make common cause with the poor, making incarnate the love of God for the most unlovable. For once, at just the right time, God, in the great divine wisdom, chose to enter the world, exchanging a heavenly throne for a manger, surrendering the powers of the cosmos for the frailties of a human body, vacating the kingdom of holiness for the dusty streets of Nazareth.

"And the Word became flesh and lived among us, and we have seen his glory, the glory as of a father's only son, full of grace and truth" (John 1:14 NRSV). The verb that the New Revised Standard Version translates as "*lived* among us," and several other versions translated as "*dwelled* among us," is literally "*pitched his tent* among us." I suppose the translators and editors thought that phrase too cumbersome, maybe a little too corny, for the Bible, out of place with John's majestic testimony to Christ's glory. And yet, John's point is just this: Christ's glory was apparent in his very lowliness, his triumph came by way of his execution on a cross. And in his incarnation—his coming into the world in human flesh—he became subject to all the things that beset and befall all human creatures. What Christmas is about is God's choice, made from before time began, not to be isolated or insulated from the hurts and disappointments and frustrations of human life, but to experience them, to be subject to them, and to live *alongside, for,* and *on behalf of* sinful and suffering humanity. He didn't just live or dwell among us, startling as that would have been. He *pitched his tent* among us, cast his lot with us, committed himself to us, even the lowliest and most despised. Perhaps that is why John decided no retelling of the story of the humble birth in a cattle stall was necessary, nor any comment on Jesus the baby who was laid to sleep in a feeding trough. Throughout his earthly life, even the poorest, even the hungriest, even the most despised, could see in Jesus a compassionate and merciful and encouraging friend, confidant, Savior. At every point of his ministry, whether helping out an embarrassed wedding host, talking to a woman gossiped about at a well, shaming the accusers of an adulteress into dropping their stones, or restoring soundness of limb and clarity of sight on the sabbath, Jesus pitched his tent wherever there was need.

No wonder John, two chapters later, says, "For God so loved the world that he gave his only Son, so that everyone who believes in him may not perish but may have eternal life" (John 3:16 NRSV). Our *perishing* was the very thing God became incarnate in order to *prevent*. So whoever would truly welcome God into our world and our circumstances, like Francis, could never despise, never ignore, never condemn, never curse another human being, but must be willing and eager to embrace, to feed, to forgive, to love without exception and without limit. Anyone who truly knows the love of Christ for him- or herself must seek to love as deeply and as broadly, to forgive as freely and as unconditionally, to minister to physical needs as completely and effectively, to welcome and befriend as genuinely and indiscriminately, as Jesus himself did—as *God* did, and *does*, in Jesus.

We would all have some candidates to nominate for sainthood—people whom we have known or witnessed quietly at work loving others in Christ-like ways. Some have made headlines with their compassion. Others will never be celebrated in this world, but, unbeknownst to them, already have a crown of glory reserved for them in heaven. But notice that, in the understanding of the New Testament, and as commonly used in the early Christian church, the term "saint" referred to *every* believer. The Hebrew equivalent for "saint"—"holy one"—referred not to a person who had achieved moral perfection (who has?), but to someone who had been chosen and set aside and dedicated to the service of God. So the Letter to the Ephesians, where we read that God has destined us for adoption as God's own children through Jesus Christ, entitled to share in his inheritance as God's Son, is addressed to "the *saints* who are in Ephesus and are faithful in Christ Jesus" (Eph 1:1b NRSV). Many of the better manuscripts actually omit the phrase "in Ephesus," raising in the minds of some scholars the possibility that this was a circular form letter sent to many churches, with instructions to fill in the blank as appropriate for each congregation. Paul's letters to the congregation at *Corinth, contentious* and *competitive* as *that* church was, are *also* addressed to "the saints."

The point is, the early Christian church understood that sainthood is not a status bestowed on the dead. It is a vocation of the living—of all of those who believe in and respond to Jesus Christ, and who, by their faithful participation in his mercy and his ministry, "live for the praise of his glory" (Eph 1:12c NRSV)—the glory not only of heavenly honor, but the glory of the *stable* and the glory of the *cross*. "In [Christ] you also, when you had heard the word of truth, the gospel of your salvation, and had believed in him, were marked with the seal of the promised Holy Spirit"—in other words, our baptism;—"this is the pledge of our inheritance toward redemption as God's own people"—saints,—"to the praise of his glory" (Eph 1:13–14 NRSV). Or, in John's explanation of the coming of Jesus into the world, "[T]o all who received him, who believed in his name, he gave power to become children of God" (John 1:12 NRSV).

The Bible often uses words, like "power" and "glory," that you and I commonly associate with marbled halls and military prowess and shining spotlights. But when we look carefully at the scriptures, we learn that God's most powerful act had to do with the cry from a manger signaling a baby's ordinary hunger and the cry from a cross signaling a condemned man's cruel pain; we learn that God's glory was attested in a flutter of wings, to the great terror of some sleepy shepherds in a sleepy place, and a stone rolled away from an empty grave, to the great distress of some despondent disciples who were hiding from the authorities. God's power was used not to crumble mountains, but to soften hearts. God's glory was not displayed in a blaze of fireworks and a blare of trumpets, but in the touch of a hand and the words, "Your sins are forgiven, your faith has made you well." To be saints, to be dedicated to the service of God, to be Christ-like, to be adopted as God's own children, to receive the inheritance for which God has destined us from before time began, is all wrapped up in the ministry and sacrifice of the one who pitched his tent among the sinful, among the sick, among the hungry, among the orphaned, among the widowed, among the foreigners, among those who had never had *anyone* say to them that they were worth God living and dying for *them*.

But it's true! They are the very ones whom God had in mind all along for the exercise of divine power and heavenly glory. "See," God testified through the prophet Jeremiah,

> I am going to bring them from the land of the north,
>   and gather them from the farthest parts of the earth,
> among them the blind and the lame,
>   those with child and those in labor, together;
>   a great company, they shall return here.
> With weeping they shall come,
>   and with consolations I will lead them back,
> I will let them walk by brooks of water,
>   in a straight path in which they shall not stumble....
> They shall come and sing aloud on the height of Zion,
>   and they shall be radiant over the goodness of the LORD,
> over the grain, the wine, and the oil,
>   and over the young of the flock and the herd;
> their life shall become like a watered garden,
>   and they shall never languish again.
> Then shall the young women rejoice in the dance,
>   and the young men and the old shall be merry.
> I will turn their mourning into joy,
>   I will comfort them, and give them gladness for sorrow.
> I will give the priests their fill of fatness,
>   and my people shall be satisfied with my bounty,
>   says the LORD. (Jer 31:8–9b, 12–14 NRSV)

In the streets of medieval Assisi, a young man named Francis threw off his fine clothes, surrendered his privileged inheritance, and went out into the streets and countryside sponging lepers and begging food for the starving and living gently with all creatures and singing praise to God for the sun and the moon, for the birds and the flowers, and restoring joy and delight to the forgotten and the forlorn. He was a saint, long before history books called him that. He fulfilled the destiny of adoption as a child of God through God's own Son, Jesus Christ. You and I can be saints, too—not only *can be*, but *are*, when we testify in our lives to the great power and wondrous glory of God who pitched his tent among real people, who understood their real afflictions, who satisfied their real hunger, who bound up their real wounds, who forgave their real sins, who showed them real love. "To the saints who are in Spanish Springs and are faithful in Christ Jesus: Grace to you and peace from God our Father and the Lord Jesus Christ."

Epiphany of the Lord
Spanish Springs Presbyterian Church, Sparks, Nevada
January 6, 2009

Isaiah 60:1–6
Ephesians 3:1–12
Matthew 2:1–12

"To Make Everyone See"

A few weeks ago, people all over the world witnessed an unusual sight in the evening sky—the near conjunction of the new moon and Venus and Jupiter. Even before they heard anything about it on the news or read about it in the paper, people were aware that they were witnessing something out of the ordinary, an aligning of the celestial bodies that might happen but once in a lifetime. In the simplicity of three shining lights against a void shading imperceptibly from blue to black, we observed a beauty that no human invention could rival. And many of us were struck with a sense of wonder. It didn't last very long each night, as the moon continued its progression toward the western horizon and as all the other stars came into view, camouflaging the two planets. And as the days went by, the two planets themselves migrated farther and farther apart. But for a few evenings, and for a few moments each evening, only the most self-absorbed person, or someone unfortunate enough to be confined indoors, could have missed the heavenly display.

Today, we know the science of it. Textbooks explain the occurrence in terms of the most natural phenomena. But the event still drew our fascination and prompted our awe. Imagine the attention we would give it if we *didn't* know that it was a natural, even a predictable, happening—the wonder it would elicit, the curiosity, the reverence, even.

In several passages in the New Testament, we are warned against astrology, against the notion that the lights in the night sky have any influence over human lives or world events. They are instances of the "powers and principalities" to which we are inclined to surrender too much authority, along with our more modern supposed determiners of fate such as economics and politics and biology and psychology. Many ancient religions were based on presumed connections between the location of stars and planets and the history of individuals and nations. In many cultures, great respect was accorded to people who studied the sky and made predictions and pronouncements based on the way the shining lights were aligned. But on at least one occasion, a bright shining star, newly appearing in the western sky, played a prominent and positive role in the story told by scripture, and in God's plans for the salvation of this world that God created along with all the other stars and planets in the universe. Wise men in the East—probably astrologers—observed the phenomenon, deemed it significant, and traveled to where the star came to rest in the heavens. Such astral events, they believed, heralded the birth of an important personage onto the world stage, such as a new king. These particular wise men made the effort to travel a good distance on the strength of their trust that the light would reveal a truth that *they* and *all* people should know about. And they brought with them gifts precious and rare.

Christians in the *twenty*-first century might not recognize as fully as the members of Matthew's *first*-century church the significance of some of the particulars of this story. We are not as well schooled in the Old Testament prophets as they were. But even our modern ears must have pricked up at tonight's reading from Isaiah, a reading that perhaps has had a part in filling in some of the details of the popular picture of the wise men's visit: not only the offerings of gold and frankincense being brought as gifts for the Lord, but the specific mention of the coming of kings to the bright light, and the reference to camels.

> Arise, shine; for your light has come,
>   and the glory of the Lord has risen upon you.
> For darkness shall cover the earth,
>   and thick darkness the peoples;
> but the Lord will arise upon you,
>   and his glory will appear over you.
> Nations shall come to your light,
>   and kings to the brightness of your dawn.
> Lift up your eyes and look around;
>   they all gather together, they come to you:
> your sons shall come from far away,
>   and your daughters shall be carried on their nurses' arms.
> Then you shall see and be radiant;

> your heart shall thrill and rejoice,
> because the abundance of the sea shall be brought to you,
> the wealth of the nations shall come to you.
> A multitude of camels shall cover you,
> the young camels of Midian and Ephah;
> all those from Sheba shall come.
> They shall bring gold and frankincense,
> and shall proclaim the praise of the Lord. (Isa 60:1–6 NRSV)

Isaiah was speaking of a glorious day in which Israel's prestige and power, obliterated by Babylon, would be restored, and Israel's God, whom Israel had disobeyed and not worshiped properly, would be recognized by the entire world as the one true God to whom all honor and all offerings are due. Matthew perceived in the coming of wise men from far away, following a star and bearing presents of gold and frankincense and myrrh, the fulfillment of the prophecy—these visitors were the first of the multitude of nations that would eventually recognize in Christ the light of truth that reveals the glory of God. And in that event, not only will *God* be glorified, but those who *worship* God will be glorified as well—*radiant*, even. The showing forth of the light of God in Jesus Christ will be the occasion for *us* to arise and shine, to reflect the glory of the Lord that has arisen not impersonally and anonymously, but upon *us*.

Isaiah bade a demoralized nation, freed from exile but languishing in despondency far from its potential, to awaken to the light and fulfill the purpose for which it was created—to give witness with its social and political and economic and religious life to the truth of God intended for all the world. Even *non*-Jews, *Gentiles*, would come to Jerusalem to worship and make sacrifices on the temple altar. So Matthew bade the *church* to rise above *its* obstacles and frustrations to be what God created *it* to be and to acknowledge with hope and gratitude the commission and opportunity it had been given to point even the *Gentiles* to the God of Abraham and Isaac and Jacob, who was also the God of its Lord Jesus Christ. So all people will come to worship him and honor him with their devotion and their obedience.

In Matthew's time, stories were told that the births of Isaac and Moses many years previous had been announced by the appearance of stars. Not long before Matthew wrote his Gospel, an embassy of Parthian magi had traveled to Naples to pay homage to the Roman emperor Nero. In the circumstances of the birth of Jesus, Matthew discerned the truth that the traditions of his people and the headlines of his own time and the sacred writings of the prophets had hinted at or shouted. The one urgent truth of eternity had been hidden under the *partial* truths of history and religious impulse. But now, the truth of eternity had been revealed fully. Not everyone had recognized it yet, not even the people who should have been most keenly attentive to it—the Jews, and their religious experts. The leader of their government even wanted to *suppress* it, to make sure that it *never* became known, to stop it before it eclipsed the lies that propped up his throne and kept his subjects subservient.

But the insight of the prophet was more potent than the blindness of scholars. The authority of God was greater than the claims of Herod. Despite human scheming and notwithstanding sinful incomprehension, everything that God had promised was in fact coming to pass. The nations were starting to come to the light—even wise men from a Gentile land—as kings coming to the brightness of Israel's dawn. They were not coming to pay homage to the despot enthroned in the palace, but to the infant laid in a crib. Perhaps the press hadn't picked up on it yet, maybe academics had not tumbled to the fact, it might not have been something that the trend-setters and jet-setters had noticed, but it was happening nonetheless. And Matthew's hope was that the people would lift up their eyes and look around, would see the light that had dawned upon the world, would glorify God by acknowledging what even these *Gentiles* had glimpsed—from little, insignificant, disdained Bethlehem was coming a ruler who would shepherd God's people Israel, the one before whom every person on earth and in heaven should kneel down and worship.

The truth that Matthew was declaring was not simply a history lesson for his congregation. It was a challenge to the whole church. Showing forth the light of God's glory in Jesus Christ, proclaiming the truth that it was none other than God's own Son whom the wise men found in Bethlehem, is the enduring work of the church—to make everyone see. The veils of ignorance must fall. The walls of division must be dismantled. The light of God's glory must be shed abroad upon every dusky corner and into every dismal abyss. The mystery must be revealed: the Gentiles, as Ephesians testifies, "have become fellow heirs" with descendants of Abraham and Isaac and Jacob, "members of the same body, and sharers in the promise in Christ Jesus through the gospel" (Eph 3:6 NRSV). No one is excluded from God's love. No one is excepted from God's forgiveness. No one is left out of God's promise. No one is to be abandoned in darkness. And therefore *everyone* should come to worship God in Jesus Christ *together*, bearing gifts of great worth to be laid before him, bowing down in homage, and—here is the essential point for Matthew's audience—sharing in Christ's glory by reflecting his light upon others. No more than the ancient nation Israel does the church exist for its own pleasure. As *Israel* was chosen to do, so the *church* exists to glorify God. And the miracle is that, as it glorifies God by showing forth to all people God's truth in Jesus Christ, the church *itself* will be, is, *glorified*, becomes a great shining star revealing the truth, lighting the way, welcoming people of every nation, of every race, of every condition, without distinction, without exception, without discrimination.

Israel's long hope was realized in Jesus Christ, though some did not know it, chose to ignore it, decided even to reject it. The grace given to the church is that it should be the agent of making the hope of Israel available to all humankind. The truth should be allowed to illuminate all people. Everyone should be given the opportunity to see. It is not just for the church, certainly not for just a few individuals who regard themselves as especially worthy or entitled. Indeed, the church's very reason for existence is to make everyone see the glory of God in Christ—even "the rulers and authorities in the heavenly places" (Eph 3:10b NRSV), as Ephesians says. And fulfilling that task is the church's, and Spanish Springs Presbyterian Church's, glory. How are *we* glorifying God in Jesus Christ?

Baptism of the Lord
Spanish Springs Presbyterian Church, Sparks, Nevada
January 12, 2003

Genesis 1:1–5
Acts 19:1–7
Mark 1:4–11

"Unwrapping the Gift"

If you are like I am, you're always hopeful that, sometime soon after Christmas, perhaps as the Christmas tree ornaments are being put away or the living room furniture is being rearranged after the tree has been taken down, you'll find one last gift, wrapped up and addressed to you and just waiting to be opened, having been overlooked on Christmas morning, stuck in the branches of the tree or pushed under an end table. And immediately, of course, you sit down, all full of anticipation, and remove the wrapping paper to see what little delight is inside. One year in Kansas, my wife and I decided to try to combat the paper-ripping, glance-at-the-gift-and-toss-it-aside-to-reach-for-another syndrome that threatened to undo our careful attempts to nurture gratitude in our children. Our plan was to parcel out the Christmas presents over the twelve days of Christmastide. We abandoned the project, however, on about the third day of Christmas. By that time, we had already been made to feel like criminals something on the scale of the Grinch, even, perhaps, bordering on being child abusers. Actually, we were feeling a little awkward even without the children's accusations. There was something about gifts sitting under the tree still wrapped, days past Christmas, that violated our sense of the season, especially as the Christmas school break began to wind down to a precious few days of playtime.

Gifts, of course, are meant to be *unwrapped*, because if they *aren't* unwrapped, they can't be used and appreciated. Wrapped gifts might be aesthetically pleasing, particularly the ones with fancy bows and bright-colored paper, but the wrapping itself, attractive and teasing as it might be, isn't the *gift*. Perhaps that is why Mark the evangelist didn't write about the birth of baby Jesus in a cattle stall, or shepherds coming to admire the baby Jesus or wise men coming to bring *him* gifts, but got right to the point in his Gospel by starting with the *baptism* of Jesus, preceded only by a very brief explanation of his importance as heralded by John the Baptizer. "In those days Jesus came from Nazareth of Galilee and was baptized by John in the Jordan. And just as he was coming up out of the water, he saw the heavens torn apart and the Spirit descending like a dove on him. And a voice came from heaven, 'You are my Son, the Beloved; with you I am well pleased'" (Mark 1:9–11 NRSV). Jesus' birth is a wonderful story, winsome and delightful. But Jesus' *baptism* was the event that launched Jesus into his ministry of defying Satan and preaching repentance and calling disciples and healing those who were sick in body and spirit.

Our children are very careful observers of everything that goes under the Christmas tree. They keep a detailed mental record of what gift is for whom, as they examine with their eyes and their fingers and sometimes with their ears and even their nose anything with their name on it. Their mother and I sometimes wonder why we even *bother* wrapping things, when the children have most of them figured out before the wrapping paper is removed. Oh, but once in a while, they really get fooled. You can't do much with a bicycle, of course, but there have been a few times that we have stumped them, when a box looks just rather square and ordinary, but, upon opening it, they find something unusual and not shaped at all like the box in which it was packaged.

Babies were born every day in Palestine, even, perhaps, in Bethlehem—nothing special, it seemed. Except for some shepherds with a lunatic story about angels and some vagabond eccentrics chasing stars, no one would have thought the birth of a baby portended anything extraordinary. But when the heavens were torn apart, and a voice announced from heaven the unique goodness of the man kneeling in the waters of the Jordan River at John's invitation, God unwrapped the extraordinary gift of his Son for our salvation. The ambiguity of a birth from a mother's womb was gone. The miracle of a birth from heaven above was confirmed. And the importance of Jesus the Son of God was manifest, not only to shepherds "living in the fields, keeping watch over their flock by night" (Luke 2:8 NRSV), charming as that was, not only to wise men from the East who came asking, "Where is the child who has been born king of the Jews? For we observed his star at its rising, and have come to pay him homage" (Matt 2:2 NRSV), impressive as that was, but, much more significant for you and me, the importance of Jesus, the Son of God, was manifest in his daily obedience to God and in his daily service to people who were in spiritual and physical need and in his daily preaching the will of his heavenly Father and in his daily love of God and neighbor.

One of the reasons that the Presbyterian Church, with the whole Reformed family of faith, strongly encourages parents to present their children for baptism as soon as practicable, is because the sacrament of baptism is not some milestone to be achieved or some reward to be bestowed upon reaching a certain number of years or a particular level of knowledge. The sacrament of baptism is a gift of God that marks the *beginning* of the life of faith, not the *attainment* of faith. It is the church's testimony to the reality of God's promise in each person's life from the moment we're born. It is the testimony of the faithful to the Holy Spirit's work within us toward God's purpose of salvation and wholeness and engrafting into Christ.

Jesus wasn't baptized *after* God expressed approval of Jesus, or *after* Jesus had resisted temptation in the wilderness. Jesus' baptism was the occasion for God's announcement of who Jesus was, and the time at which Jesus received empowerment for his life of obedient ministry. So far as Mark is concerned, Jesus' life up to that point, while it might have been interesting, did not signal the identity of who Jesus was, did not demonstrate the significance of what Jesus did, did not testify to the crucial importance of Jesus for every human being in the world. Jesus might have been a beautiful baby. But the importance of Jesus was that he was the Christ, *is* the Christ, the one to whom the law and the prophets point, the one who *fulfills* the law and the prophets, the Messiah, God's very own Son. And it was in the swirling waters of the Jordan River that his life was stamped with God's imprint. It was in baptism that his destiny was confirmed—the gift of the baby in the manger was unwrapped, if you will—and, by the descent of the Holy Spirit upon him and the voice of God attesting his favor, he was marked and set aside and empowered to teach, to preach, to forgive, to heal, and to die for the salvation of the world. The baptism of Jesus, Mark tells us, was the event in which Jesus' identity was established and made known.

According to Paul, it is in *our* baptism that *our* identity is made known. It is in the event of water poured on our heads in the name of the Father, Son, and Holy Spirit that we are known for who we truly are. Jesus was who God *said* he was—God's own Son. And *we* are who God says *we* are—in Christ Jesus, God's own sons and daughters. Our Christian baptism is our unwrapping—when what we are is declared to all the world—an identity that is unfolded, that gains meaning, as our lives as children of God unfold in our actions and our speech, until our earthly story comes to a close at our Christian funeral. Christ was God's great gift to all humankind, once for all, complete, unique. But the way people today *know* of that gift, understand the *meaning* of that gift, its *importance* and its *significance*, is through the lives *you and I* lead as baptized people, the witness *you and I* give by way of our generosity and our kindness and our compassion and our mercy and our love and our hope—qualities not native to us as an earthly inheritance, but gifts of the Holy Spirit to be exercised in Christ's name. Our birth was an ambiguous event insofar as determining what we would grow up to be like. The people we would become would depend upon *God's* choice of *us*, and *our* choices in response to *God*. As children of God, we are new creations, born *not* just of the *flesh*, but also of the *Spirit*. No wonder Paul was in such a hurry to baptize in the name of the Lord Jesus the people he found in Ephesus whose experience of faith had been limited to John's baptism of repentance! The gift that they were *from God to the world* was yet to be unwrapped!

Until our identity is revealed in the waters of baptism, even the good things we do or might do and the truth we speak or might speak are ambiguous. Even our *best* deeds, unless we do them at Christ's command and in Christ's name, are ambiguous; they might be done to serve our own reputation, they might be done for the sake of our personal profit, they might be done in order to make us feel good. But to do them as people baptized in the name of the Lord Jesus puts them in a whole new, and much clearer, light. All murkiness and amorphousness are gone. Mark and the other Gospel writers, in reporting Jesus' baptism, well remembered the Bible's testimony about God's *first* creation. "In the beginning when God created the heavens and the earth, the earth was a formless void and darkness covered the face of the deep, while a wind from God swept over the face of the waters" (Gen 1:1–2 NRSV). Until God's Spirit moved over it, the watery sphere, by itself, was an incomplete creation, indefinite at best, ominous at worst—desolate, unproductive, threatening. But then God gave shape to what was a "formless void." God made something of it by divine word and divine will. Water and Spirit together brought forth a new creation according to God's purpose.

The writers of the New Testament saw in the creation of the world a way of explaining what happens to *us* when *we* are *baptized* in water and the Spirit of God descends upon *us* as it descended on Jesus, declaring his relationship to God and authenticating his words and his actions and empowering him for his life of sacrifice for our salvation. In baptism, our lives are marked for goodness. In baptism, we are set aside for service. In baptism, our destiny of producing works of faith and love, of peace and hope, of righteousness and mercy, resistive to Satan and dedicated to God, is proclaimed. In baptism, at whatever age, our identity is declared as being God's own person, a brother or sister of God's Son, Jesus Christ. The ambiguity is over. The gift is unwrapped. God reveals who we truly are. And, if we are receptive to God's Holy Spirit, our lives will be a clear and consistent *testimony* to our identity, and, at life's end, our baptism will be completed in God's pronouncement, "Come, my child, my joy and my delight, into your heavenly home; I recognize you—you are mine. With you I am well pleased."

At the end of his Gospel, when he told of Jesus' death on the cross, Mark used the very same word to describe the tearing of the curtain of the temple in two as he had used at the beginning of his Gospel to describe the tearing apart of the heavens when Jesus was baptized. And a Roman centurion, of all people, who stood facing him, who must have seen for himself or heard from others what Jesus had done during his earthly life, and what Jesus had said, confirmed the identity of Jesus that God had declared at Jesus' baptism: "Truly this man was God's Son" (Mark 15:39b NRSV)!

It is past Christmas now. The delightful and intriguing wrappings of the shepherds and the manger and the wise men are gone—must be torn off and cast aside as the nativity set is packed safely away until next Christmas—so that Jesus can be revealed as God's Son, and get on with the crucial work of salvation. And in our baptism, the time of ambiguity in our lives comes to an end, whether as an infant or a youth or an adult, as our identity is declared and we are acknowledged to be who we really are, apart from all the *world's* judgments, apart from all the *world's* titles, apart from all the *world's* demands, apart from all the *world's* expectations: we are God's own children, bathed in the water and empowered by the Holy Spirit to fulfil our calling as new creations born from above. What a waste it would be to leave the gift all wrapped up.

Second Sunday in Ordinary Time
Spanish Springs Presbyterian Church, Sparks, Nevada
January 18, 2009

1 Samuel 3:1–20
1 Corinthians 6:12–20
John 1:43–51

"Come and See"

Today is the second Sunday after the feast of the Epiphany. "Epiphany" comes from a Greek word that means to "show forth" or to "manifest." The day of Epiphany on the Christian calendar commemorates the revealing of Jesus as the Christ to the wise men, Gentile visitors who came from faraway lands in search of Jesus, or, rather, how on their arrival they knelt down and paid him homage, some of the first people to recognize his divine identity. They perceived that Jesus was the *true* king of the Jews, fulfilling the scriptures. Epiphany is "Twelfth Night," January 6th, the end of the twelve days of Christmas. And the Gospel passages we will be reading between Epiphany and Lent all have to do with the Epiphany theme—the revelation of Jesus as the Son of God.

In the story of scripture, all sorts of people are coming to see that Jesus is no ordinary person—not even an ordinary teacher or healer or miracle-worker. The signs he does, the wisdom he possesses, the words he says—all of these are so *extra*ordinary that they could *only* come from God. For no *ordinary* teacher or healer or miracle-worker could know and say and do the things *Jesus* does. And no *ordinary* teacher or healer or miracle-worker requires of *us* a reaction, a decision, about that person's identity, the way *Jesus* does. Scripture makes it clear it cannot be a matter of *indifference* to us what Jesus knows and says and does.

But in our modern, twenty-first-century marketplace of ideas, a lot of people seem to regard Jesus as just one of *many* options for authority in their lives. To many folk, Jesus is like the roast beef that finds a place on the buffet table between the ham and the chicken: a lot of people these days assume they can take a little bit of this and a little bit of that and make a meal that satisfies their appetite for the moment—take some of the nice teachings of Jesus and mix them with a dab of astrology and perhaps a smattering of transcendental meditation, for instance. "It doesn't matter what you believe," some people say, "just so long as you believe *something*." "When you get right down to it," some people say, "Hinduism, Buddhism, Christianity—they all get us to the same place." "God is just an idea," some people say, "a nice, good, wonderful idea."

Those of us who have been in the Christian faith for many years are rightly appalled to realize that people think that the truth can be designed to suit by selectively sampling this and that, or that the truth can change from person to person. But even long-time Christians have a certain tendency to borrow some ideas from here and borrow some ideas from there and mix them all up on our platter of middle-class American Christianity, while ignoring completely much of what Jesus said and did and commanded *us* to do. Of course, it is nothing new. But the *freedom* with which it is happening today, in the *name* of personal freedom, is unprecedented. And the notion that one can *sort of* follow Christ while keeping one's religious options open, that Christ can *sort of* be Lord of one's life while we cling to comfortable prejudices and pleasurable indulgences and accustomed allegiances, runs the risk of making the term "Christianity" meaningless in our time. Is the truth of Christ absolute, or is it valid only until something less demanding comes along? Is Jesus the Son of God for us, who speaks and acts with the *authority* of God, or was Jesus just a *thinker* about God, whose ideas and behavior were suggestions and possibilities with no more ultimate claim on us than a Greek philosopher long dead or a cultic priest off on some remote South Sea isle? Are the words and deeds of Jesus no truer than those of any *other* wise and compassionate person?

The day after John baptized Jesus, Jesus again came by where John was, standing with two of *his* disciples, and John said to them, "'Look, here is the Lamb of God!' [John's] disciples heard him say this, and they followed Jesus. When Jesus turned and saw them following, he said to them, 'What are you looking for'" (John 1:36b–38a NRSV)? They asked Jesus where he was staying. "'Come and see'" (John 1:39a NRSV). And they did so, and *stayed* with Jesus. "The next day Jesus decided to go to Galilee. He found Philip and said to him, 'Follow me'" (John 1:43 NRSV).

It seems that Philip did so, and by watching and listening, and remembering what John the Baptizer had said about Jesus, Philip came to perceive that he was the Messiah. And "Philip found Nathanael and said to him, 'We have found him about whom Moses in the law and also the prophets wrote, Jesus son of Joseph from Nazareth.' Nathanael said to him, 'Can anything good come out of Nazareth?' Philip said to him, 'Come and see'" (John 1:45–46). And Nathanael did so. "When Jesus saw Nathanael coming toward him, he said of him, 'Here is truly an Israelite in whom there is no deceit'" (John 1:47 NRSV)! Nathanael, who seems to have been skeptical by nature, asked Jesus how he knew anything about him. "Jesus answered, 'I saw you under the fig tree before Philip called you'" (John 1:48b NRSV). Sitting under a fig tree was the place that rabbis said was the best place to study the Torah, the law of God, so Nathanael must have been sitting reading the scriptures when Jesus first noticed him—noticed that Nathanael was a person eager to understand the things of God. Nathanael was astounded that Jesus had spotted him and now possessed such knowledge about him. And Nathanael, no longer the skeptic, replied to Jesus, "Rabbi, you are the Son of God! You are the King of Israel" (John 1:49 NRSV)! What the wise men from the East had recognized years before in Jesus' infancy, now his own countrymen were only just beginning to discover. Jesus answered, "Do you believe because I told you that I saw you under the fig tree? You will see greater things than these" (John 1:50 NRSV). And in the very next scene, in the presence of the disciples at the wedding feast in Cana, Jesus performed the first of what John's Gospel called his "signs"—he turned water into wine. "Jesus . . . revealed his glory," the Gospel says, "and his disciples believed in him" (John 2:11 NRSV).

Just as the *doubts* of *Thomas* at the *end* of John's Gospel gave way to a burst of confession that the *risen* Christ was his Lord and his God, so here at the *beginning* of John's Gospel *Nathanael's skepticism* gave way to a burst of confession that the *earthly* Jesus was the Son of God. We can perhaps forgive Nathanael's first incredulous reply, "Can anything good come out of Nazareth" (John 1:46a NRSV)? After all, if Nathanael was indeed a student of the scriptures, he knew that Nazareth—that little village hidden among the hills of Galilee—was not mentioned *anywhere* in the Bible, had figured *not at all* in the prophecies of the Jews, and had never had *anything significant* happen in it, so far as the writers of scripture were concerned. So what could possibly be so remarkable about "Jesus son of Joseph from Nazareth" that Nathanael's friend Philip declared Jesus to be the one written about by "Moses in the law and also the prophets?" What made *him* different from anybody *else* who was so-and-so's son from the boondocks? What made anything *he* said more important than any self-help book on the library shelf, or any seller of secret potions, or any pretender to be something unique? What made *him* someone so special that Nathanael would want to set down his scrolls about the promises of God and follow? Scripture doesn't say Jesus had a halo around his head, or any other physical clues that gave away his divine origin. Only *faith* can lead a person to understand that Jesus is the Son of God. And it is Jesus *himself* who *awakens* such faith, by his words and his deeds, by his truth and his majesty—not just his words and deeds back *then*, but the words he speaks and the deeds he performs even *now*, through his *church*, that *continue* to reveal his truth and his majesty.

No one can be coerced into believing in Jesus. No one can be argued into faith in Jesus. Philip merely invited Nathanael to do what Jesus himself had invited Andrew and the other disciple of John to do: "Come and see" (John 1:39a NRSV). And when they came and saw, and observed and listened, they understood that in spite of all his earthly lowliness, in spite of his insignificant home town and unimpressive human parentage, even, Jesus came from *God*, Jesus *spoke* and *acted for* God, Jesus, in fact, in a miraculous way, *embodied* God. And those who were willing to leave all other allegiances behind, and those who were willing to see with clear vision, chose to *follow* Jesus and become *his* disciples.

A person's decision whether or not to be a disciple of Jesus cannot be separated from the decision he or she makes about who Jesus *is*—about Jesus' *identity*. And to recognize that Jesus is indeed God's own Son, and then to give oneself up to Christ's lordship, requires *more* than just a mental nod to him. It requires *more* than being able to recite the facts of his life and repeat the story of his death. It means an active *engagement* with Jesus—a committing of oneself to his truth, a risking of oneself on his call, a depending on him in every instance of life as the living and perfect expression of the will and wisdom of God. "What are your looking for?" Jesus had asked the people who came to him. If they weren't looking for the Son of God—the very *embodiment* of the *truth* of God—they probably wouldn't recognize him as such. This king of the Jews wasn't born in a palace, didn't have an army, never levied taxes. But he transformed every moment into a taste of eternity, turned every sorrow into joy, redeemed every defeat into triumph. He searched every human heart and, for those who were *open* to his truth, he satisfied their deepest yearnings. "Rabbi," said Nathanael, "you are the Son of God" (John 1:49a NRSV)!

Last Sunday morning, we began an adult class focusing on developing our ability to speak easily about our faith, to share the good news, and last Wednesday evening we offered the first installment of an introduction to the Christian faith. As we look around on Sunday morning, we see that evangelism is going to be necessary if we are to grow as a new church. But it's not only a matter of *survival* for a new congregation. It is also a special *calling* for a new congregation. Older churches tend to become preoccupied with the maintenance of their organization and, perhaps unintentionally, it is easy for them to put on the back-burner the task of communicating the gospel *outside* the church. For a new church development, communicating the gospel to others has to be of front-burner importance. And the simplest way of doing that, I think, is the invitation that Jesus gave to the disciples, and which the disciples, in turn, gave to their friends and acquaintances: "Come and see."

It all begins with "Come and see." For it is not you or I who bring other people to faith, but Jesus himself, at work through the Holy Spirit. But people first need to be invited to where Jesus can be found. ("Rabbi," the two disciples of John said, "where are you staying" (John 1:38b NRSV)? And Jesus said to them, "Come and see" (John 1:39a NRSV)). Jesus has promised to be present and at work in and through the church. The people of this congregation, most of us anyway, keenly sense Christ alive and at work here in this place, among us. And when people come to where Jesus is present and at work, and if their hearts and minds are open to his majesty and power, his words and his deeds, they will discover that Jesus meets their needs and fulfills their yearnings. But, first, someone has to say to them, "Come and see"—someone who has already *found* Jesus to be the Messiah, someone like you or me. Our task is not to *argue anyone* into faith in Jesus. Our task is not to *threaten anyone* with damnation or misfortune if they *don't* have faith in Jesus. Our task is not to compel *anyone* to do something against his or her will. Our task is simply to give witness to our belief that the living Christ is the Messiah, the Son of God, and to invite others to come and see. And whoever has eyes to see and ears to hear is promised a ringside seat at great things. "Very truly, I tell you," said Jesus, "you will see heaven opened and the angels of God ascending and descending upon the Son of Man" (John 1:51 NRSV). In the ministry of Christ through his church, the followers of Jesus will witness the glory of God.

"Can anything good come out of Nazareth?" That's another way of asking, "Can anything important come out of Spanish Springs? Can anything extraordinary be happening in a rented storefront on a Sunday morning?"

Come and see.

Third Sunday in Ordinary Time
Spanish Springs Presbyterian Church, Sparks, Nevada
January 26, 2003

Jonah 3:1–5
1 Corinthians 7:29–31
Mark 1:14–20

"Leopard's Spots"

Mark is not only the *shortest* of the four Gospels in the New Testament. It is also the most *compact* of the Gospels. As we are seeing in our Sunday morning adult class that is an introduction to the book, one of the literary techniques Mark frequently uses is summary sentences that compress a lot of activity over a long period of time into a very short statement. Many miles and many days are sometimes condensed into a few words, giving the gist of the matter. That doesn't mean that the subject is unimportant; in fact, the summary sentence often serves as a guide to understanding the events that Mark does report in greater detail. One such example is the first part of our Gospel reading today: "Now after John [the Baptizer] was arrested, Jesus came to Galilee, proclaiming the good news of God, and saying, 'The time is fulfilled, and the kingdom of God has come near; repent, and believe in the good news'" (Mark 1:14–15 NRSV).

How often, and in how many settings, Jesus preached about the fulfillment of time and the presence of God's kingdom and the need to repent and the invitation to believe the goodness of it all, Mark doesn't enumerate. The point is this was what Jesus was doing not only on the occasions Mark *doesn't* report, but this is what Jesus was doing on the occasions Mark *does* report. Mark then goes on immediately to tell about Simon and Andrew and James and John being called to follow Jesus and become fishers of people, and how these men immediately stopped what they were doing and did so.

The word "repent" means literally to turn around from the direction you're headed. Among other things, that means to *stop* doing what you're *doing* and *start* doing something *else*. We usually think in terms of stopping some pattern of sin, of evil, of wickedness. Very often, it involves just that—turning away from habits of wrongdoing and adopting the ways of virtue. But Jesus frequently linked repentance to belief. As Jesus used it, the term "repentance" seems to have as much to do with an overall *attitude* as with specific *actions*. Repentance is a way of seeing and perceiving, not just an abandonment of certain behaviors. Repentance is a matter of priorities and allegiances, not just a way of avoiding punishment. Repentance involves changing one's mind, not just bringing an end to certain activities. Repentance, in other words, has to do with rejecting everything that hinders a person from turning fully toward God. And, the time being fulfilled and the kingdom being at hand in the person of Jesus Christ, repentance becomes not only a stern demand; it is also a real possibility. Adages about old dogs learning new tricks are no longer true. The most amazing result of the teaching and preaching of Jesus Christ was to demonstrate that, by the grace of God, hearts *can* be changed and spirits *can* be righted. What seems *im*possible in terms of *human* effort and *human* achievement is *possible* with *God*. Leopards *can* change their spots.

Mark understood that to mean, among other things, that people who all their lives had baited hooks and cast nets into the sea could be Jesus' disciples, leaving behind their occupations—legal and honorable and with nothing at all sinful about them—to turn their attention fully to the kingdom of God. But to *follow* Jesus required having *faith* in him. And *faith* and *repentance* are two sides of the same coin—no one can genuinely *repent* without at the same time genuinely trusting Christ. No one can turn their backs on what they have known and been accustomed to and banked upon, unless they have faith that what they are turning *toward*, what is unfamiliar and untried, is better, is truer, is more important. It takes *faith* to abandon our previous securities. And of course Peter, Andrew, James, and John did so. Faith gave them the ability to repent, to turn around. Otherwise, surely, they could not have left behind in an instant their accustomed livelihood, their considerable investment, their family responsibilities—abandoning any and all of which was probably regarded by their relatives and neighbors as irresponsible in the extreme, even sinful, doing what everybody assumed was the wrong thing to do. Repentance, turning *toward God*, in the case of the *disciples*, meant turning *away from* the common notions of respectability and duty, not just the easier choice of turning away from something you and I would identify as *sin*.

Christians have sometimes misapprehended what Christianity and discipleship are all about. Christianity is not just a matter of turning away from obvious wickedness and toward the middle-class American way of life, motherhood, and apple pie. The summons to repent and believe more frequently comes to us as a call to turn away from something that is *good* toward something that is *better*, away from that which is *important* to that which is *ultimate*, away from overriding preoccupation with the *world* to life in the kingdom of *God*. And to *recognize* that is perhaps the key to recognizing that Jesus' call to repentance and belief is directed as much at *you* and *me* as at the most abject sinner.

Consider the story of Jonah going to Nineveh, identified by God as "that great city" (Jonah 1:2 NRSV) as well as wicked. The story told in the book of Jonah is a story of two cases of repentance, and the need for a third. After the episode of Jonah being swallowed by the big fish while he was trying to turn away from God, literally running in the opposite direction from where God told him to go, Jonah did as God commanded him to do, though without much interest or enthusiasm, it seems. He was to tell the people of Nineveh, the capital city of Assyria, that the city's days were numbered, that she was doomed because of her wickedness. Now, remember that Assyria was the nation that conquered the Northern Kingdom of Israel and dispersed many of its people into exile. Clearly, this was not a comfortable assignment for Jonah—going into the heart of the enemy's territory, though he might have otherwise relished the thought of Nineveh's destruction. The reluctant prophet went only about a third of the way into the city, and uttered a prophecy consisting of only five words in Hebrew. His whole attitude suggests that Jonah's warning of Nineveh's utter doom and destruction went something like this: "Forty days, Nineveh will fall." But what an effect those few words had! The people of Nineveh believed and repented—here those two things are joined already, long before Jesus' preaching about them—and the Ninevites proclaimed a fast and everyone put on sackcloth, the clothes of mourning. And when the king of Nineveh heard of it, he took off his robe and covered himself with sackcloth and sat on a pile of ashes. Talk about a leopard changing its spots! The king decreed that no one was to eat, no one was to drink—even the livestock were enlisted in the great show of sorrow, having no feed and no water and being draped with sackcloth. And everyone, the king decreed, was to turn from evil ways and from violence. "Who knows?" the king said. "God may relent and change his mind; he may turn from his fierce anger, so that we do not perish" (Jonah 3:9 NRSV). And when God saw the seriousness with which the Ninevites were taking the words of Jonah, how they believed God and turned themselves around so utterly, "God changed *his* mind about the calamity that he had said he would bring upon them; and he did not do it" (Jonah 3:10b NRSV).

So the king of Nineveh and all the residents of the city changed their ways—repented—and God changed *his* mind about their *destruction*—*God* repented. But Jonah, meanwhile, who had already judged Nineveh as worthy of whatever destruction God could throw at it, and even more, was *angry* at God's change of heart and *pouted* about God's salvation. Though he himself had earlier defied God's command by trying to run away from his appointed task, and showed no signs of repentance about *his* sinful disobedience, he was miffed by *God's* repentance, which was occasioned by *Nineveh's* repentance. He didn't *want* the leopard to change its spots. But *heathen Nineveh* had done *instantly* what *Jonah the Israelite* refused to do even *now*—to repent and believe *good* news.

Most of us know we must not commit sins like murder and adultery and theft, and, thankfully, most of us don't do these things. But all of us, to some degree or another, at some time or another, adopt priorities, fall into habits, and become enmeshed in the concerns of the world in ways that take our focus off of the kingdom of God. Often, it involves matters that sound reasonable and respectable, even pious. But they are penultimate, they are only subsidiary, to Jesus Christ. And some of the world's best people are capable of building family, occupation, patriotism, even volunteer service, into a barrier against readiness to answer Christ's call immediately and without question. You can well imagine that even ministers can erect such barriers with our routine of sermon-writing and program-administering and scheduling hospital visitation on Tuesday and Thursday (or is it Wednesday and Friday?), and offer the excuse of our very faithful ministry to nice people as a reason for *not* answering, in faith, Christ's call to follow him into the alleys where the addicts and the prostitutes and the beggars are, or as a reason for *not* answering, in faith, Christ's call to follow him by preaching against things we know to be wrong but which might upset our congregations and the important givers in them. It's not easy to throw the light of Christ upon the headlines, placing Jesus' command above opinion polls, heedless of the effect this will have on the security of a comfortable pastorate.

And yet scripture declares that none of us has the luxury of putting off repentance, putting off a change in our direction, putting off the choice to drop our nets and follow Christ. "I mean, brothers and sisters," wrote Paul,

> the appointed time has grown short; from now on, let even those who have wives be as though they had none, and those who mourn as though they were not mourning, and those who rejoice as though they were not rejoicing, and those who buy as though they had no possessions, and those who deal with the world as though they had no dealings with it. For the present form of this world is passing away. (1 Cor 7:29–31 NRSV)

Pretty harsh language. Irresponsible, some might even say—wives and husbands acting as if they weren't married, the bereaved putting off their grieving and the joyful putting off their gaiety. The point Paul was making, perhaps overstating somewhat in his fervent belief that Christ would return immediately, is that, good as marriage is, appropriate as mourning or joyfulness may be, they mustn't be the focus of our lives, certainly not our obsession. Nothing in the present world must be allowed to take our attention away from Christ's call and our readiness to respond to Christ's summons; nothing about life in the world must distract us from the infinitely *greater* importance of living in the kingdom of God. There have been too many cases of thieves and murderers and embezzlers and even perpetrators of securities fraud whose lives have been turned around, former scoundrels who have abandoned their old ways and charted a new course, to believe that leopards can't change their spots. The much *tougher* task of repentance is for you and me, good, respectable, responsible citizens, church-goers, spouses, children, parents, teachers, employees, employers, to repent and believe—to put our work and our family and our patriotism and even our church involvement, good and important as they are, into proper perspective so that we are always ready to follow immediately Christ's command to be his disciples, giving witness in everything we do to the kingdom of God, and to rejoice whenever someone else makes that same decision.

Can a leopard change its spots?

> Jesus came to Galilee, proclaiming the good news of God, and saying, "The time is fulfilled, and the kingdom of God has come near; repent, and believe in the good news."
>
> As Jesus passed along the Sea of Galilee, he saw Simon and his brother Andrew casting a net into the sea—for they were fishermen. And Jesus said to them, "Follow me, and I will make

you fish for people." And immediately they left their nets and followed him. As he went a little farther, he saw James son of Zebedee and his brother John, who were in their boat mending the nets. Immediately he called them, and they left their father Zebedee in the boat with the hired men, and followed him. (Mark 1:14–20 NRSV)

Fourth Sunday in Ordinary Time
Spanish Springs Presbyterian Church, Sparks, Nevada
February 2, 2003

Deuteronomy 18:15–20
1 Corinthians 8:1–13
Mark 1:21–28

"Yield to the Right"

I am a child of the sixties. My conscience and consciousness were formed by images of marches, of sit-ins, of boycotts, of bombings, of assassinations, of riots. I remember the picture on the front page of *The El Paso Times* of a minister being kicked in the face by a policeman in Little Rock, Arkansas, because the white minister gave witness to his conviction that public schools in the land of the free should be open to all, regardless of race. I remember the picture in *The Denver Post* of the owner of a chicken restaurant standing in the doorway of his establishment with a shotgun to bar entrance by people who were not of his color, and how that same man was later elected the governor of his state. I remember how difficult it was to get laws passed to guarantee equal pay for equal work despite one's gender. I remember the threats against a man who was trying to establish a union to secure the simplest tokens of human decency for Hispanic people who toiled in the fields. The decade began when I was nine years old, and it ended when I was nineteen. I am a child of the sixties.

So I am someone who heard and participated in a lot of discussions about rights—rights granted under the Constitution of our nation, but which had long been denied to African-Americans, to Native Americans, to women, to the poor, to those who did not agree with the prevailing political views or economic theories, and the inherent rights that are the heritage of each person created in God's image—and that's *everyone*—to be treated with dignity, with fairness, with compassion, with an acknowledgment that that person is to be cared for by each one of us as deeply as we care for ourselves. And, recognizing that whole classes of people have been denied those constitutional rights and God-given rights in the past (and, indeed, some are *still* being denied such rights *today*), I can't begrudge preferential treatment intended to make up for lost time, whether it be in the employment office or the admissions office.

But, in recent years, the term "rights" has become cheapened, has been trivialized. It is being invoked promiscuously by those who are already in a position of privilege, by those whom life has treated really rather well, on the whole, by those who can't even begin to *imagine* what it would be like to be excluded from hotels, from restaurants, from workplaces, from schools, from neighborhoods, from churches, from spiritual vocations, from sporting events, from the voting booth because of something over which that person has no control—his or her race, his or her gender, his or her economic class, his or her pedigree, maybe his or her sexuality. And so, the right to "free speech" is being appealed to in order to interrupt us with telemarketing calls repeatedly during the dinner hour, or to justify the emblazoning of every sort of vulgarity on T-shirts and bumper stickers, and freedom of thought and expression are appealed to in order to achieve new levels of shock and offense in art galleries and music recordings and movie theaters and on television, often, sadly, to rave reviews and high ratings. The fulfillment of any desire or impulse, it seems, is now considered to be a "right." And the seriousness and sacrifice of people like Dr. Martin Luther King are cheapened, are trivialized, in the process.

For the Christian, the solemn rights of our fellow creatures are, or should be, of utmost importance. We must promote them. We must never deny them. But, for the Christian, the assertion of our *own* rights is not, and must *never* be, superior to doing what is *right*. And sometimes that means refraining from exercising our rights out of deference to the welfare of others. Our rights, like every other gift from God, were given to be used always and only for the purpose of blessing others. When our assertion of our rights is rooted in our selfishness, or our greed, or our lust, or simply in our spite or our petulance, then the whole *concept* of rights is degraded, and God's loving purpose is mocked. When our demand to exercise *our* rights is more important to us than the well-being of our *neighbor*, then we have abandoned any possibility of having God as an ally in our cause, no matter how just we imagine it to be.

This seems to have been much at the heart of the problems in the church at Corinth. The basic self-centeredness that was afflicting the

Corinthian congregation manifested itself in many ways, one of which was an issue that might strike us as trifling and quaint, but in which the apostle Paul detected a real danger. There was apparently a great difference in the levels of sophistication among the Corinthian Christians, and it fell largely along the lines of social class and economic status. And there was also the strong influence of the various schools of Greek philosophy present among the privileged class, that tended to put a premium on thought and tended to disregard behavior. The members of the privileged class in Corinth were inclined to vaunt their superior knowledge—not just their command of facts and figures, but their perception of reality. In their congregational life, their emphasis on knowledge tended to manifest itself in their assertion that, since there is only one true God and therefore the idols of the pagans have no power, the various social and artistic and cultural reminders of paganism pose no problem for Christians.

Paul agreed with the substance of their knowledge. To put it in the modern context of discussions current among some fundamentalists, Paul would have had no problem with Harry Potter books or movies, recognizing that they are stories of fantasy, since we are well aware that there are no such things as wizards or sorcerers, and those people who pretend to be such have no power. They are immensely entertaining, and, by now, we know what special effects can do. But the situation would be different if, in our reading the books or going to see the movies, another Christian, perhaps new to the faith, was led to believe in wizards and sorcerers and to think they had real power. In the case of Corinth, the circumstance that had raised the issue was the eating of meat that had been sacrificed in the temples of the pagan gods. The well-heeled Corinthian Christians traveled in social circles in which they were often invited to dinner parties that were sometimes held in the dining rooms of the temples, where meat was served that had been barbecued on the altars. Presumably, not to eat what was offered would have been an offense to their hosts. So, they reasoned, since they knew the pagan gods weren't real, what difference did it make if they took part in the meal? And then there were the cultic festivals that were central to the social life of Corinth; to maintain one's social prestige, and to be a good citizen, was thought to require attending and participating in the various festivities held in conjunction with these observances. No harm there, either, they thought, since, again, they knew there was nothing real about the pagan gods.

Again, Paul agreed with them—they had a perfect right, as Christians who knew there is but one true God, to eat whatever they wanted to, to attend whatever parties they wanted to. The problem was, *some* of the members of the congregation thought such behavior served to acknowledge the *claims* of the pagan gods. More specifically, it seems that, in their defense of their visits to pagan temples and participating in pagan festivals and eating meat that had been offered to pagan idols, the more-sophisticated church members were encouraging their *less*-sophisticated Christian friends to do the same thing. Perhaps they justified it as a way of proving to them that food was food and wouldn't harm them. Paul agreed that, as far as *God* is concerned, food *is* food; what we eat makes us no less or no more holy. But, under the circumstances, it *might* harm them, Paul observed. It might be like the drink that is, by itself, modest in its effect, but, when offered to an alcoholic, could be his or her ruin. It might be the very thing that would start a slide away from Christ and back into paganism for that person who didn't have the intellectual strength or experience to distinguish between simply eating *meat* offered to an idol and investing *belief* in the idol. A reversion to paganism would be the spiritual ruin of *any* Christian. If it came to a choice between exercising his right to eat meat at all and the possibility of endangering the soul of a brother or sister for whom Christ died, Paul declared, he, for one, would rather give up his rights entirely than risk another's destruction. For the welfare of his brother or sister, Paul's personal rights must yield to what was the right thing to do—to refrain from his own desires, for the sake of his neighbor.

For the Christian, talking about one's own motives for doing something should focus not on *rights*, but on what is *right*, not on one's *knowledge*, but on one's *love*. Judging from the shows that seem to dominate daytime television these days—people screaming at each other in courtrooms, people screaming at each other in studios, people screaming at each other in bedrooms, asserting their selfishness and demanding their gratification, *our* culture is as mired in pagan concerns as Corinth *ever* was. Headlines and our own experience demonstrate that Christ-like humility and Christian servanthood are little in evidence on our streets or in our boardrooms. "Knowledge puffs up," wrote Paul, "but love builds up" (1 Cor 8:1c NRSV). Knowledge is not bad, not evil, not undesirable—certainly it is better than ignorance. But knowledge, as Paul contended and as the situation in Corinth proved, has limitations. It is useful only when it is fruitful, and the proper and only commendable fruit of knowledge is love. Paul didn't want Christians to be know-nothings, to deny the discoveries of science or the lessons of history. He certainly didn't disparage the knowledge that there is only one God, and that therefore the deities of the pagans are unreal and powerless. But those who claim to *know everything* tend to make *themselves* the measure of *all things*, which is its own denial of the one true God and an embrace of the world's standard. And when knowledge is used as a status marker or is used to place others in jeopardy of their souls, then knowledge has replaced love, and truth has gotten turned upside down.

Jesus' knowledge—the knowledge of God's will—caused him to shed every human right he could claim, let alone his rightful treatment as the Son of God—and submit, in humility and humiliation, even, to the cross for the sake of our salvation. In God's judgment, love trumps knowledge every time. Our focus should not be on *our* rights and privileges, but on the well-being of our sisters and brothers, even those who are weak in their apprehension of the oneness of God. Christ died for the weak. We must not do anything that would cause them to stumble. As one commentator on this passage puts it, whether Bible-thumping certainty about revealed truth, or serene confidence in the latest scientific findings, or passionate discernment of the right social cause, any knowledge that divides the community and causes the knowledgeable ones to despise those who are ignorant or uncertain is not being used in the service of God—in fact, it is being used in just the opposite way.

But he goes on to note that that doesn't mean the entire Christian community is to be held hostage to the standards of the most narrow-minded and legalistic members of the church. That wasn't Paul's point at all. Paul's concern wasn't about causing offense to the legalistic; his very ministry to the Gentiles was an offense to the conservatives. Paul's concern was that the weaker believers not be destroyed by being drawn away from faith in the one true God. Idolatry *can* lead to destruction. And that is why the Christian church should be wary of adopting the symbols and vocabulary of wealth, of ease, of nationalism, of military power, of self-gratification, of entertainment. It should inform every discussion from flags in sanctuaries to forms of church music to methods of evangelism to language about God. Do they point to the ways of the world and draw us away from allegiance to the one true God who is *above* all race and class and gender and nation, or do they risk confusing those who are less sophisticated in their faith, perhaps simply less experienced, so that Christianity looks to them only like a mishmash of patriotism and familyism and capitalism and moralism, any *one* of which can easily become our *idol*?

"[I]f food is a cause of their falling," Paul wrote, "I will never eat meat, so that I may not cause one of them to fall" (1 Cor 8:13 NRSV). Christian truth, whose supreme principle is love, involves humility, forbearance, restraint, even sacrificing now and then our *rights* for the far greater reward of *doing right* by our sister and brother. Above the din of voices asserting the right to do this or that, those whose knowledge consists in knowing that *they* are known by *God* hear Jesus' command to *love*. And, hearing that, they are content that their *rights* should yield to what is *right*.

Fifth Sunday in Ordinary Time
Spanish Springs Presbyterian Church, Sparks, Nevada
February 6, 2000

Isaiah 40:21–31
1 Corinthians 9:16–23
Mark 1:29–39

"The 'Whole' Gospel"

This morning's Gospel reading from the lectionary covers in a few brief verses a whole series of events in and near Capernaum on the shore of the Sea of Galilee, the town where Peter lived and where Jesus began his ministry. Among the things that Jesus did while in Capernaum were healing Peter's mother-in-law of a fever, curing others of their diseases, and casting out demons.

The subject of miraculous cures and exorcisms always raises questions in people's minds today. We don't live in a time or place where faith healing is a common experience. The whole subject may make us uncomfortable, especially those of us who come from the more rationalistic traditions of the Christian faith, like Presbyterianism. Our clan puts a lot of emphasis on education and reason. Over the centuries, we have been professors and doctors and jurists and scientists. And, as fairly sophisticated and intelligent people, our thoughts about miracle cures and exorcisms may be shaped as much as anything by our suspicions of charlatans and by headlines about scandals. We do not *discount* the importance of prayer and the effects of prayer. But, if we have ever prayed for a person who was ill and that person did *not* get better or perhaps even *died*, it may be confusing to us that the Gospels and the book of Acts speak so much about something that is so different from the way *we* have generally experienced the faith. Still, we mustn't deny the testimony of scripture. Of the 678 verses in Mark, for instance, *almost a third*—just under 200—are about *miracles*. And of the eighteen miracles reported in Mark as having been specifically worked by Jesus, thirteen of them are some sort of healing or other, including four exorcisms. And Mark is not unique. *All* of the Gospels report miracles of healing. So it is difficult for us to *ignore* such episodes, even if we would *like* to. But it is also *irresponsible* for us to *try* to ignore such episodes, because the writers of the Gospels were telling us something important about *Jesus* by including these stories. And, as Christians, we need not only to try to understand what they tell us about Jesus for the sake of our *own* faith, but we need to *pass on* that truth to *others* as *we* seek to be faithful *witnesses* to *Christ*.

But I suspect that the issue is more than just a matter of understanding about Jesus and about being faithful to our calling as Christians. I suspect a large part of the issue is that we, many of us, feel *cheated* in our faith. Why aren't such miracles of healing happening with *our* loved ones who are sick and perhaps dying? To say that God works miracles today through expensive wonder medicines and advanced but imperfect technology is not really very satisfying, compared to stories of Jesus just touching someone and they were well again. Jesus simply took Peter's mother-in-law by the hand and lifted her up from her bed, and the fever was gone and she was feeling well enough to serve them dinner! Aside from any discomfort with sexist stereotypes, that sure beats days and weeks and months of tests and therapies and surgeries, doesn't it? And dismissing demons with a word sure beats a dozen sessions with a psychiatrist. If God or Jesus only has to *will* it and a person is *cured*, why doesn't God or Jesus seem to want *our* parent well, or *our* child, or *our* friend, or even *us*? What is wrong with *our* faith that *we* aren't cured, or our *spouse*, or our *sibling*, when Mark doesn't say a *single word* about the faith of Peter's mother-in-law or most of the *other* people whom Jesus cured, either before or after they were made well? Is the lack of instant healing miracles in *our* experience due to *lack of faith*? Is faith *necessary* for healing? And if so, *whose* faith is *essential*? The sick person's? The healer's? Or the relatives' and friends' of the person who is sick? Is there any hope for patients who don't *accept* the healer?

Perhaps it would help if we stopped a moment to see *why* Mark and the other Gospels are telling us about these miracles at all. Perhaps it would help to ask the questions *they* were attempting to *answer*—questions not so much about "Exactly what really happened and exactly how did it happen?," but "What did this happening really mean and why is it important?" As always, we need to take the time to look at the *context* of the verses with which we are dealing.

In the Gospel of Mark, most of the miracles of healing come in the first half of the book. This is the part of the book in which Jesus is ministering in Galilee, before he goes to Jerusalem, before the religious authorities there plot to have him arrested. The Gospel of Mark is very much interested in exploring the question, "Who is Jesus?" Like all of the books of the Bible, Mark has its *own* questions and concerns, and to allow scripture to speak on its own terms we need to be cautious about imposing on an ancient writing *our* questions and understanding of the world and its natural processes and history. The Gospel of Mark is a *theological* statement, not a medical text or a how-to manual. It is concerned with revealing the truth of God in Jesus Christ. Think about it—just a few verses earlier, Mark has said, "Now after John was arrested, Jesus came to Galilee, proclaiming the good news of God, and saying, 'The time is fulfilled, and the kingdom of God has come near; repent, and believe in the good news'" (Mark 1:14–15 NRSV). And immediately, Mark shows us that Jesus began teaching and exorcising demons and healing sick people.

That word "epiphany" needs to be in our minds. Jesus' wondrous works in these chapters are showing forth God's merciful, mighty presence and gracious, wise governance. *This* is how Jesus is *proclaiming* the *nearness* of the *kingdom of God*—a realm that can be entered only by those who repent and believe the message about the good news Jesus is proclaiming. The miracle stories during Jesus' ministry in Galilee are stories that reveal Jesus' power, and questions about how Jesus came to *have* such power, and how and why Jesus *used* such power, are ways of exploring the *bigger* question of who Jesus *is*. The miracles of Jesus are deeds of compassion—this is not just another wizard, not just a magician, who is amazing people for his own financial benefit. He orders the demons he exorcises to be silent, and he commands his disciples not to run around trumpeting the miracles—this is not some publicity hound, someone out to stoke his own ego. Many of the miracles come about, Mark tells us, when Jesus has *pity* on the person who was sick or blind or lame or possessed. That says something about Jesus, and about the reasons behind his power.

But Mark implies that everything Jesus says and does all remains centered on the kingdom of God, a place where *God* is *sovereign* and where *God's* decisions are *final*, and upon the God who, free to work *miracles* even where faith is *un*voiced or even *absent*, must be free also *not* to work miracles even where faith is *proclaimed* and *fervent*. Jesus invites people to repent, to believe the gospel, and to follow him, and Mark is communicating that invitation to his readers. Anyone who *responds* to the invitation enters the gates of the kingdom of God and can expect to be infused with a strength that is beyond him- or herself. But such strength is not given to us simply to meet our *own* desires—not even the compassionate desires to heal our friends and our relatives. Jesus himself did not use his powers to avoid his *own* suffering and death. If anything, his *curing* people hastened his own *crucifixion*.

There was more to Jesus' ministry, of course, than his healing. And at about the time he seems to have been in danger of being thought of simply as a healer, however wonderful, he knew it was time to leave that place behind and get on with his broader ministry. He could have stayed there in Capernaum, no doubt, healing one person after another, and then healing them again when they had their *next* ailment, and their *next*, beloved and safe from the Jerusalem authorities in the relative obscurity of a little fishing village. And the people of Capernaum would have been some of the healthiest people in the world, but the rest of us would still be left chained in our sins without any assurance of forgiveness and doomed to death without any hope of eternal life. And so,

> [i]n the morning, while it was still very dark, [Jesus] got up and went out to a deserted place, and there he prayed. And Simon and his companions hunted for him. When they found him, they said to him, "Everyone is searching for you." [Jesus] answered, "Let us go on to the neighboring towns, so that I may proclaim the message there also; for that is what I came out to do." And [Jesus] went throughout Galilee, proclaiming the message in their synagogues and casting out demons. (Mark 1:35–39 NRSV)

And the nearness of the kingdom of God was proclaimed and shown forth—the place where God's will reigns not only in the matter of *health*, but also in the matter of peace and plenty and forgiveness and never-ending communion with all creation through Jesus Christ, God's own Son.

And if Jesus is the Son of God who healed the fever of Peter's mother-in-law so that she could get on with her role of serving—which is the task of *every disciple*—and if Jesus is the Son of God who banished the demons from people who were haunted by convulsive fears and tortured nightmares so that they could once again perceive reality clearly and respond to God's grace freely, then what does that tell us about the power of the Son of God to hold sway over the *host* of fevers that infect *our* lives—anxiety about popularity and nonstop moneymaking and the quest for the ultimate thrill—and to *tame* and *silence* the demons of drugs and alcohol and promiscuity and possessions in *our own* time?

The Bible is saying that such things are not the goals or the rewards that are worthy of the kingdom of God. But Mark is not pointing a finger at *anyone* whose relative is sick or whose child is obsessed with gangsta rap (or whatever this year's equivalent is). Mark does not provide any support for preachers anywhere to say that illness or marital discord or wayward children or unemployment or addiction is all your fault because you just don't have enough faith, and Mark certainly isn't saying that if you just *had* faith, or if you just had *more* faith, you wouldn't have any physical problems or family problems or financial problems or problems at work or problems at school or problems with your social life. *That is not the gospel.* The gospel does not support any notion that Jesus is our personal genie to be manipulated at our will and if we just rub the Bible hard enough he'll pop out and grant us three wishes.

But Mark *is* giving witness to the truth that Jesus has the power, and on specific occasions during his earthly ministry *used* it, and used it *generously*, to restore people to wholeness and to grant them peace by healing and exorcising, and by forgiving and feeding, and by encouraging and befriending, all demonstrating in *actions* what he was proclaiming in *words*—the nearness of the kingdom of God *for those who believe in him*, a kingdom where the will of God is supreme over microbes as well as dementia, just as the will of God is supreme over pride as well as self-reproach, and just as the will of God is supreme over greed as well as poverty, and just as the will of God is supreme over gluttony as well as hunger, and just as the will of God is supreme over sin as well as death.

"[R]epent," Jesus said—turn around from marching to the drums of the kingdoms of *this* world—the drums of the bad news of anxiety and war and tyranny and lust and materialism and every sort of idolatry and pagan desire—"and believe in the good news" (Mark 1:15c NRSV). Those things are not the will of God, and God is bringing a new kingdom whose reality is open to everyone who believes in the good news that Jesus is demonstrating. And, stretching out his hand to touch the fevered brow of an old woman, and searching deeply into the mind and heart of a man who was mad with hateful thoughts and destructive urges, the Son of God showed that the time is fulfilled indeed, and the kingdom of God has come near.

Sixth Sunday in Ordinary Time
Spanish Springs Presbyterian Church, Sparks, Nevada
February 15, 2009

2 Kings 5:1–14
1 Corinthians 9:24–27
Mark 1:40–45

"To Be Made Clean"

"Lord, I am not worthy to receive you," goes the Roman Catholic liturgy of the Mass, "but only say the word and I shall be healed." Those words, adapted from the story of Jesus' encounter with the Roman centurion who asked that he cure his servant, are spoken by the people before they receive the bread and the cup. It reminds communicants of the faith of the Gentile soldier that Jesus could make well again his servant even from a distance, even without touching the man or even seeing him, and the Gentile soldier's sensitive concern that Jesus not have to break the taboo about a Jew entering the house of a non-Jew. In the context of the eucharist, the Lord's Supper, it reminds communicants that none of us is worthy to receive God's gracious gifts, blemished as we are with sin, but that Christ's very word of mercy can and does cleanse us and render us welcome guests at his table. In the context of our weekly confession of sin and of the weekly pronouncement of forgiveness, it reminds us that Christ has healed us, has made us acceptable in his words from the cross, "Father, forgive them" (Luke 23:34a NRSV).

As we have seen from the Gospel readings over the past few weeks, healing and salvation are two aspects of the same gracious and merciful ministry of Jesus. Indeed, in Greek they are the same word, so it's a rather narrow judgment call by translators and editors which English word to use in a particular verse, depending upon their understanding of the context. But even to have to *make* the *choice* does some violence to the scope of what the *gospel* means by being made *whole*. Sickness was commonly thought to be the work of demons. And so, to be sick was to be considered ritually unclean, so that others could not come in contact with the person, and the person certainly could not take part in religious ceremonies, could not enter the temple. With some diseases, the ritual uncleanliness seemed to be confirmed by visual unsightliness.

That was especially the case with leprosy, a term which probably covered a whole variety of skin disorders. So serious was the disease considered to be, so strong the taboo against any contact with a leper, that people who were afflicted were supposed to announce their approach so others could keep their distance. "Unclean!" they were required to shout, or, in some cultures, to wear a bell that would signal they were nearby. The taboo seemed justified by the fact that those who came in contact with a leper often developed the illness themselves. And so the life of a leper was not only one of excruciating pain and unsightly ulceration and grotesque deformity, but of acute stigma, insult added to injury as the victim was cut off from family and friends, losing all social contact except the company of other sufferers just as miserable and just as bitter. "Lord, I am not worthy to receive you"—to receive you under my roof for hospitality, to receive your hospitality in the bread and the wine,—"but only say the word and I shall be healed"—only utter the word of forgiveness, of acceptance, of hope, and I shall be made whole, saved from being shunned and despised and avoided, saved from being cut off from everything beautiful and meaningful and loving. Rabbis regarded lepers as living corpses, and, bandaged as they sometimes were, their flesh ashen or black, so they must have appeared. To cure a leper was thought to be as difficult as raising a cadaver—in other words, a virtual impossibility.

So it was very remarkable, this encounter between Jesus and a leper who "came to him begging him, and kneeling he said to him, 'If you choose, you can make me clean.' Moved with pity"—some manuscripts say "anger,"—"Jesus stretched out his hand and touched him, and said to him, 'I do choose. Be made clean'" (Mark 1:40–41 NRSV)! The man himself broke a sacred taboo—broke through the rules of both social convention and religious obligation—by coming up to Jesus rather than warning Jesus away. And *Jesus* broke a sacred taboo—broke through the rules of both first-century hygiene and ritual prohibition—by touching the man and presuming to do what only *God* was thought able to do.

The priests were authorized to examine lepers who had somehow recovered from their disease and certify them fit to reenter society and synagogue, but *no* human being could presume actually to make someone clean, *no* human being was authorized to cancel someone's unholiness. What Mark is suggesting is that the leper, in some way or other, recognized, had faith, that Jesus was God. He didn't merely *ask* for *healing*. He affirmed that *Jesus* had the ability, the power and authority, to do what only *God* can do, and laid it before Jesus to decide whether he would: "'If you choose, you can make me clean'" (Mark 1:40b NRSV)—"you can make me acceptable again, Jesus, you can give me a life worth living again, you can return me to my family and my friends, you can save me." "'I do choose,'" Jesus replied. "'Be made clean!' Immediately the leprosy left him, and he was made clean" (Mark 1:41b–42 NRSV)—not merely a statement about the restoration of smoothness and color to the man's skin, but profoundly and even more importantly, the restoration of the man's spirit to the land of the living. If others were to find out, Jesus would be opening himself to severe criticism and punishment on the one hand, and being swarmed with the sick and the infirm on the other. But, tired as he was from the crowds that had been clamoring for his attention, wary as he was that his miracles of healing had caused people to misunderstand or not care about the truth of who he was and what he was teaching, Jesus could let no taboo of custom or prejudice stand in the way of the love of God, not even for a leper, or, perhaps, *especially* for a leper. The *healthy* people—the people who thought therefore they had committed no sin in their lives—would be *appalled*. But the *sick* and the *maimed*—the *desperate* ones—perceived that the *healer* was also the Savior. The touch of his hand, the word of his mouth, his very presence, made holy what had been unclean. The leper had to do nothing but recognize who Jesus was, rather like our approach to the table—"only say the word and I shall be healed."

Taboos bring to mind pagan practices, even primitive animistic religions, and the notion of elaborate rituals meant to safeguard against curses and undo the penalty for transgressions. The Aramean general Naaman was incensed that the prophet Elisha prescribed such an unceremonious cure for his skin disease as bathing seven times in the Jordan. Perhaps it wasn't so much a matter of taking a certain number of baths in a certain river, but seeing whether the pagan general had enough faith actually to humble himself by splashing in the waters of Israel. He was probably expecting some complex recitation of formulas, some intricate choreography of sacrifice and genuflection. After all, he didn't have to come all the way from *Damascus* just to take a bath! But, at the urging of his servants, he finally did what Elisha prescribed, and his skin was restored. Jesus' work of healing the leper was even simpler still. He did what the poor man *said* he could do, without incantations, without an "Abracadabra," but by the simple compassionate gesture of a gentle touch and an encouraging expression of acceptance—"'I do choose. Be made clean!'"—and "[i]mmediately the leprosy left him, and he was made clean" (Mark 1:41b-42). And I think those are two separate but related things—the disease vanished, which was well enough, but more importantly, and more to the point of who Jesus is and why he is unique, the taboo was broken, the stigma was removed, the man was restored to fellowship. He was healed. He was made whole. He was saved.

I think it can only be because he was tired and irritated by all the misunderstanding of his miracles that Jesus then said something that I believe was really rather nonsensical (stand back, a thunderbolt may strike me at any minute): "See that you say nothing to anyone" (Mark 1:44a NRSV). To cure a man of leprosy, to relieve him of his pain and his humiliation and his crushing sense of guilt, and then command him not to *tell* anyone? Did Jesus think people wouldn't *notice* that the man's skin had been falling off one day and was perfectly normal the next? Did Jesus think people might not say, "Couldn't help but noticing, old boy, that you're not a leper anymore"? Did Jesus think that people wouldn't ask, "How did you get well?" "[G]o, show yourself to the priest, and offer for your cleansing what Moses commanded, as a testimony to them" (Mark 1:44b NRSV). "The offerings of birds and lambs and cedarwood and hyssop and everything else that Leviticus 14 prescribes—do all those things and maybe the priests won't ask questions but just pronounce you clean like Leviticus scripted it. The fact that you're already clean, because I said so—that'll just be our secret."

Eventually, the man might have gone to Jerusalem and made his offerings and taken baths and shaved his hair and done everything else that Leviticus says to do, but of course, in the meantime, he couldn't keep quiet about the fact that he had been given a second chance at life, had been born again by the cleansing pronouncement of Jesus, and so "he went out and began to proclaim it freely, and to spread the word" (Of course he did!), "so that Jesus could no longer go into a town openly, but stayed out in the country; and people came to him from every quarter" (Of course they did!) (Mark 1:45 NRSV). They wanted to be made well. And some of them, maybe, even wanted to be *clean*, to be accepted again, *really* to be healed, to be saved. Jesus was not interested in merely restoring people *physically*, though he detected that would satisfy the crowds. Jesus came to restore people *spiritually*, which required restoring them *socially*. Jesus came to remove not only *disease* but *taboo* and *estrangement* and *rejection*. Jesus came to make people clean, with a touch and a word—a *compassionate* touch and a *forgiving* word. And when he gave *them* the power to heal, he was commissioning his *disciples* to do the same.

Those crowds that flocked to Jesus to see the spectacle, to be entertained, to have something to talk about, even those who came just to have their pain relieved or their stamina restored, were an embarrassment to Jesus and an obstacle to his ministry. But those who came to have their relationship with God and their neighbors—with the Creator and his creation—restored, *they* were the *very* reason Jesus came into the world.

For what reason have *you* come *today* to seek out Jesus? Is it to be made clean of the world's judgments about you and your judgments about yourself? To slip loose the taboos of pride and custom and even religiosity that have stood in the way of knowing yourself to be acceptable *to* God and accepted *by* God, and genuinely accepting of *yourself* and *others*? Are you here to encounter him and say, "If you choose, you can make me clean?" "Lord, I am not worthy to receive you," goes the preface to the great feast of reconciliation, "but only say the word and I shall be healed."

Seventh Sunday in Ordinary Time
Spanish Springs Presbyterian Church, Sparks, Nevada
February 23, 2003

Isaiah 43:18–25
2 Corinthians 1:18–22
Mark 2:1–12

"A New Thing"

I have never been in any Bible study discussion of the Gospels in which the question hasn't come up, "Why didn't those people understand who Jesus was?" "Why didn't they believe?" "Why did they reject him?" "How could they listen to his words and watch his deeds and admire his miracles and not realize that he was the Son of God?" And yet, it seems to me there would be just as many people today—including a lot of good, solid church members—as there were back in the days of the earthly Jesus who would regard him with skepticism, jealousy, envy, maybe even hatred, as a disturber of order, an upsetter of the status quo, a toppler of long-cherished traditions and assumptions.

If we consider the ways we have treated prophets in our own time— the Martin Luther Kings, the Caesar Chavezes, the Ralph Naders, even, with ridicule, with denunciation, with bullets,—what makes us think that Jesus would be treated any differently in twenty-first-century America than he was in ancient Israel? Or, for that matter, that he would be treated any differently in our churches than he was in their synagogues? The issues of judgmentalism are still with us, perhaps even more intensely. The issues of authority are still with us, perhaps even more assertively. The issues of God's purpose for creation are still with us, perhaps even more profoundly. And, whenever the church becomes comfortable with the prevailing order, whenever the church becomes dependent upon public approval, whenever the church becomes accustomed to privilege and prestige, it acts very much like the Sanhedrin, the council of elders that ruled the religious and social life of Israel and judged Jesus to be a menace.

So the healings Jesus was performing in Galilee were a threat to the authority and prestige of the people of power and tradition. Of course, they didn't express it that way. Some of them at least did not interpret it that way at all. *They* spoke in terms of blasphemy and law-breaking. Some of them at least genuinely feared that Jesus' miracles were undermining the religious and social system that God had ordained and that seemed to them to work so well—in other words, that confirmed their worldview and satisfied their desires. Some of them at least genuinely feared Jesus' popularity would provide an excuse for the Romans to crush their nation and destroy their religion altogether, and so, even if the immediate effect of Jesus' healings was good for a few sick individuals, it was certainly disastrous for children of Abraham in the long run. Add to that his quick forgiveness of people that everybody just *knew* were sinners—even people whose sins were sexual! "He's destroying public morality!" a lot of good people must have complained. Can't we just hear much the same arguments being raised if Jesus were to come among us today, and do the same things he did two thousand years ago? I think so.

So let us be honest enough to see a little bit of us in the them when we shake our heads about the bad guys in incidents like the paralyzed man brought to Jesus by some people who hoped the healer they had heard about would be able to cure their friend. Jesus' fame had spread broadly by then because of the other healings and exorcisms he had performed in and around Capernaum. A huge crowd had come to the house where he was, and he was speaking to them, teaching them. Those who had brought the paralyzed man, apparently on a mat or a stretcher, were no doubt tired, whether they had carried the man a few blocks or several miles. Imagine how discouraged they must have been to arrive in the neighborhood of Jesus' house and find that the street was clogged with people and they couldn't get anywhere *near* Jesus. Think of the desperation that caused them to concoct the plan of climbing up on the roof and dismantling it in order to lower their friend down to where Jesus could see him and hopefully speak to him or touch him or do whatever Jesus needed to do in order to make him well.

The common assumption about illness in those days, especially debilitating illness, was that it indicated the sick person had committed some sin. The illness was considered a punishment, a public sign of God's judgment. That that was not necessarily the case is clear from what Jesus said on some other occasions. Here, apparently, Jesus perceived that the man's paralysis *was* connected with some sort of sin, though it is not clear whether his condition was a result of *God's* judgment upon the sin or the result of the man's *own* judgment upon *himself*. At any rate, when Jesus saw the faith that had prompted the man's friends to such determination, "he said to the paralytic, 'Son, your sins are forgiven'" (Mark 2:5b NRSV).

How the man reacted, or his friends, we don't know. Was that what they were expecting, a word about the man's sin? Or were they surprised or disappointed by it, that Jesus had not simply touched him and made him well? Did the man in fact feel strength return to his arms and legs the moment Jesus announced his forgiveness? The Gospel doesn't say. Mark immediately shifts our attention to the reaction of the legalists who were present—the scribes, schooled in the interpretation of the laws of Moses. They were thinking to themselves that what Jesus had said was blasphemy, an impudent usurpation of the power and authority that belonged only to God, this business of forgiving sins, and which justified, by the way, their own judgmental attitude toward sick people. Jesus, Mark tells us, knew what they were thinking. Perhaps that didn't even require a miracle. "'Why do you raise such questions in your hearts?'" (Mark 2:8c NRSV) he suddenly turned and asked them. Undoubtedly, they were surprised, perhaps embarrassed, at this exposure of their inner thoughts. And then, something more surprising yet: "'Which is easier, to say to the paralytic, "Your sins are forgiven," or to say, "Stand up and take your mat and walk?" But so that you may know that the Son of Man has authority on earth to forgive sins'—he said to the paralytic—'I say to you, stand up, take your mat and go to your home'" (Mark 2:9–11 NRSV). And the man did so—he "stood up, and immediately took the mat and went out before all of them; so that they were all"—well, probably not the *scribes*—"amazed and glorified God, saying, 'We have never seen anything like this'" (Mark 2:12 NRSV)!

The reaction of the people in the crowd here, I think, is key to the whole issue of accepting the authority of Christ. They all thought they knew the way God worked—not just the scribes, but the rest of the crowd as well. The men who brought the paralyzed man to Jesus probably had thought *they* knew, too, but their *hopes* were greater than their *knowledge*, their *faith* was stronger than their *sophistication*, and their *love* for their *friend* was greater than the offense of his *sins*, whatever they were. They trusted that God was able to do something new and different from what they had *known* before, what they had *expected* before, what they had been *taught* before. And, as it turned out, they were *right*. God was working in Jesus Christ, who possessed, they found out, an authority, a compassion, a mercy, a power that no other human being ever had, demonstrating an insistence on God's *love* that none of their teachers had ever told them about. The friends and the spectators rejoiced. The scribes must have fumed. And, a few verses later, when Jesus, on the sabbath, restored to soundness a man's withered hand, the Pharisees, who themselves were legalists, self-appointed guardians of the law, started to plan how to destroy Jesus.

The scribes thought that God's story was finished. They assumed they knew everything that God was capable of, understood the way God worked, recognized the limits of God's grace, that God had no *further* mercy to bestow than what was reported in the scriptures. Oh, they talked about the coming of the Messiah—that was part of their religious creed, like talk about the second coming is part of *our* religious creed—but they didn't govern their daily activities or make their long-range plans with any urgent expectation of the Messiah's coming, just like most of *us* don't seem to take the second coming into urgent consideration. There had been plenty of testimony to God's new and continuous work of redemption—miracles of salvation, like the Red Sea and water from a rock and manna from heaven and walls falling down at the blast of a trumpet and a mighty warrior toppled by a little boy's slingshot. And, in one of the grimmest periods of Israel's history, the prophecy of God's way out of exile in a far-away, pagan land.

> Do not remember the former things,
>   or consider the things of old.
> I am about to do a new thing;
>   now it springs forth, do you not perceive it?
> I will make a way in the wilderness
>   and rivers in the desert.
> The wild animals will honor me,
>   the jackals and the ostriches;
> for I give water in the wilderness,
>   rivers in the desert,
> to give drink to my chosen people,
>   the people whom I formed for myself
> so that they might declare my praise. (Isa 43:18–21 NRSV)

Long before, God had chosen Israel, had promised to make Abraham and his offspring great, had promised an everlasting throne to David, just like, long *before*, God had created humankind and called it good and vowed to cherish it and provide for it as the crowning achievement of creation. Carried off to Babylon because of their sins, the Israelites didn't see how God was going to accomplish the salvation that had been promised. It would take too big a miracle. Yes, there had been the exodus long back in hoary history. It was in the books. But this was *now*, and no *book* offered a recipe for God's miraculous solution to *today's* problem. And yet God *did* what God *promised*—worked a return of the people from exile to their homeland, and *this* time, even the animals along the way rejoiced at the scale of God's salvation—a redemption whose *superiority* over the exodus through Sinai had been symbolized by the promise *this time* of miraculous "rivers in the desert," compared to just a spring of water spurting out of a rock.

Here is the message: God reserves the right to do even greater acts of salvation in the *future* than God has done in the *past*. God reserves the right to do a *new* thing today, tomorrow, and the day after that. Our past, our present, are not the full measure of God's future. And when God broke into our world in the person of Jesus Christ, the boundaries of salvation fell, the limits of mercy disappeared, and every attempt to *ration* the grace of God became a sin. Jesus Christ was not *soft* on *sin*; Jesus Christ *forgave sins*. Jesus Christ did not deny the *severity* of God's *judgment*; Jesus Christ declared that God's *judgment* falls *most* severely on those who dare to judge *others*. Jesus Christ is not the *end* of God's story of salvation; Jesus Christ is the door through which God's miracle of salvation is to spread and broaden through the radical mercy and reckless love of people who *believe* he is the Messiah, the Son of God. "I am about to do a new thing; now it springs forth, do you not perceive it" (Isa 43:19a NRSV)?

The scribes heard Jesus' words of forgiveness, crossed their arms, frowned, and thought to themselves that what Jesus had said was blasphemy.

> "Why do you raise such questions in your hearts? Which is easier, to say to the paralytic, 'Your sins are forgiven,' or to say, 'Stand up and take your mat and walk'? But so that you may know that the Son of Man has authority on earth to forgive sins"—he said to the paralytic—"I say to you, stand up, take your mat and go to your home." And he stood up, and immediately took the mat and went out before all of them. (Mark 2:8c–12a NRSV)

The miracle of the man being *healed* was a wonderful thing, but it was only proof of the yet *more* wonderful thing—the *forgiveness* of *sins*.

"A New Thing"

The crowd that saw this thing was amazed and glorified God. What is the reaction of *you and me* to such mercy, we who say we believe that Jesus is the Christ, the Messiah, the Son of God? What is the message about the issues of judgmentalism, the issues of authority, the issues of God's purpose for creation that are still with us and much in the headlines and much in our daily lives? How do we testify to the *reality* of the *new* thing God has done in Jesus Christ and is doing through the *body* of Christ, which is the church, *today*? Did the boundaries of salvation *stop* at the people Jesus forgave in the *Bible*? Have the limits of mercy been set at the sins that Jesus pardoned in the *Gospels*? Does being faithful to Jesus Christ mean that we are to *ration* the grace of God? Jesus commissioned *us* to do what *he* did, and even *greater* things than he did. We individuals, our congregation, our denomination, the whole church of Jesus Christ, are ever faced with challenges and opportunities to practice the merciful love of God, to extend the experience of God's grace beyond the boundaries of our own prejudices and presumptions. Every day, in ways that will make the headlines and in ways that the world will never know, we have the choice either to cross our arms and frown, or to participate in a miracle. "Do not remember the former things, or consider the things of old," God said long ago. "I am about to do a new thing; now it springs forth, do you not perceive it" (Isa 43:18–19a NRSV)? "And [the paralytic whose sin Jesus had forgiven] stood up, and immediately took the mat and went out before all of them; so that they were all amazed and glorified God, saying, 'We have never seen *anything* like *this*'" (Mark 2:12 NRSV)!

Eighth Sunday in Ordinary Time
Spanish Springs Presbyterian Church, Sparks, Nevada
February 27, 2000

Hosea 2:14–20
2 Corinthians 3:1–6
Mark 2:13–22

"A Passion for Salvation"

The Bible is a passionate book. It contains images and scenes every bit as graphic as some of the more modern books that people have sometimes, ironically, crusaded against in the name of the Bible. Scholars and mothers of teenagers sometimes puzzle over how the erotic Song of Solomon ever got *into* the Bible. It's pretty clearly a very secular piece of writing. But even the most spiritual and theological books of the Bible can and do draw on romantic imagery and contain sexual overtones. And in all of the Bible, perhaps there is not a better example of how romantic passion provides an illustration for theological truth than the book of Hosea.

The book of Hosea tells us how God directed Hosea the prophet to take a prostitute for a wife—Gomer was her name. In the course of time, Gomer bore Hosea a son and a daughter and another son. But Gomer would not submit herself to the discipline of domestic life; she continued her promiscuous ways, now adultery, throwing herself after other lovers as easily as she did before she was married. Her adulterous prostitution, the Lord explained, was like the unfaithful nation of Israel, throwing itself after other *gods* despite the covenant of faithfulness it had made with the Lord.

How would Hosea deal with the harlotry of Gomer? How would *God* deal with the harlotry of *Israel*? In the book of Hosea, the gut-wrenching experience of *Hosea* is made to stand for the gut-wrenching experience of *God*. The heartache and discouragement of *Hosea* mirror the heartache and discouragement of *God*. Pride and propriety gave *one* answer to the adultery—Hosea should *abandon* Gomer, just as *God* should abandon

Israel. Legally speaking, and perhaps also from the standpoint of psychological health, Hosea had the right and even the moral duty to *abandon* Gomer—to cast her out and send her packing. But Hosea's *love* for Gomer was greater than his *pride*, more *profound* than his *disgust*. She was his wife. He would do whatever he could to frustrate her waywardness. And then he would turn his efforts to winning her love to him, wooing her again like he wooed her once before, even when he knew what sort of woman she had been, renewing his commitment to her in spite of her many infidelities.

Just so, no one could have blamed God for washing his hands of Israel entirely after the nation had run after this Baal and that, after the people had made sacrifices to this idol and that, after the chosen race had vowed allegiance to this deity and that, often engaging in the gross sexual acts that were a part of the cultic rituals of these false religions. But God could not forget his passionate love for this people that had prompted God to gamble on their loyalty when he first chose them for his own and raised them up out of slavery in Egypt and led them through the wilderness of Sinai, when he entered into an eternal covenant with them to be their God. "Therefore," said God, "I will now allure her, and bring her into the wilderness, and speak tenderly to her. From there I will give her her vineyards"—vineyards that God had laid waste in a fit of jealousy—"and make the Valley of Anchor"—where the Israelites had sinned as they were first entering the promised land—make that place of sad memory "a door of hope. There she shall respond as in the days of her youth, as at the time when she came out of the land of Egypt" (Hos 2:14–15 NRSV).

If you or I had been standing by, watching what Hosea was doing, we would have called him a fool; his misguided experiment to make a fair lady out of a sordid wench would culminate in the only way it could. "Do your best to forget her," we would have advised him. "Cut your emotional losses and give up on such an immoral creature." And if any one of us had been advising *God* regarding the behavior of *Israel*, we would surely have said the same thing—noble attempt, but doomed from the beginning. "Quit wasting your time on such an unfaithful race as humankind. Get a dog."

But anyone who has ever been passionately in love with someone who did not *value* that love knows that forgetting about an unworthy lover is much easier said than done. Love is not rational, and it cannot be turned off like a light switch. We might have expected that God, surely, would cast Israel aside on the basis of principle and propriety. But the affections of God's heart, it seems, are more powerful than any resolution God could make to stop loving us. God could not give up hope, God could not forget the passionate love that aches to have the lover return. "On that day, says the LORD, you will call me, 'My husband,' and no longer will you call me, 'My Baal.' . . . And I will take you for my wife forever, I will take you for my wife in righteousness and in justice, in steadfast love, and in mercy. I will take you for my wife in faithfulness, and you shall know the LORD" (Hos 2:16, 19–20 NRSV). All of creation will be restored in that day to the pristine harmony in which it was first brought into being—the birds will sing again, we might say, the sun will shine again, everything will be right again.

Perhaps you have known that kind of feeling, if you have ever been in such a situation with someone you loved deeply but who was unfaithful, or who simply had lost interest in you. Perhaps you have known that kind of hope that makes you set aside all pride and go begging for that person's love. It seems hardly the proper thing for a God of righteousness and majesty to do. And yet it was *God* who was the one who told Hosea to go take a prostitute for his wife to begin with. And several centuries later, it was God, in human form, who sought out and fraternized with the most unsavory company Israelite society had to offer.

"Jesus went out again beside the sea," Mark tells us. "As he was walking along, he saw Levi . . . sitting at the tax booth, and he said to him, 'Follow me.' And he got up and followed him" (Mark 2:13a, 14 NRSV). Now, aside from being despised because they collected taxes, which meant squeezing as much money as they could from people, the men who collected taxes and tolls and customs fees in the Israel of Jesus' day were despised because they were doing it in the service of the *Romans*. They had sold out to the *enemy*, and the *enemy* was a *pagan*. The Romans had conquered God's chosen people and now went where they liked, took what they wanted, did as they desired, defiling holy places and ignoring religious sensitivities. Tax collectors were classed with the "sinners"—people who deliberately rejected or flouted the law of Moses, like prostitutes did. They were considered unworthy beneficiaries of the sun God made to shine on the righteous, of the rain that fell on the fields of the righteous, of the fruits that sprang forth from the earth to sustain the righteous. They were unfaithful to God, running instead after the gods of their bellies, the gods of their greed, the gods of their lusts. No self-respecting person would have had anything to do with either tax collectors or sinners. So it was very difficult for the religious people of the day to see Jesus as a godly person, much less the *Son* of God, when he not only said to Levi the tax collector, "Follow me," but then went to Levi's house for dinner and ate at the same table where tax collectors and sinners were eating.

Houses in Galilee weren't very large, and the front door usually opened directly into the only large room in the house, so it was easy to know what was going on inside someone's house simply by walking up and down the street as the doors were opened and closed or sometimes, on warm evenings, simply left open. "When the scribes of the Pharisees saw that [Jesus] was eating with sinners and tax collectors, they said to his disciples, 'Why does he eat with tax collectors and sinners?' When Jesus heard this, he said to them, 'Those who are *well* have no need of a physician, but those who are *sick*; I have come to call not the *righteous* but *sinners*'" (Mark 2:16-17 NRSV). Jesus came to pursue not just those who, like cute and cuddly but inexperienced lambs, had innocently wandered away from the flock. Jesus came to pursue those who knew exactly what they were doing by ignoring the law of God and all decency. It was scandalous! Every bit as scandalous as running after the most undeserving, most adulterous, most faithless spouse. And Jesus would endure the disapproval of the religious and the reasonable, their ridicule, even their cross of execution meant to put an *end* to such impropriety, all because of his passion for salvation—the same passion that burned in the heart of God when God resolved to woo back Israel the unfaithful, Israel the disloyal, Israel the harlot.

Do we find this whole business a bit sordid, rather impolite, somewhat uncomfortable? We all know of times in the history of the church—maybe we have been in congregations that fit this mold—when the sanctuary was only for decent, respectable folk who turned up their noses at a good number of people they passed on their way to worship. The organizing pastor of the church I served in Dodge City was a Presbyterian minister named Ormond Wright, way back in the 1870s. Over the years I was there, I looked into the archives from time to time. It seems that the decent folk of old Dodge City—there *were* a few—wanted a church in their frontier town not so much to *save* people like Levi and his friends, but to put up a *fence* between themselves and the tax collectors and sinners of the world. When Reverend Wright began spending time among the people who were literally on the other side of the tracks in South Dodge, his congregation came down on him like a hammer. We can just hear him trying to explain that, like Jesus himself, so Jesus' *disciples* were here to call not the *righteous* but *sinners*; those who are *well* have no need of a *cure*. His explanation was not well received. Reverend Wright eventually had to go back east after suffering a nervous breakdown. I am not sure that everyone who admires Reverend Wright today, laity and clergy alike, would find it easy to welcome into the sanctuary and sit beside a prostitute, much less accept a dinner invitation from the modern equivalent of a tax collector.

Jesus had a passion for salvation, and so must we. Otherwise, why does the church even exist? It made no earthly sense for the holy one of God to pursue those who had so absolutely turned their *backs* on God, when he *could* have so *enriched* the faith of those who were already *interested* in the law of Moses. Surely, it would have been easier to swap God-talk with the scribes and the Pharisees, and perhaps more pleasant to dine with *them*. Just so, it would be a lot easier and more pleasant, perhaps, for a new church development to be spending all of its resources gathering people who are already churchly-minded, rather than spending—some might even say wasting—time and money pursuing people who don't seem to know or care that Sunday is the *Lord's* Day, or people who don't seem to know or care that we should give thanks for our blessings (blessings which, by the way, are not our hard-earned *reward* but God's gracious *gift*), or people who don't seem to know or care that God expects us to live according to the ways *God* considers wise and just, rather than living according to our appetites and our greed and our lusts.

Jesus' passion for salvation is the personal expression of *God's* passionate love for humankind, and indeed, for all of God's creation. Jesus' tireless interest in the lowly and most despised reflects the stubborn commitment of a God whose pride does not even prevent him running after a notoriously faithless spouse, no matter what the neighbors think, no matter what our friends advise, no matter what even the religious establishment considers proper and wise. Jesus' passion for salvation is the reason we are here in Spanish Springs—not to create a comfortable space for people just like us, but to proclaim and demonstrate the unquenchable love of God for *every* person, even the most sinful, even the most resistant, even the most profane. Can *you* feel that passion, a passion for salvation?

Transfiguration of the Lord
First Presbyterian Church, Ponca City, Oklahoma
February 15, 2015

2 Kings 2:1–12
2 Corinthians 4:3–6
Mark 9:2–9

"Make Way for the Cross"

In the age of "seeker services," when, in desperation it seems, many Christian organizations are trying anything that will bring people out of their homes and into the church, we are advised that whatever might turn people off should be dispensed with. So, many churches no longer have a prayer of confession, because people don't like to be reminded that they are sinners. Many churches no longer have an offering during worship, because people might not come if they think that they are expected to part with some of their money. Many churches no longer have any symbols of the faith in their sanctuaries which in fact are not to be called "sanctuaries," but "auditoriums" or "worship centers," and which are virtually indistinguishable from high school auditoriums or concert halls, because it makes the faith too churchy. Indeed, some churches no longer have visible in their meeting places even the ancient symbol of the cross, because it might be a turn-off to people. Church growth experts tell us that getting people connected to Jesus is more important than any of these incidentals, which they can later grow into as they mature in their faith.

The issue *is*, of course, what faith is it that they are maturing *into*? Is it the faith that was handed down by apostles, the faith that was testified to by martyrs, the faith that turned barbarians from their paganism, the faith that humbled emperors and kings, the faith that was preached by the Reformers, the faith that ended slavery and brought education and health care and child labor laws to the poor and the powerless and the dignity of equal rights to women, the faith that sustained our parents and our grandparents and our great-grandparents through dark days of depression and war? Or is it a faith that finds easy accommodation with the spirit of the times and promotes consumerism, a faith that makes few demands and extracts little cost, a faith that is comfortable and convenient, a faith that has as its sole purpose making us feel better about ourselves and blessing the status quo, a faith that can be designed and redesigned to fit preferences and tastes? Ultimately, of course, the *real* question is: Who *is* the Jesus Christ who is calling us to have faith in him? Who *is* it that we are called to worship, to whom we are to give our absolute devotion and who insists that, if we are to follow *him*, we must *accept* him as Lord of our lives and every aspect of them? And that is the *very* question that permeates the Gospel of Mark: *Who is Jesus?*

Mark knew that, finally, each of us must answer that question for ourselves. But he wrote his Gospel in order to provide us with the relevant evidence for arriving at the correct answer, starting with the testimony of the baptizer John, the herald and forerunner of the Messiah. And our reading from Mark today, standing as it does at the very *middle* of his book, is the high point, literally as well as figuratively, of the revelatory witness of the oldest Gospel. Six days after Jesus had taught his disciples that he must suffer and be rejected and be killed and rise again, six days after he said to his followers, "If any want to become my followers, let them deny themselves and take up their cross and follow me. For those who want to save their life will lose it, and those who lose their life for my sake, and for the sake of the gospel, will save it" (Mark 8:34b–35 NRSV),

> Jesus took with him Peter and James and John, and led them up a high mountain apart, by themselves. And he was transfigured before them, and his clothes became dazzling white . . . . And there appeared to them Elijah with Moses, who were talking with Jesus. . . . Then a cloud overshadowed them, and from the cloud there came a voice, 'This is my Son, the Beloved; listen to him!' Suddenly when they looked around, they saw no one with them anymore, but only Jesus.
>
> As they were coming down the mountain, he ordered them to tell no one about what they had seen, until after the Son of Man had risen from the dead." (Mark 9:2–3a, 4, 7–9 NRSV)

There is a special genius about the Christian calendar, and that includes each year placing the Gospel accounts of the transfiguration of the Lord at the end of the weeks following Epiphany—during which the episodes that we read make manifest the divine identity of Jesus—as the transition into Lent—the liturgical season in which Christians are summoned to accompany Jesus on his journey to the cross of shameful death. For several weeks now, we have read of crowds witnessing the miracles of healing that Jesus performed and giving praise and glory to God for what they have seen Jesus do, while some questioned among themselves what sort of a person could perform such wonders: "Who is Jesus?" In the *Fourth* Gospel, Jesus is exalted—lifted up—not by being seated on a cushioned throne, high and lofty, but by being hoisted up on the cross. So Mark here wraps the glory of Christ—his clothes become dazzling white "such as no one on earth could bleach them" (Mark 9:3b NRSV), while standing in the presence of the great figures of the Law and the Prophets, he to whom all the commandments and the prophecies point, and the cloud of God's presence descending upon the mountain and enveloping them all, and the voice of God proclaiming Jesus to be his very own Son—Mark wraps all of this in the context of Jesus first declaring that he will soon suffer and be rejected and be put to death, and then descending again from the mountain of divine approval to serve the crowds that are sick and needy. In the very middle of his Gospel, Mark juxtaposes the amazing splendor and awesome grandeur of Christ with the lowly servanthood and agony of Jesus, and so makes way for the cross.

Why was it that Jesus pledged his disciples to secrecy about what they had seen and heard on the mountain? What could be *better* than that they would publish afar and aloud the fact that Jesus kept such impressive company as Moses and Elijah, and that God had specially identified Jesus as his own Son whose words should be heard and heeded? Then *everyone* could just praise the Lord all the time. Then Jesus would have been *acclaimed* instead of *arrested*. Then the scribes and the Pharisees and the Sadducees and the priests and even the Roman governor might have been put in their place and their criticism silenced and their plots foiled. Then, maybe, all of that *cross* stuff could have been *avoided*. But then we would have no understanding of the radical *obedience* that lies behind Christ's glory. Then we would have only a *rumor* of God's passionate love. Then our sins would be *unatoned*. It would doubtless make for a more cheerful *Lent*; in fact, we wouldn't have Lent at *all*. But it would not be true to who Jesus Christ is, and so we would not see who *God* is—a God who is willing to *suffer beyond imagining* rather than see the beloved creation *lost* in the fatal enormity of its *sin*.

Much is at stake in the way we go about worship, in the language we use to speak of Christ, in the decision to follow Jesus back down from the mountaintop instead of remaining there in little tents like Peter proposed in a moment of frightened babble and misguided enthusiasm. Less than a week earlier, Peter had *rebuked* Jesus for saying that the destiny of the Son of Man had to do with suffering and rejection and death. *Jesus* had rebuked *Peter* in *turn*, saying *he* was looking at things from a too purely *human* perspective of what would be good and worthy and pleasant and logical. Peter's understanding of who Jesus was still had no room for the cross. But *without* the cross, Peter and the others, and the world in general, could never understand what Jesus was all about. So Jesus warned the disciples who had been privileged to glimpse his heavenly glory against talking about it until the whole story was known, including the shame and defeat of a criminal's execution, and even Peter's own fear and embarrassment about the crucifixion.

No, without the cross and without the resurrection that it would make possible, the testimony about Jesus could only be a *half*-truth at *best*. The identity of Jesus would not be fully known. The sober reality of God's merciful love could not be appreciated. The full meaning of allegiance to Jesus Christ as Lord could not be comprehended. And the daily demands upon the followers of Jesus could not be assessed. As quickly as the transfiguration had happened, it was over; Moses and Elijah were gone, the dazzling whiteness of Jesus' garments was faded to a homespun ordinariness, the cloud of divine presence had vanished, and Peter, James, and John saw again only Jesus, who beckoned them down off the dizzying summit back to the grimy world where he ministered again to people burdened with sickness and sin, and was himself finally made to feel the full force of human hatred and vengeance.

At the place where the Mexican state of Chihuahua and the American states of New Mexico and Texas all meet, there is a mountain called El Cristo Rey, and atop it stands a cross, thirty feet in height, and the cross bears in relief a statue of Christ, arms outstretched on the cross beam and facing a metropolitan area of more than two million people. At the foot of the mountain, on the Mexican side, is a squatter's village several miles in length and width, with thousands of shacks and shanties, where the poorest people in North America live. On the American side are a major freeway, a race track, a country club, and the busy truck crossing where commerce flows twenty-four hours a day, seven days a week, mostly from the low-wage factories and workshops and farms south of the border to the affluent consumerist society north of the border. Sometimes, the smog of a winter-time temperature inversion obscures the mountain and the cross on top of it from view from downtown El Paso and downtown Juárez. But for three-quarters of a century, the light of the rising sun cresting over Mount Franklin has instantly and brightly illumined the sculpted face of Christ every morning, and the fading glow of the sunset has made the silhouette of the cross the last visible feature on the western horizon every evening. It is not a billboard advertisement marketing Jesus and the Christian faith, certainly not any particular church or renowned preacher. It is a benediction upon the day's beginning and upon the day's ending and a judgment upon each moment in between.

Some in this congregation wear a cross on a necklace, not, I think, as another piece of jewelry, interchangeable with any other, for I have seen that some wear it not just on Sunday, but as a daily reminder of who it is they belong to, who is their Lord—the one who was *crucified*, and who is *risen*—not just *one* of those, but *both*. And every time we worship here, we worship under the sign of the cross in testimony of who this Jesus is in whose name we have been baptized, in whose name we gather, in whose name we go back out into the world not as *products* of our *culture* but as *servants* of *Christ*, and who, following the way of the cross, may be called upon to suffer, maybe even to die. For the cross takes us beyond any comfortable dwelling place in the glow of the Mount of the Transfiguration to the painfully dark truth of the Mount of Calvary, where faith is not easy, where faith is not simplistic, where faith is not a matter of taste and preference, but where faith leads to crucifixion and then is answered with resurrection.

The testimony of the apostles brings us from the manger to the bright shining moment of splendorous confirmation that Jesus is the beloved Son of God to whom all the Law and the Prophets point, but then the testimony leads us back *down* from the mountain to learn what *being* the Son of God, and what being a *follower* of the Son of God, truly *means*. If we would be faithful to the Christ of the Gospels, and not merely attracted to the Jesus of the bumper sticker, we cannot stop and dwell in booths perched pristinely above human need and safely distanced from Gethsemane. The Jesus Christ of the scriptures, the Jesus Christ proclaimed by the apostles, pushes on toward Jerusalem. In the Christian faith that the Bible has known for two thousand years, the question "Who is Jesus?" is not *fully answered* at any comfortable resting stop short of Good Friday and Easter. The testimony of the *Gospels* is that *God's glorification* of Jesus makes way for the *cross*.

Ash Wednesday
First Presbyterian Church, Ponca City, Oklahoma
February 18, 2015

Joel 2:1-2, 12-17
2 Corinthians 5:20b—6:10
Matthew 6:1-6, 16-21

"Trying it Again"

A few years ago, there was a phrase that was very popular—a sort of slang expression that reflected the material affluence of the time and raised images of world travelers who had just about exhausted all of the planet's attractions and amusements: "Been there, done that." In its very overuse, the phrase demonstrated the sense of ennui that it represented. We can just picture the indolent rich, bored with all the things their money has bought, whose most urgent decision in life is where to spend the next vacation—a repeat trip to the Riviera or a repeat visit to Fiji. "Been there, done that." Or maybe it calls to mind the more middle-class goal of going to Disneyland and squeezing the whole experience into a single day, trying to make it to all of the rides on one admission price, and mentally checking off each one as it is conquered. "Been there, done that." In that case, it's as if the experience is just for the sake of putting another notch in our belt; the family with the most at the end wins the prize.

When you add the "Been there, done that" attitude to our modern tendency to regard faith and ethics as primarily a matter of thought and knowledge, the notion of the Christian year seems completely out of place in our time. The annual cycle of holy days and liturgical seasons is surely a concept bound to prompt *boredom* in a culture that always demands the new, the bigger and better, the exciting and expensive. Christmas may be an exception, but even there, many people turn the holiday into a competition, if not with their neighbors and friends, then with their own previous Christmases—a prettier tree, a finer dinner, more thrilling presents. Easter may be an exception, but even there, many congregations turn the holiday into a competition, if not with other churches, then with their own previous Easters—a more spectacular anthem, a more wonderful sermon, a bigger attendance than last year. How easy it is for all of us to get sucked into our culture's premium on overcoming the objection of "Been there, done that."

Perhaps *most* problematic of all the days on the liturgical calendar, and of all the seasons of the Christian year, are Ash Wednesday and Lent. Already at disadvantage by not being associated with presents or bunnies—thankfully, the greeting card industry has not attempted to induce a practice of wishing everybody a "Happy Lent" and the appliance stores have refrained from advertising "Ash Wednesday Sales,"—if we look forward to Ash Wednesday and Lent every year, it must be for purposes solely related to faith, unless we are expecting to compete with our neighbor in a public show of piety. That, of course, Jesus forbade in our Gospel reading for today. But really, if we admit that we are sinners, and that, despite our best intentions, we will most certainly be sinners again tomorrow, what is the point of this annual repetition of introspection, of intensified prayer and Bible reading and even fasting, and of this yearly exercise of ashes on the forehead? What more will we learn that we haven't known before? What prospect is there that we can have a better Lent—whatever that may mean—than last year? Why shouldn't we just sit back and sigh and say, "Been there, done that"?

The apostle Paul experienced many afflictions, many insults, many criticisms in his ministry of spreading the gospel through Asia and Europe. The temptation to give up and leave people to their chosen fate must have been very strong at times. The temptation for Paul to abandon his own faith in the face of beatings and stonings and imprisonments must have been very real. I won't flatter myself by supposing I know that *I* would be steadfast in such circumstances. I pray that I will never be so tested. And then there was the frustration of the grumblings and inconstancies in the congregations of people who *had* heard Paul and believed and turned to Jesus Christ.

The church at Corinth was one such particular case, though clearly not the only one. "As we work together with him, we urge you also not to accept the grace of God in vain. For he says, 'At an acceptable time I have listened to you, and on a day of salvation I have helped you.' See, now is the acceptable time; see, now is the day of salvation" (2 Cor 6:1–2 NRSV)! Paul wasn't saying that to passersby in the square; he wrote it to an existing church. The apostle wasn't appealing just then for unbelievers to become Christians; he was addressing a believing Christian congregation. These people had already professed faith in Jesus Christ. It is even likely that many were already paying a high price for their Christianity—rejection by friends and family members, perhaps loss of jobs and income because of employers who objected to their faith or because they had decided to abandon occupations that had involved them in heathenish practices, perhaps forsaking plans for a career in government service or some other mark of prestige, the door to which was now closed to them because of their allegiance to Jesus Christ.

The price that the apostles had paid had been too great for their converts to render it pointless by yielding again to the ways of sin and paganism. More important, the price that *Christ* had paid had been too great for *anyone* to take her or his salvation for granted, to think it a little thing. Believers must be diligent in their faith, in their prayer and behavior and hope. All that God has done, and all the labors of the apostles, will be of no avail unless believers are sincere and steadfast, committed in their faith and constant in their devotion. See, *every* moment is the acceptable time; see, *every* day is the day of salvation!—not just the day on which we *first* accepted the offer of Jesus Christ, but every *subsequent* day, too. Being a Christian takes constant effort, requires a daily commitment. Salvation is an ongoing way of life, is an ongoing turning not only from what is *evil*, but even from what seems *good*, and turning toward what is *best*. As God places before us daily new opportunities of serving Jesus Christ by serving others, often in simple, unglamorous ways, we are being called again and again to faithfulness. Again and again the substance of salvation is being actualized. And again and again we are made aware of our total dependence upon God's grace, because we become again and again mindful of our sinfulness—our tendency to prefer *ourselves* over our *neighbor*, to choose *our desires* over *God's will*, to assert *our wants* over *other people's needs*, to make *ourselves* the center of all meaning rather than *God*. "See, *now* is the acceptable time; see, *now* is the day of salvation" (2 Cor 6:2c NRSV)!—no matter how humble the service, no matter how simple or tedious or inconclusive; no matter how great the sacrifice, no matter how costly or self-effacing or anonymous. When it comes to responding to the call of Jesus Christ, there is no "Been there, done that."

And so, Ash Wednesday, the day each year on which Christians acknowledge together our need of God's merciful grace, individual and corporate, ongoing and constant, is an acknowledgment that our sinfulness is habitual, that our need is permanent, that God's forgiveness is available, that God's mercy is always fresh. Whatever deeds of piety and devotion we performed *last* Lent or *any other* time were not sufficient to earn us salvation. Whatever resolutions we made *last* Lent or *any other* time are not sufficient to keep us from sinning. Thought and knowledge are not the substance of faithfulness. And there is nothing *magical* about ashes on the forehead as a protection from pride and greed and lust and hatred. *Ashes* are not a demonstration of our laudable *piety*. *Lack* of ashes is not a sign of other people's contemptible *impiety*. The ashes are a *reminder* to *us* of our constant tendency to value ourselves above others and serve our own desires rather than God's purpose, a *reminder* to *us* of our mortal creatureliness that makes us totally dependent upon God's grace, a *reminder* to *us* that spiritual discipline is not a need from which we can ever graduate or which we can ever outgrow in our earthly life, a reminder that we must never relax our attempts to live in Christ-likeness, never abandon our vigilance against our own sin, never forget the costly sacrifice made for our salvation, and that compels *us* to live sacrificially for *others* for whose salvation, also, Christ died. Being faithful to Jesus Christ requires diligence. Discipleship requires persistence. "Been there, done that" is not the attitude of people who recognize that *every* day is a miracle of God's creation and a gift of God's love.

So here we are, trying it again, this reminder, and knowing that, once more *next* year, we will have to try it yet again, confident always that God's victory is greater than our defeats, that God's triumph is mightier than our failures, that God's salvation is more decisive than our sinfulness. The ashes mark our recognition of our unworthiness. But the message of Lent is that our unworthiness isn't the deciding factor of our destiny; in fact, it is our unworthiness that is the whole reason for Good Friday and for Easter.

Will you try it again, this exercise that never quite seems to take, this ritual that we repeat year after year, this admission that we, left to our own devices, have failed once again in our resolve? Will you try it again, this acknowledgment of our dependence upon the All-Wise, All-Knowing, All-Giving, this sign of our hope in the All-Forgiving, All-Merciful, All-Loving, this exercise of remembering in deed as well as in thought our constant need of God's salvation and God's constant readiness to save? God's love endures forever. Let us try, once again, to live out *our* love for *God*.

First Sunday in Lent
Spanish Springs Presbyterian Church, Sparks, Nevada
March 9, 2003

Genesis 9:8–17
1 Peter 3:18–22
Mark 1:9–15

"Never Again"

It had taken very little time before the first man and the first woman disobeyed God and committed sin. It was almost as if it were in their nature, what happened in Eden, despite the fact that God had judged the whole creation to be good. It had taken very little time before one person killed another—in the very first generation to be born on earth, Cain murdered Abel. It was almost as if it were in their nature, what happened between brothers out in the field, despite the fact that the entire world was theirs to share. And as humankind multiplied, so did the wicked deeds, Genesis says, "[a]nd the Lord was sorry that he had made humankind on the earth, and it grieved him to his heart" (Gen 6:6 NRSV).

Things had not gone the way that God had intended—a fact that we need to remember when we make sweeping statements about God's being all-knowing. Presumably, had God *foreseen* the wickedness of humankind, men and women would never have been created in the first place, just as some parents may regret having brought into the world children who grow up to commit crimes or cause constant heartache. But, having *brought* them into the world, parental love hopes for the best, looks for the good, agonizes over the hurt and the injury. It is almost impossible for a parent to stop hoping, to give up, to abandon. We have family friends whose alcoholic daughter, now nearing age sixty, has broken her parents' hearts so many ways, has squandered their loving sacrifices so many times, has hurt so many other people along the way. All logic says, "Give up, you've done all you can, you've no more to give." And yet, for the umpteenth time, they seek her out yet again when she has failed to report to a good job, has failed to show up at a family gathering, has failed to respond to calls and letters. A parent's love.

God once finally decided to give up on human beings and do away with them all, and, in the process, animals, too—to just be done with the whole experiment of creation as a waste of time and labor and, we are led to believe, emotion. "So the LORD said, 'I will blot out from the earth the human beings I have created—people together with animals and creeping things and birds of the air, for I am sorry that I have made them'" (Gen 6:7 NRSV). But even then, a parent's love, and a Creator's hope, prevailed over the logic and the pain and the disgust. God decided *not* to destroy *Noah*, for, the Bible says, "Noah was a righteous man, blameless in his generation; Noah walked with God" (Gen 6:9b NRSV). Would Noah be obedient enough to trust the outlandish task God summoned him to perform?

We know the story—Noah passed the test. '[H]e did all that God commanded him" (Gen 6:22b NRSV). One little shining ray in the gloomy mess the world had become—but it was enough to make God decide that creation was worth another try. And so there came the flood of God's judgment, but Noah and his family, and two of every species on earth, floated high above the destruction and the chaos in the big boat that God had told Noah to build. The same waters that destroyed all other life were the means by which some were saved. It rained forty days and forty nights, and on the seventh day, the flood came, "[a]nd the waters swelled on the earth for one hundred fifty days. But God remembered Noah and all the wild animals and all the domestic animals that were with him in the ark. And God made a wind blow over the earth, and the waters subsided" (Gen 7:24—8:1 NRSV). Eventually, the waters dried up. God told Noah to come out of the ark with his family and the other creatures, and life began again on the face of the earth.

Interesting as the story of the flood is, vivid as the images that come to our minds when we hear this tale, the Bible's main interest in the event isn't the size of the ark or the age of Noah or the number of days the rains fell. The very fact that we are here to listen to the story is testimony that the most important part of the story comes at the end.

> [T]he LORD said in his heart, "I will never again curse the ground because of humankind, for the inclination of the human heart is evil from youth; nor will I ever again destroy every living creature as I have done.

> As long as the earth endures,
>> seedtime and harvest, cold and heat,
> summer and winter, day and night,
>> shall not cease." . . .
>
> Then God said to Noah and to his sons with him, "As for me, I am establishing my covenant with you and your descendants after you, and with every living creature that is with you, the birds, the domestic animals, and every animal of the earth with you, as many as came out of the ark. I establish my covenant with you, that never again shall all flesh be cut off by the waters of a flood, and never again shall there be a flood to destroy the earth." (Gen 8:21b–22; 9:8–11 NRSV)

And God set a bow in the clouds to be a sign of the covenant that God made with Noah and his children and with every living creature, for all future generations.

"Never again!" God's grief at the destruction caused by the very natural divine anger was greater even than the grief God had felt at the wickedness of human beings. And God felt remorse, even revulsion, as when a parent spanks a child too hard, or sees that some administered punishment has alienated a child, justified though it may have been. It has achieved the very *opposite* of the purpose for which the parent brought that child into the world. And the mother or father thinks, "Never again!" But there is a difference, of course. A *human* parent may *forget* the vow that he or she has made. God *never* breaks a promise, no matter how one-sided the covenant may be.

That was not the last of human disobedience, of course—of evil, of wickedness, of sin, of doing harm to self and others. The righteousness of Noah was not a genetic trait that was passed on to all posterity. Nothing about humankind had changed; the only thing that changed was *God's* attitude *toward* humankind. God acknowledged that the human heart is inclined to evil; that is a hard fact God had to accept. But God's *purpose* did *not* change—the purpose of loving community that prompted God to bring order out of chaos in the first place; that moved God to care about rocks and trees and fish and birds and you and me in the first place; that persuaded God to bear with human sin after the flood, and ultimately to make the supreme sacrifice of his own Son to rectify sin's disastrous effect. Given our natural makeup, *we* weren't going to make everything right. So *God* determined to make everything right by taking upon the divine soul the judgment *we* deserve, that any court of law would render, that any *other* god would impose who did not love the offender as a parent loves a child. Judgment there would be after the flood, but never again would God give up on creation and blot it out. Judgment there would be after the *cross*, but *always* for the purpose of *redemption*, of bringing back the wayward child to the open arms of the loving parent. God would enter the pain and frustration of the human situation, even face the most seductive of human temptations, even suffer fearsome death, out of love for you and me and all creation. No terrible two's, no adolescent rebellion, no unwise choice in young adulthood, will turn the heavenly parent away from the earthly children. "Never again!" The pain in the heart of God only makes God more determined to save, restore, and take delight in God's creation.

A lot of people have a hard time with such a notion of unqualified, unconditional, unending love. Their prescription of judgment upon the wrongdoing of others calls for every sort of wrathful punishment God could conjure. There are still some Christians who pray a cure will *not* be found for AIDS. There are actually Christians who pray *for* war with Iraq. There are even Christians who pray *for* the destruction of Muslims and Buddhists and Hindus. The story of God's change of heart *away* from *destruction* and *toward* faithfulness to the *purpose* of creation is our assurance that, while God responds to prayer, God will never again abandon the purpose for which the world was created in the first place.

A lot of people have a hard time accepting the notion that God could love *them* with an unqualified, unconditional, unending love. And they therefore have a hard time accepting even the *imperfect* love of family and church members, of would-be friends and would-be lovers. The story of God's Son suffering rejection and ridicule and torture and death on the cross is our assurance that, while God is grieved by *sin*, God is willing to go to the fullest length to avoid the *greater* grief of losing *us* forever. Fortunately, the Creator of all that is is not near so proud and narcissistic as the mortals he has created. Fortunately, the Source of our salvation is not near so damning of human wrongdoers as we are, either for the wrongs others do to us, or for the wrongs we do to others, or for the wrongs we do to ourselves.

All of God's wrath was unleashed upon the earth once upon a time, Genesis says, and the face of the earth was destroyed by a great flood. It was the original weapon of mass destruction, the mother of all devastation, like a giant bow shooting a volley of arrows from heaven. The lightning must have crackled and boomed almost constantly through the ether as the torrents fell, like a Midwestern thunderstorm that just wouldn't quit. Think of the fear and panic, and nowhere to escape. And then, finally, after forty days and nights, the last rumble of thunder died away, and all was quiet, deathly quiet, as there was nothing but water anywhere—no talking, no singing, no sounds of industry or transport, no birds, no dogs, no rustle of breeze in the leaves and the grass. Nothing. Except the gentle lapping of water on the hull of a lone boat bobbing up and down slightly—the only little sign left of all of God's work and all of God's hope and all of God's love on the face of a watery ball.

Loneliness.

Loneliness.

Lonely for Noah and his family and his anxious cargo. Lonely for God. And God must have said to himself, "This isn't what I wanted. This isn't why I created. This isn't going to be the end." And God made a wind to blow over the earth, and the waters subsided. And God caused the waters to give way to dry ground. And God told Noah to come out of the ark, with his family and two of every kind of animal, and God said, "Never again." And as a sign to creation of that one-sided promise, and as a reminder to the loving parent of all creatures of that one-sided covenant, God set a bow in the clouds, not aimed threateningly at the earth, but turned away. And as a sign to humankind of God's enduring purpose, and as the unequivocal confirmation of the Creator's willingness to bear the full cost of fulfilling the covenant, God now has climbed up on a cross, not to pronounce death on us all, but to work our salvation to everlasting life.

Second Sunday in Lent
First Presbyterian Church, Dodge City, Kansas
February 27, 1994

Genesis 17:1–7, 15–16
Romans 4:13–25
Mark 8:31–38

"Radical Faith"

Poor Peter. He had just done the boldest, bravest, smartest, noblest thing in all his life. He had just declared that Jesus was the Messiah when everyone else who had an opinion and was willing to voice it had missed the mark, rather obtusely speculating that Jesus was John the Baptist or Elijah or one of the prophets raised from the dead. Poor Peter. He was probably feeling rather proud that he alone had given the right answer to Jesus' question, "[W]ho do *you* say that I am?" (Mark 8:29a NRSV)—that *he,* of *all* people, possessed both the insight to *know* and the confidence to *proclaim* what he knew. Poor Peter. The truth was so new to him that he could not believe his ears when Jesus began to talk about suffering and rejection and death in Jerusalem. Poor Peter.

That was when he did something stupid.

If Peter believed that Jesus was the Messiah, surely he should have drunk in everything Jesus had to say, no matter how it contradicted his accustomed ways of thinking and challenged his habitual ways of acting. But instead, Peter took Jesus aside and began to rebuke him for talking that way.

> But turning and looking at his disciples, [*Jesus*] rebuked *Peter,* and said, "Get behind me, Satan! For you are setting your mind not on divine things but on human things."
>
> He called the crowd with his disciples, and said to them, "If any want to become my followers, let them deny themselves and take up their cross and follow me. For those who want to save their life will lose it, and those who lose their life for my sake,

and for the sake of the gospel, will save it. For what will it profit them to gain the whole world and forfeit their life? Indeed, what can they give in return for their life? Those who are ashamed of me and of my words in this adulterous and sinful generation, of them the Son of Man will also be ashamed when he comes in the glory of his Father with the holy angels." (Mark 8:33–38 NRSV)

Poor Peter. He was an honest and decent human being, very likely a good father and a good husband and a good citizen. He had come to faith that *Jesus* was the *Messiah*, but he did not have faith in what the Messiah *was*, and so he could not accept the revolution in wisdom and values that Jesus demanded. And in so many ways, Peter is us.

Most of us learned in Sunday school about the popular view of the Messiah among Jews of Jesus' time—how the Messiah was expected to be a political and military hero, someone with the power and the authority to set everything right, ridding Palestine of Romans, ridding the streets of prostitutes and tax collectors, ridding the temple of corruption and impurity. *That* was a social program *every* true patriot, every moral champion, every devout worshiper could support. The Messiah had been awaited for centuries.

What had triggered Peter's faith that *Jesus* was the long-expected one, Mark does not *tell* us. Perhaps it was Jesus' way with *people*, perhaps it was Jesus' way with *demons*, perhaps it was Jesus' way with *words*. But whatever prompted Peter to his confession, Peter still did not have it right, for though Peter had *faith* in *Jesus*, he continued to put faith in many *other* things, *too*—physical safety, popular approval, intellectual reasonableness. Peter still did not have faith in a Messiah who must suffer and be rejected and be killed—a Messiah who quite literally said that his *followers* must *likewise* be willing to suffer and be rejected and be killed for his sake and for the sake of the truth which he proclaimed. Peter still did not have faith in the God of Jesus Christ alone. And when that's what it all came down to, starting on the night of Jesus' arrest—suffering, rejection, and death—Peter denied that he even *knew* Jesus. Loyalty to *Jesus* required *dis*loyalty to too many *other* things in which Peter *also* had faith—security, prestige, tradition, and privilege. He was unwilling to trust completely and unconditionally. Faith in the God of Jesus Christ *alone* was simply *too radical*.

Martin Luther, who put his *own* life in jeopardy for the sake of his convictions about the truth Jesus taught, *knew* the cost of allegiance to Christ. Luther once wrote: "Whatever your heart clings to and confides

"Radical Faith"

in, that is really your god."[1] In theory, at least, or in the safe arena of theological talk, I am sure all of us would agree with Luther without hesitation, as would Peter. We know that idols can come in forms other than bronze statues and marble mosaics. But when we begin to examine what it is that we genuinely rely on in our lives, what we are truly devoted to as measured by our time and our treasure, what we really *believe* about the way the world *is* and the way the world *should* be, most of us, if we are honest, will discover that our single-hearted devotion to the God of Jesus Christ falls apart under the scrutiny. We *have* put and we *continue* to put our faith in things that pass by such familiar names as common sense, fiscal prudence, and self-preservation. One of the greatest Reformed theologians of the twentieth century, H. Richard Niebuhr, put it this way: "Whatever be our relation to the official monotheism of our religious institutions"—that is, our churchly claim that there is only one God,—"the *private* faith by which we *live* is likely to be a . . . thing with *many* objects of devotion and worship."[2] Niebuhr observed that, in terms of our *devotion*, we bow deeply before ourselves, our children, our homes, sex. As the ancient Greeks had a whole collection of gods on Mount Olympus, so we have *our* Olympian gods:

> our country, our ideologies, our democracies, civilizations, churches, our art which we practice for art's sake, our truth which we pursue for truth's sake, our moral values, our ideas and the social forces which we personalize, adore, and on which we depend for deliverance from sheer nothingness and the utter inconsequence of existence.[3]

Many of the idols Niebuhr listed sound sacred and we assume they are fully compatible with our professed single-minded faith in the God of Jesus Christ. It may seem like sacrilege indeed for Niebuhr to suggest that family and nation and even moral convictions are capable of becoming gods for us, but so they are, and so they do. And Peter could not imagine that comfort and safety and long life were not part and parcel of a right relationship with God.

But Jesus said, "If any want to become my followers, let them deny themselves and take up their cross"—the cross, the instrument for execution of criminals, shameful and humiliating and disgraceful—"and follow

---

1 Lenker, *Luther's Large Catechism*, 44.

2. Niebuhr, 119; emphasis added.

3. Niebuhr, 120.

me" (Mark 34b NRSV)—even to *death*, for faithful obedience to God. Jesus was not simply talking about maintaining a stiff upper lip in spite of the little annoyances and frustrations that are an inevitable part of life. He was talking about *your* deliberate choice and *my* deliberate choice to take up a burden voluntarily and without any compulsion except the determination to be faithfully obedient to God the Father of Jesus Christ who will not let us off the hook when we piously object that we have family responsibilities or patriotic sentiments or financial policies or personal reputation to think of. He was talking about taking up a burden that puts all our worldly securities and virtues at risk, perhaps, but that is necessary for us because we have but one God and none beside him and, above everything else, we must be faithful to that God.

We are part of a generation that has made a religious virtue of preserving itself—preserving its looks, preserving its money. And what is true of us as individuals has become true of us as churches. We are too untrusting of the God who appeared to Abram when he was ninety-nine years old, and Sarai, his wife, was elderly as well, and said, "I am God Almighty; walk before me, and be blameless. And I will make my covenant between me and you, and will make you exceedingly numerous. . . . You shall be the ancestor of a multitude of nations" (Gen 17:1b-2, 4b NRSV). And Abram was incredulous for a moment but then did what God told him to do, and God did as God had promised, implausible as it was and impossible as it seemed. A child in such old age, through whom nations and kings would come and all the families of the earth would be blessed? That was faith. That was *radical* faith, faith beyond reason, foolish faith, faith even worthy of the world's ridicule, faith that will draw the *anger* of *good* people and *wise* people and will *perplex* people who are a little bit *better* and a little bit *wiser*. And that is the faith—the complete and absolute and undivided trust—to which Jesus Christ calls anyone who would become a stranger to one's own self and one's own self-interest, and to take up the burden, knowing well the risks involved to security and health and family ties and fortune and reputation, and to respond obediently to Jesus' call to the opportunities for ministry that God puts before us, even if they pave a path that leads up the slopes of Calvary.

It takes faith in God alone to recognize and act upon the truth that our life is not for saving, our fortune is not for keeping, our time is not for hoarding. It takes radical faith. And it takes radical faith for a church to model such risky self-abandon for the world around it and for its own members. Or is *our* faith in God something *less* than that, and so we join

Peter in rebuking Christ for talking about a cross, and insist instead on a painless, undemanding, sensible faith that requires neither that we make any real sacrifice nor that we surrender any of our other allegiances, and ends up being no genuine faith in God at all? "What do you mean by talking about suffering and rejection and death, Jesus?" Peter might have asked. "You're the Messiah! Get on with the program! This sacrifice business isn't going to get us ahead in life. It's not going to score any points. What kind of parent would I be? What kind of spouse would I be? What kind of American? What kind of employee? What kind of church member? What kind of elder or deacon or pastor?" If we reduce our Christian discipleship to a matter of popular wisdom and common reasonableness, it is hard to see how we are putting *faith* in the God of Jesus Christ who won our salvation by the foolishness of the cross. By putting safety first, and security, and comfort, and convenience, by whatever virtuous names we choose to disguise them, Satan will have *triumphed* in setting our minds on human things rather than divine. And then we will have lost our life indeed.

H. Richard Niebuhr wrote,

> [O]ur gods [of self, sex, family, patriotism, ideology, whatever] are unable to save us from the ultimate frustration of meaningless existence . . . . [But to] attach faith, hope, and love to [the one true God], this source of all things and this slayer of all, is to have confidence which is not subject to time, for this is the eternal reality . . . . To have hope of this One is to have hope that is eternal. . . . [F]aith in God involves us in a permanent revolution of the mind and of the heart, a continuous life which opens out infinitely into ever new possibilities. [Such faith] does not, therefore, afford grounds for boasting but only for simple thankfulness. It is a gift of God.[4]

"If any want to become my followers, let them deny themselves and take up their cross and follow me" (Mark 8:34b NRSV). That is faith. That is absolute faith. That is radical faith in God alone.

---

4. Niebuhr, 120, 123, 126.

Third Sunday in Lent
First Presbyterian Church, Ponca City, Oklahoma
March 11, 2012

Exodus 20:1–17
1 Corinthians 1:18–25
John 2:13–22

"Only the Cross"

When you read or hear the term "Death Row," what comes into your mind? I suspect that, at the very least, most of us would consider anybody who has been sentenced to be executed as being disreputable. Even those of us who regard capital punishment as incompatible with the gospel don't deny that anyone *rightly* convicted for a capital offense has acted reprehensibly; such people are unsavory, deserving of the ultimate punishment that is *morally* permissible. No one thinks of such people as heroes. No one considers such people to be role models. No one wants his or her children to grow up to be like them.

When you read or hear the term "Death Row," do you also imagine an electric chair, or a hangman's rope, or a gas chamber, or a lethal injection? Not very pleasant things to contemplate. Certainly nothing to celebrate in paintings or jewelry or giant replicas alongside the highway. And the last place we would think of seeing it would be atop a building where nice, decent, respectable people gather regularly, even bring their spouses and children and grandchildren.

When you read or hear the term "Death Row," do you remember Jesus? Do you think of the cross? If that association is in any way upsetting to you, or disturbing, or causes you to be angry, you might begin to understand why, as Paul noted in a letter to the Christian church at Corinth, in Greece, the apostles' proclamation of "Christ crucified" was considered to be "a stumbling block to Jews and foolishness to Gentiles" (1 Cor 1:23 NRSV)—and why so many *modern* Christians, conditioned by hymns dripping with syrupy sentimentality and familiar shapes

"Only the Cross"

illuminated with neon lights and easy use of the word "cross" as a shorthand for having a confirmed ticket to heaven, and nearly all of whom consider being on Death Row a sign of a prisoner's obvious guilt and wickedness, tend to ignore the profound *scandal* of declaring Jesus to be the Christ, the Messiah, the Son of God. No person relying on common sense and reasonableness could possibly call Jesus "Lord." And so, I think, unbelievers can hardly be *criticized* for being unbelievers—it *could* be that they understand more about Jesus than a lot of people who call themselves *Christian* and who have always supposed that *being* one is part of the package of being a normal, respectable, decent human being, none of whom could ever imagine having as the image of one's faith an electric chair, or a hangman's rope, or a gas chamber, or a needle full of poison. And so, indeed, many modern places of worship, acknowledging that the cross, properly understood, is not just the best marketing tool for attracting consumers for the product they are selling, don't have one visible anywhere on the premises.

And yet, Paul was insistent on preaching "Jesus Christ, and him crucified" (1 Cor 2:2b NRSV). Just a few verses after our reading this morning, Paul, addressing a church in which many people considered themselves wise and sophisticated above and beyond any sort of folly, said he had come to bring the gospel to them, having decided "to know nothing among you except Jesus Christ, and him crucified" (1 Cor 2:2 NRSV). Neither in his letters to the Corinthians nor in any other correspondence does Paul say anything about a virgin birth. Neither in his letters to the Corinthians nor in any other correspondence does Paul say anything about Jesus' parables. Neither in his letters to the Corinthians nor in any other correspondence does Paul say anything about Jesus working miraculous cures or feeding thousands with a paltry few loaves of bread. For Paul, faith all centers on the cross, this first-century Roman equivalent of an electric chair, or a hangman's rope, or a gas chamber, or a lethal injection.

Now, obviously, Paul did not consider the world's salvation to be dependent upon *every* death of *every* person who was *ever* hoisted up on a cross. It was, in fact, the cruel and gruesome death, plotted by the establishment and cheered by the crowds and ordered by the governor, of the Jesus who had been born in unique but humble circumstances and who healed people considered incurable and even untouchable, and who had transformed limited resources into adequate and more to satisfy human hunger, that Paul understood to be necessary for himself and anyone else to have genuine life. But if we don't understand the absolute scandal of the Christ of God being considered by nearly every pious person who knew about him to be a worthless scoundrel who undermined the foundations of society by healing the sick and feeding the hungry and befriending the outcast and championing the poor, whom everybody else in society had given up on or written off or said if they're sick or hungry or outcast or poor it's their own fault and so he was condemned and put to death for it, *then we don't get it*. "For the message about the cross is foolishness to those who are perishing, but to us who are being saved it is the power of God. For it is written"—and here Paul quotes from the Greek translation of the prophet Isaiah,—"'I will destroy the wisdom of the wise, and the discernment of the discerning I will thwart.' Where is the one who is wise? Where is the scribe? Where is the debater of this age" (1 Cor 1:18–20b NRSV)? Where is the reasonable person, he was asking. Where is the respectable person? Where is the person who has his or her fingers on the pulse of contemporary culture, with its tastes and preferences and fads? "Has not God made foolish the wisdom of the world" (1 Cor 1:20c NRSV)? Has God not made the key to and symbol of salvation, of blessedness, of obedience to him, the ancient equivalent of the electric chair, of the hangman's rope, of the gas chamber, of the lethal injection, administered to some prisoner whom every reasonable person and virtually every government official and religious authority judged to be a criminal of the worst kind, deserving of the worst possible punishment for the things he said and did? "For since, in the wisdom of God, the world did not know God through wisdom, God decided, through the foolishness of our proclamation"—that is, the proclamation of Jesus Christ executed on the cross,—"to save those who believe. For Jews demand signs and Greeks desire wisdom, but we proclaim Christ crucified, a stumbling block to Jews and foolishness to Gentiles, but to those who are the called, both Jews and Greeks, Christ the power of God and the wisdom of God. For God's foolishness is wiser than human wisdom, and God's weakness is stronger than human strength" (1 Cor 1:21–25 NRSV).

This is a tough tonic to swallow, and, as I was writing this sermon this week, I rather astounded myself how shocking it sounds, how shocking it would sound to my congregation! But we are all adults, or nearly so. More to the point, we have all declared that we believe in, have faith in, Jesus Christ, or are in process of preparing to decide whether to do so. So sober honesty is in order. Can we really swear absolute loyalty to this person whom the prevailing wisdom judged to be wrong, whom the vast majority of good and respectable people considered to be utterly detestable? And—and here's the really disturbing part of all of this, for me—if the world, even our friends and business associates and public officials, consider *us* to be reasonable and acceptable and respectable, are *we* really being that *loyal* to, do we really even *know*, Christ *crucified*?

In essence, that was the question Paul was putting before the Corinthians. It seems they wanted both—to be Christians, and to be well thought of by society; to be Christians, and to be considered wise; to be Christians, and to retain their accustomed privileges of class and status and prestige. Because of that, they were habitually quarrelsome, they were often divided, they were invariably prideful in asserting prerogative and superiority over one another. And they seem to have thought that it was all about how much or what one *knew*. They thought their salvation was a matter of their own achievement, ultimately—their own commendable assent to particular beliefs, their own admirable agreement with this or that teaching,—and had turned salvation into a contest, a rivalry, yet another occasion to determine winners and losers. In fact, they had merely exchanged their *old* philosophies for what they now considered to be a *newer* philosophy, and it really had nothing to do with the sacrifice of God's own Son on the ugly instrument of execution that poets and songwriters and painters and jewelers and greeting-card designers over the years have sentimentalized into acceptability. But, judged by the standards they applied to everyone else, Jesus was the world's biggest failure, and justly so. Had their attitudes about people in dungeons awaiting execution changed at all because of the cruel death of Jesus? Had their acceptance of the way society judges people and their actions modified in the least bit because of the reasons Jesus was arrested and tried and condemned and sentenced? Had they changed at all their self-justifying dismissal of their own sins and all their self-righteous denunciation of others' wrongdoing? Had the scandal of the cross set them in the way of Jesus Christ? Or had it merely confirmed their determination to avoid any such disrepute for themselves? If anybody but *Jesus* had come into their sacred places and dared to cleanse them of idolatry and false worship and profiteering, what would their response have been? What did they think of Paul's exposing their communion meal as gluttonous and an excuse for getting drunk, for reinforcing distinctions and mistreating the poor? What did they think the crucifixion was all about?

Midway through Lent, the death of Jesus begins to loom large over our faith, judging our pious speech, our pious behavior, with the stark truth that forces us to decide whether we will think thoughts that the *world* considers *reasonable*, whether we will conform to the *world's* code of what is *proper*, whether we will avoid upsetting the *status quo*, whether we will take the cross in *stride*—or whether we will provoke the world's *wrath* and perhaps earn a place *alongside* Jesus on *Calvary* by feeding the world's hungry and thereby judging its selfishness, by championing the world's poor and thereby judging its greed, by healing the world's sick and thereby judging its insensitivity, by befriending the world's lonely and thereby judging its verdicts, by comforting the world's bereaved and thereby judging its threats, by forgiving the world's sinners and thereby judging its vengefulness, by reconciling the world's enemies and thereby judging its war-making.

"For the message about the cross is foolishness to those who are perishing," Paul declared, "but to us who are being saved it is the power of God" (1 Cor 1:18 NRSV). Salvation is not a commodity that can be acquired. It is not an award that can be earned. It is not a distinction that we can use to divide or exclude or elevate or promote. It is not a result of right thoughts or even right behavior. Indeed, it is not something that is yet complete in anyone. It is all about the cross—what God has done through this ugly and shameful instrument by which the world pronounces *its* judgment of worthless failure. Jesus, the Son of God, was hung on a cross. And, ironically, by its own instrument of doom, God is working the world's salvation to life. The world's wisdom isn't smart enough to do that. The world's strength is powerless to do that. Only what the world ridicules and condemns and rejects. Only God's foolishness. Only God's weakness. Only the cross.

Fourth Sunday in Lent
First Presbyterian Church, Ponca City, Oklahoma
March 15, 2015

Numbers 21:4-9
Ephesians 2:1-10
John 3:14-21

"Looking Up at Love"

In the middle of the noisy traffic and bustling hubbub of Honolulu, Hawaii, there is a sanctified circle of green and quiet. It is the National Memorial Cemetery of the Pacific, located in the shallow crater of an extinct volcano known locally as "The Punchbowl." There, laid out in neat and even rows, are the grave markers of thousands of soldiers and sailors and airmen and, in some cases, their spouses, many of them killed during the war in the Pacific, many during the war in Korea, many during the war in Viet Nam, some, now, perhaps killed in wars in the Middle East. At the west end of the cemetery is a large white stone monument. On it are inscribed these words first written by Abraham Lincoln to a mother who lost five sons in battle during the Civil War, now addressed to thousands more parents and grandparents, brothers and sisters, and sons and daughters: "The solemn pride that must be yours to have laid so costly a sacrifice upon the altar of freedom."

About forty years ago, I first stood before that monument, having earlier visited the sunken tomb at Pearl Harbor which was the USS *Arizona*, and having read, at the cemetery, the accounts of the various Pacific battles of World War II written alongside large mosaic maps of the theatres of war, and I wept, thinking of the pain of mortal wounds, thinking of the pain of profound grief. "The solemn pride that must be yours to have laid so costly a sacrifice upon the altar of freedom." Heartbroken, but proud—the image came to mind of mothers and fathers and widows and widowers and orphaned children being handed a folded American flag.

What a high price answering the call to commitment can sometimes exact! Seventy-five years ago, a dark pall had fallen over Europe and Asia, and in order to save a desperate world, people gave their money, their toil, and even the sons and daughters on whom they had centered their hopes and dreams, believing that the cause of liberty for people the world over was worth the risk involved in sending their children off to battle. And many of them paid the *full price* of *saving* the world from the curse of enslavement, the bane of perpetual darkness. "The solemn pride that must be yours to have laid so costly a sacrifice upon the altar of freedom."

That must be the closest *human* analogy to what happened on the *cross*. The God who created the world to be a pleasant and bountiful home for us, who witnessed in agonizing astonishment the self-destructive behavior that is human sin and wondered if the creation would all be lost, took a last desperate step to right the wrongs by sending his own Son into the field of battle armed with words of truth and deeds of compassion, and his Son was killed; worse, he was killed through the treachery of his own comrade. But *his death* was the *turning point* of the whole war, and by his sacrifice, which was the sacrifice of the one who *sent* him, creation was redeemed, and the many were set free.

"What do you think happens at Calvary?" asked Scottish theologian James Denney of an acquaintance a century ago. And the other replied:

> If I had a [child], and [the child] went wrong, dreadfully wrong, I couldn't give him up. But to redeem him a heart would need to break—my heart; and perhaps his as well. And at the Cross comes home to me that I have broken my Father's heart; and yet that he can't give me up. And I can't bear it; grow sick of myself; and long to be quite different; and there and then begin to be it.[1]

Another theologian, many centuries earlier, said it this way: "For God so loved the world that he gave his only Son, so that everyone who believes in him may not perish but have eternal life. Indeed, God did not send the Son into the world to condemn the world, but in order that the world might be saved through him" (John 3:16–17 NRSV). By sin's ugliest instrument of destruction—the cross—we are saved from sin's ugliest consequence—eternal death. Through the heartbreak of God's supreme sacrifice, God's broken dream for creation is repaired. By nurturing with grateful devotion the seed of *faith* which God has implanted *in us*, we discover God's limitless *love for us*.

---

1 Quoted in Gossip, "Gospel According to St. John, Exposition," 510.

The cross is the altar upon which God was willing to lay the costly sacrifice of *his own Son* for *our freedom*—freedom from fear, freedom from meaninglessness, freedom from self-indulgence, freedom from sin, freedom from death. The cross of Jesus should speak to us daily of God's great hope for us. We stand before *it* as I stood before the monument in the Punchbowl, pondering with teary amazement the price willingly paid for the salvation of humankind, and of each one of us. We picture the cross ornamented with the body of him who was perfectly obedient to God and completely devoted to the eternal well-being of every person, and we wonder how human hearts can turn so cruelly against unlimited goodness. We look up at it, and we see the love of God. And suddenly, if we have any sensitivity to spiritual things at all, there must flood in upon us the realization that we, each of us, have had a part in nailing Jesus to the cross, and we still do, with our little mutterings of prejudice and our little rushes to judge others and our little twinges of pride and our little plans for revenge and our little stirrings of greed.

But there must *also* flood in upon us, if we have any sensitivity to spiritual things at all, the realization that God's great sacrifice to *save his creation* was also God's great sacrifice to save *you* and *me*, and that it surely calls for a fundamental response of thankful devotion with every breath and every expression and every movement of our lives.

The Bible tells us that when the people of Israel were journeying through the wilderness from Mount Hor toward the Red Sea and then around Edom they became impatient. They grumbled among themselves and complained against God and Moses. Fed up with their whining about the trivialities incidental to their escape from slavery, it seems, God decided to give them a *real* reason to complain. God sent venomous serpents among the people which bit them, and many died.

> The people came to Moses and said, 'We have sinned by speaking against the LORD and against you; pray to the LORD to take away the serpents from us.' So Moses prayed for the people. And the LORD said to Moses, 'Make a poisonous serpent, and set it on a pole; and everyone who is bitten shall look at it and live.' So Moses made a serpent of bronze, and put it upon a pole; and whenever a serpent bit someone, that person would look at the serpent of bronze and live. (Num 21:7–9 NRSV)

The dangers remained; the serpents still sank their fangs into the heels of the people, and the people still became sick and were in danger of death.

But if they would look up at the bronze serpent hanging on the pole, the power of God would heal them.

As the snake-bitten Israelites were healed by looking up at the bronze serpent lifted high on a pole, and they lived, Jesus tried to explain to the befuddled Nicodemus, "so must the Son of man be lifted up, that whoever believes in him may have eternal life" (John 3:14b–15 NRSV). With our eyes of faith lifted up and trained on Jesus hanging on the cross, we will be healed, by the power of God, from the evils that plague and bedevil us—we will have the gift of eternal life, the inheritance of the kingdom of God. By training our gaze on the one who was crucified because of his loving obedience to God and his loving service to humankind, by seeing through *his* life and death what it means for *us* to be obedient to God and to serve humankind, we discover what salvation is, what it *means* to have *eternal life*—the quality of life that flows from God through Christ to all who believe, truly believe, in him.

The cross of Jesus transforms the humiliation of lowly passion and sacrificial death into glorious triumph. The cross of Jesus is no longer a sign of ignominious scandal but a majestic beacon of salvation. Jesus raised up on the cross is the guidepost to eternal life, and no matter how many poisonous serpents may be loosed about our feet—gossip, illness, self-concern, mean-spiritedness, jealousy, injustice, oppression,—biting at our heels, menacing us with their venomous threats, they cannot overcome God's promise of eternal life, life as it is meant to be, life lived in the close companionship of God himself, if we will but keep looking up at the cross of Jesus Christ, the cross that is the altar upon which God has laid his costly sacrifice for our freedom from sin and from death.

A Presbyterian pastor in Texas told of the encounter in a church sanctuary between a minister and a young man, rebellious in attitude and crude in manner and vulgar of speech. I don't quote to offend anyone, but only in order to give you the full picture of the young man's show of total disdain for everyone and everything. The exchange went like this:

"Jesus Christ died for you," said the minister.

"And I don't give a damn," answered the youth.

"Really?" the minister responded. "Then you won't mind an experiment."

"What do you mean?" asked the young man, stiffening his back.

"I want you to look up at that cross hanging in the front of the sanctuary," said the minister, "and repeat a dozen times, 'Jesus Christ died for me, and I don't give a damn.'"

The young man gave a sneer, at once cocky and contemptuous, and turned toward the cross and began his recitation. "Jesus Christ died for me, and I don't give a damn."

He glanced smugly at the minister to gauge the effect, and then he turned again toward the cross and repeated the words.

After about half a dozen times, with his eyes still gazing up at the cross, the young man's speech began to slow, and then it slowed some more, and then it slowed some more. And finally, the twelfth time, the young man started, "Jesus Christ died for me, and I—" and he sank to his knees, sobbing.

The minister put his hand on the boy's shoulder. "You see?" he said gently.

Just as looking up at the *serpent* raised on the pole in the wilderness meant *bodily* life for the grumbling and self-consumed and then terrified Israelites, so looking at the cross on which *Jesus* was lifted up means *eternal* life for the most wretched, for the most abused, for the most unlovely, for the most hateful, for the most prideful. How can *we* not then have eternal life—a new and vibrant and everlasting relationship of obedience to God, of thanksgiving to God, of loyalty to God, of love for God? How then can *we* not understand that God cares for us—cares for us so much that God has laid such a costly sacrifice upon the altar of our salvation?

Look up at Jesus on the cross. Look up at love—the unreasonable, stubborn, boundless love that God has for you and for me. "For God so loved the world that he gave his only Son, so that everyone who believes in him may not perish but have eternal life" (John 3:16 NRSV).

Fifth Sunday in Lent
Spanish Springs Presbyterian Church, Sparks, Nevada
April 6, 2003

Jeremiah 31:31–34
Hebrews 5:5–10
John 12:20–33

"This Side of the Covenant"

All through Lent, our Old Testament readings have been about the covenants that God made with God's people—the covenant God made with Noah never again to destroy the earth; the covenant God made with Abraham to give him and Sarah a great and numerous progeny and to be their God; the covenant God made through the law that was delivered to the people through Moses. We have seen that God's continuing purpose through all the covenant-making has been to redeem creation back to the purpose God had in mind for it from the beginning—an arena for God to shower the great divine love upon all creatures, and to enjoy a loving fellowship with them.

For the past three Sundays, our lectionary texts have been encouraging us to reflect on the meaning of the cross, not only for Jesus, but for us. We have seen that the cross is not a memento of sentimentality, but an insistent reminder of the cost of our salvation—Jesus' gruesome death, shameful and foolish in the eyes of the Jews and the Greeks—and the best possible indication of the measure of God's love for the world, and God's loving intention of redeeming the world, and a claim upon our lives, if we would be faithful. Today's passages, it seems to me, round out the relationship of cross and covenant by putting the crucifixion in the perspective of God's promise made long before Jesus' birth, and they serve to interpret the events of Holy Week in the light of that promise.

Paul tells us that, on the night before his crucifixion, the night when he was betrayed, Jesus "took a loaf of bread, and when he had given thanks, he broke it and said, 'This is my body that is for you. Do this in remembrance of me.' In the same way he took the cup also, after supper, saying, 'This cup is the new covenant in my blood. Do this, as often as you drink it, in remembrance of me'" (1 Cor 11:23c–25 NRSV). On Maundy Thursday, in less than two weeks, we will hear those words again as the supper is spread before us, and we once again give thanks, take, eat, and drink in remembrance of him. The words are familiar to us. We hear them frequently. But within the rubric language of the meal is a sentence of Jesus that we may sometimes hear without thinking much about it: "This cup is the *new covenant* in my blood" (1 Cor 11:25b NRSV).

To the other symbolisms of the cross, Jesus, on the night before his death and in fellowship with his friends, added that it would be a sign of a new covenant, much as the rainbow was a sign to humankind and a reminder to God of the covenant made with Noah that never again would God destroy the earth. Surely, Jesus recalled, and his first disciples, all of them Jews, would have recalled, what is perhaps the most pivotal passage in all the prophets—the centerpiece of Jeremiah's prophecy to the Israelites who had been punished for their constant failures and persistent transgressions by being taken captive to Babylon:

> The days are surely coming, says the LORD, when I will make a new covenant with the house of Israel and the house of Judah. It will not be like the covenant that I made with their ancestors when I took them by the hand to bring them out of the land of Egypt—a covenant that they broke, though I was their husband, says the LORD. But this is the covenant that I will make with the house of Israel after those days, says the LORD: I will put my law within them, and I will write it on their hearts; and I will be their God, and they shall be my people. No longer shall they teach one another, or say to each other, 'Know the LORD,' for they shall *all* know me, from the least of them to the greatest, says the LORD; for I will forgive their iniquity, and remember their sin no more. (Jer 31:31–34 NRSV)

A *new* covenant. Not just words on cold stone, but a flowering of gratitude and faith. That ancient promise of God, Jesus declared, was being fulfilled, was being realized, was coming to fruition, in his death on the cross, his body broken, his blood shed. As the making of ancient covenants had been sealed in blood, so the gravity, the solemnity, of this *new* covenant was now to be manifested in the shedding of blood—not of a sheep or a goat, dear as such creatures are to God, but of a human being, who was also God's own Son—the most valuable sacrifice that could possibly be made.

The making of covenants in the Bible was a *communal* act—an act that involved *all* the people. Even if it was an arrangement with an *individual*, it was binding upon *everyone* and was for the benefit of the *whole community*, those whom God had chosen to be a blessing to *all* nations—the house of Israel. The new covenant promised in Jeremiah was God's declaration that *all* people could know God directly and intimately. God would grant them an inner power and motivation towards obedience—no longer the threat of punishment posed by a law that had been chiseled on rock, but a habit of the spirit born of and nurtured by fellowship with God, restored and made perfect. Now, people could know God's purpose and desire by an inner testimony rather than an outward compulsion. It was not a promise that people would be *sinless*, but a promise that *God's forgiveness* would *cover* their sin. No more would salvation be merely an uncertain *possibility* that could be achieved only by presenting just the right sacrifice on the temple altar, if *then*. A long history of sacrificing innocent animals had done nothing to change the human heart. Salvation would now be a sure reality achieved by God's own sacrifice of the only true unblemished lamb, God's own sinless Son—a sacrifice that would work the most profound change in the heart of God. "I will forgive their iniquity," God promised, "and remember their sin no more" (Jer 31:34c NRSV).

And yet anyone who looks upon the cross, who really sees God's sacrifice of his own Son there, cannot but be changed in his or her *own* heart, cannot but feel established there an intimacy with a God whose love for us is so great, cannot but share God's hope for creation and every creature in it in a way that the *written* law can only *hint* at. And, with *our hearts* so changed, with an unending gratitude, with an awareness of God that reaches deep into our soul, the law of God is no longer a matter of words that *pre*scribe and *pro*scribe. The law of God is now God's own purpose *in*scribed on our hearts and demonstrated in every deed, and so every deed becomes an act of faith. To be Christians, to live on *this* side of God's new covenant, is to act, daily and in everything, on the basis of the cross—with selfless love, with humble obedience, with unflinching faith. The evidence of our salvation to eternal life is that we live in a way that reflects Christ's death—that we are willing, with Christ, to set aside interest in worldly gain and advantage; that we are willing, with Christ, to take on the world's ridicule and insult for the sake of healing and forgiving the broken and the sin-burdened; that we are willing, with Christ, to suffer even death for the sake of the truth; that we are willing, with God, to sorrow at injustice and oppression and, with God, to rejoice in mercy and wholeness.

The Letter to the Hebrews testifies that faith does not exempt us from the pain of the world—the pain of suffering, the pain of other people's sins. Obedience to God is not rewarded by opportunities for prestige and riches, but by opportunities to give witness to God's merciful love, perhaps even from a cross. Being God's Son did not exempt *Jesus* from suffering and death, and *he* was the most faithful and obedient of *all*. None of the Old Testament covenants required God's people to sacrifice them*selves* in any way. But the new covenant established in the crucifixion death of Jesus Christ in fact raises the real possibility of *our* sacrifice, *too*, if indeed God's law is now a matter of heart-felt conviction, if indeed God's eternal purpose is now the overriding motivation in our lives. The new covenant is not a promise of earthly bliss, and it certainly destroys any notion that earthly suffering must be the result of *dis*obedience to God; Jesus the crucified was the most obedient of all, the most deserving of earthly glory and honor. As he knew God intimately, so, because of his sacrifice on the cross, *we* have the possibility of knowing God intimately, not through legal commands and threats of punishment, but through God's faithful vision of the world and every person in it, through faith's understanding of God's purpose and God's ways, through faith's assurance that the *crucifixion* is the *only* and *inevitable* route to the *resurrection*.

The cross was not an *optional* method for the salvation of the world. And every Christian should understand, and the church must clearly declare, that the willingness to suffer for the sake of God's truth, even to the ultimate sacrifice of death on some cross of public opinion or family disapproval or financial insecurity or physical peril, is a constant reality of faith in Jesus Christ. And the right understanding of the cost of salvation—the price God paid two thousand years ago and the claims *that sacrifice* makes on *us today*—is why it is so critical for every Christian to attend to the disciplines of Holy Week. There are some pulpits and PowerPoint projections out there from which there is being preached a promise of health and wealth and every sort of happiness if you just have enough faith, if you just obey adequately, if you just give enough of your fortune to a post office box advertised on a television screen.

That is a lie.

That is not the gospel of Jesus Christ.

That is not the truth of the cross.

Since the time of the Enlightenment, there has been a tendency to neglect making a pilgrimage through Holy Week. In some churches, Lent is never mentioned, and the *risk* involved in taking up the cross and following Christ is never acknowledged. I have to tell you that I've received complaints from some congregation members in other churches for the soberness of the music during Lent. "I don't want to have to think about pain and sacrifice on Sunday," one lady in a former church told me one day. "This is where everything should be upbeat. I come to church to be happy." Well, there are some churches out there that will celebrate Palm Sunday a week from now without a hint of the passion, will talk much about the cross of Jesus without ever mentioning that Jesus told us we must be willing to be crucified along with him, will ignore Good Friday as a quaint Romanism that has been made irrelevant for anyone who knows about Easter.

But the meaning of Easter is incomplete at best, and totally perverted, at worst, if the joyful news of the empty tomb is divorced from the grim reality of the bloodied cross. And the resurrection of Jesus Christ has no power to raise us up with him if the new covenant in Christ's blood hasn't transformed us by writing the law of God on our hearts—the law of forgiveness, the law of peace, the law of trust, the law of love. How can anyone think that life can still be an individual effort, that life is a climb up the ladder of promotions and possessions and power, that life is something to be grasped and hoarded and held onto, who also truly believes that our salvation was worked by the obedient sacrifice of Jesus Christ, the Son of God, on the cross of shame and cruelty? How can anyone think that faith is just a matter of rule-keeping and creed-spouting who has clearly heard the words of Jesus Christ, the Son of God, on the cross, saying, "Father, forgive them, for they do not know what they are doing" (Luke 23:34a NRSV)? He who then appeared to his disciples and commanded them, "If you forgive the sins of any, they are forgiven them; if you retain the sins of any, they are retained" (John 20:23 NRSV), having said to them before his death, "I give you a new commandment, that you love one another. Just as I have loved you, you also should love one another" (John 13:34 NRSV).

But the resurrection was not just one possible outcome of the crucifixion. And every Christian should understand, and the church must clearly declare, that the same faith that leads us in the way of the cross also yields us the joyful intimacy with God that was promised when Jeremiah spoke of the new covenant so long ago. Being with God forever, knowing God face to face, letting ourselves go from our worldly securities to fall gently into the waiting arms of God, is what lies at the root of the promise of the resurrection and is the everlasting reality of faith in Jesus Christ.

On which side of the covenant do *we* live? God has established a new covenant through the blood of Jesus Christ sacrificed for us and for all creation on the cross. And if we are living in faithful response to the obedience of Jesus Christ on the cross, if we are giving witness in everything that we say and do to God's loving purpose, living our lives in the service of others and exhibiting the truth of God's redemption, then God has put his law within us and has written it on our hearts, and he is our God and we are his people. No longer do we just teach one another, or just say to each other, "Know the LORD" (Jer 31:34b NRSV), for we all know him, from the least of us to the greatest, and God will forgive our iniquity, and remember our sin no more.

Palm/Passion Sunday
Spanish Springs Presbyterian Church, Sparks, Nevada
April 13, 2003

Isaiah 50:4–9a

Philippians 2:5–11

Mark 11:1–11

"Putting the Pieces Together"

Lucius Gaius Gallus stood motionless as a statue. He could scarcely believe what he saw. Suddenly, all of the pieces came together in his mind, and he was struck with a mixture of fear and anger and pity and awe. He remembered, now, clearly, the breezy day, not quite a week earlier, when he had been sitting on a bench outside a tavern on the outskirts of Jerusalem along the Jericho road. He was returning to the city and the Roman army compound at the Fortress Antonia after having been dispatched to Jericho by the legionary commander to check out rumors of a public commotion over some healer, a wizard or something. As it turned out, there wasn't much to it; apparently, as he was able to piece together the situation, some local religious leaders had gotten excited and tried to rouse public opinion against the man after he had spoken to a blind man who then regained his sight, but they had been unsuccessful, and that had been the end of it. There had been some accusations that the man pretended to be the king of Israel, but the evidence was vague.

Ordinarily, it would not have merited any investigation, but the military was on edge, with the approach of a Jewish festival. It was always a time of potential trouble, his superiors had explained. And when he heard that more than a hundred thousand people were expected to flock into Jerusalem during the next week, he easily understood how things could get out of hand, both in the city and along the roads leading up to it. It would be a ticklish situation—managing to keep an eye on the crowds and being prepared to respond quickly to any disturbance, while yet not *provoking* disorder by their very *presence*. He had learned quickly upon his arrival in Palestine how much the Roman legion was despised by the majority of these strange people. Not that he blamed them, much. Perhaps *their* aspirations had nothing to do with Roman law or Roman goods or Roman gods or Roman *anything*. When his military discipline occasionally relaxed and allowed him to entertain private thoughts, he wondered what Rome wanted with this barren strip of land, anyway. It was so dry and dusty. Compared to Italy, the place seemed backward and worthless, and, compared to his ancestral homeland in Gaul, at the other end of the empire, this landscape was positively sterile and its inhabitants were, well, to put it politely, unkempt.

But it had not been questions about imperial politics that had occupied his mind as he sat outside the tavern. He had been reading a letter that had arrived for him the day before—a letter from his wife,—describing the illness of his son Marcus, a fever that had seized him and had been raging for three days by the time she wrote the letter. What had happened after that? he wondered anxiously. It had been more than two weeks since she had written the letter. Was Marcus now well and back at his studies and his sports? Or had the fever left him weak and listless? Or was his beloved son now . . . ? He shut his eyes hard, trying to force the thought from his mind, trying to banish the image of death from the realm of possibility. Tears blurred his vision when he again opened his eyes. His hand reached, reflexively, for the cup of wine that he had set down on the bench alongside him.

It was just then that he had become aware of a sound in the distance, borne on the wind, faint at first, but slowly growing in volume as it came closer. His horse, tied up at a stone post, pricked up its ears, shifted its weight, and snorted. Looking up and glancing back down the road toward Jericho, Lucius wiped his eyes with the back of his hand. As his vision cleared, he saw a crowd of people emerging from behind a hill, shouting as they made their way toward the city along the steep and winding road, many of them waving something in the air. Weapons of some kind, perhaps? Sensing the possibility of danger, he stood up, one hand instinctively finding the handle of his sword while the other picked up his helmet. What would a shouting mob do if they came upon a Roman soldier alone in an isolated place?

And yet, as the crowd slowly came up the road, the sound of their shouts suggested not anger, but mirth. Amid the rise and fall of their voices, he detected a cadence that still conveyed no meaning to him, although he had learned some of the local dialect during the six months or so that he had been stationed at Jerusalem. It was a chant of some sort, he guessed, perhaps a slogan. And, as they drew closer, he was able to see that it was not clubs or spears they were waving in the air, but branches covered with leaves, glistening now and then as the breeze turned them toward the sun. Stranger still, when they were yet a hundred paces distant, he saw that some of them were taking off their outer garments and, it appeared, throwing them down on the road. As the branches became more distinct, he could see through them the head of a man elevated somewhat above the others in the crowd, located, in fact, at about the middle of the throng. The people, as they walked along, were turning toward the man and directing their shouts toward *him*.

Lucius relaxed his grip on his sword and set his helmet back down on the bench. He didn't notice that a gust of wind had blown the little scroll that his wife had sent him onto the ground. He walked to where his horse stood to calm it as the parade passed by. As he stroked the nose of his horse, it tugged on the reins, catching a whiff of some familiar smell. Just then, Lucius was able to see that the man whose head was above the others was sitting on a donkey that shuffled slowly along amidst the throng of people, and that, in fact, none of them had even noticed the Roman soldier standing alongside his horse.

"Hosanna!" they were shouting—a word that meant nothing to him. But he did catch the name "David," which he instantly identified with the great king of ancient times who had managed to weld the ancestral tribes of Israel into a powerful little nation. Again, his hand found the handle of his sword.

The leading edge of the crowd was passing in front of him now, and he could see the man on the donkey more clearly. He was not answering their shouts, except to smile at the people. A few of them would pick up the cloaks at the rear of the parade and then run back the length of the crowd and lay them down again on the road. One of those who had run back to the head of the procession now stood still in the road as the crowd, and the man on the donkey, pushed past him. He seemed to be reading something that he had picked up from the ground. Then, quickly, he pushed his way up through the crowd to the man on the donkey, who stopped as he bent over to hear the man excitedly shouting something in his ear.

Lucius saw that the man on foot was holding a small, unrolled scroll. He looked back at the bench he had been sitting on, and realized that the letter from his wife was not on it. A gust of wind must have carried it from the open pouch out onto the road. The man on the donkey was now looking directly at Lucius, and, as their eyes made contact, he slid from the back of the animal, took the letter from the man who had retrieved it, and walked the dozen or so paces to where the soldier was standing. He held the letter out to Lucius. Lucius was just able to make out his Aramaic words: "Do not be anxious. Your son is alive." Then the man smiled, and turned back to his donkey. The crowd, which had fallen silent, resumed the slow but festive march toward the city.

Lucius had just stood there, his helmet in one hand and his wife's letter in the other, watching the throng round the Mount of Olives and disappear from his sight as the sound faded from his ears. Finally, he reread the letter and rolled it up and stuck it in his breastplate. He mounted his horse, and started up toward the city just ahead of another group of pilgrims headed to Jerusalem for the festival.

During the week, Lucius had dispersed the hundred troops under his command inside the city with orders that they should be alert but should in no way provoke the crowds. Their specific location was in the streets to the west of the temple. From time to time, they reported to him references to a messiah, which, when he in turn reported such talk to his superiors, seemed to make them concerned. He had learned enough about the sacred books of the Jews to know that they foretold the coming of a great hero, not unlike David, but that there was *always* such talk around the time of the festival. But there seemed to be people in Jerusalem who were suggesting some specific individual attending the festival might in fact be this "Messiah." The governor was coming up from Caesarea in honor of the festival and in order to keep an eye on things. Surely, he would know the appropriate response to any such "Messiah." In truth, Lucius was *more* anxious to receive another letter from his wife, and yet fearing to read it when it came.

As the week went on toward the day of the festival itself, Lucius grew more anxious about his son and more uneasy about the situation in the city and more troubled by thoughts critical of Rome's occupation of Palestine to begin with. He was loyal to the empire and to the emperor, but the army was doing nothing about the sick people near the pools nor the beggars on the streets, nor, for that matter, did any of the *local* authorities seem particularly interested in their plight. Well, what *could* they do? And yet, it seemed that somebody should do *something*. Perhaps the crowded condition of the city just made things seem worse than they really were. The governor arrived in due course—a man whom Lucius had heard that the local people despised and who seemed to govern with little imagination and not much success. He had met him once, and judged him to be disengaged and self-consumed. On the other hand, if he had been a more talented administrator, he would not still be stuck in a place like Palestine.

Actually, things rather quieted down on the night of the festival itself—the people were all occupied with eating the sacred meal that was at the heart of their festival in homes and rented dining halls, and, as they had finished their business in the streets with a flurry of marketing toward sundown, their mood seemed to change from festive to reflective. There had been some disturbances here and there, including, he had understood, at the temple, where some zealot or other had set loose some of the animals that were for sale there for sacrifice on the altar. Some had said it was the same fellow who had been involved in the business of the blind man at Jericho. But there was much confusion in the stories Lucius had heard, and the temple incident had gotten somewhat lost in the more pressing concern of looking out for any threats against Roman authority rather than worrying about internal religious squabbles.

But when he had reported for duty this Friday morning, Lucius had been ordered to stand by to head a detail in charge of keeping order at an execution. He had been assigned such duty a few times before, and had found it distasteful, but a necessary part of administering justice in this far-flung part of the empire. He was a soldier. He would follow orders. He would draw his pay, and look forward to the day that he would return to his wife and his son . . . his son—was he even still alive?

The sun had not been up in the sky more than an hour or so when the entire cohort was called to assemble at the Antonia. The condemned men were in the custody of the guard, who were in the habit of taunting the criminals as they were being held prior to execution. Lucius himself was not in the courtyard; he was receiving his instructions from the cohort commander to assemble his men at a hill just beyond the city where the executions always took place—public enough to make an example of the criminals, but outside the city walls and therefore less offensive to the local officials. Before departing on his mission, he inquired whether there was any letter for him from Italy, and mentioned that he was anxious to hear news from home. No, none had arrived.

It was approaching noon when Lucius and his men came to the place called Golgotha, and he relieved the centurion who had been on duty as dark clouds began to fill the sky. He did not look at the men hanging on the crosses, but he was aware that there were three in all. There was a little crowd gathered to witness the spectacle, including some of the local religious leaders, their fine robes a stark contrast to the total nakedness of the men on the scaffolds, their taunts and jeers an indication that the crucifixions were having the intended effect. But the gloomy day matched Lucius's mood. He reminded his men to do their duty and not provoke any trouble. Now and then, the men on the crosses replied to the crowd or spoke among themselves; Lucius paid little attention to the words, most of which he could not understand anyway. But at one point, a soldier approached him and held out a courier's pouch, saying, "I have orders to bring this to you, sir."

Lucius opened the pouch, removed a small scroll, unrolled it, and read it. "My dear husband," it began,

> What joy fills my heart to tell you that our son Marcus, who was so near death, is well and strong again. His cure came quickly this morning, Sunday, after the physicians had given up hope and even my offerings to the gods had had no effect. I must get this off hurriedly, as I understand a ship is sailing for Caesarea later today. If I only knew what god is responsible for such a miracle, I would devote the rest of my days to him. Be safe, and return to us as soon as you can.

Tears of joy came to Lucius's eyes. The ship's journey had been a quick one—there must have been favorable winds and a strong set of oarsmen. Sunday—what had he been doing at the moment his son was cured? Wait—that was the day, yes, *that* was the day that the man on the donkey had . . .

Just then, Lucius overheard someone in the crowd speak the word "messiah," and a shout from one of the dying men caused him to look up into his face—the one on the middle of the three crosses. And Lucius Gaius Gallus stood motionless as a statue. He could scarcely believe what he saw—it was the very man whom the crowd had been cheering as they came up the road from Jericho, the man who had stopped when he heard of a father's anguish, the man who had told him that his son was alive. But, just then, the man sighed deeply and his head dropped low. He was dead. And the pieces all came together in the mind of Lucius the centurion. "Truly," he said, his tear-filled eyes fixed on the man's bloodied face and his hand grasping his wife's letter, "this man was God's Son!"

Maundy Thursday
Spanish Springs Presbyterian Church, Sparks, Nevada
April 9, 2009

Exodus 12:1–14
1 Corinthians 11:23–26
John 13:1–17, 31b–35

"Remembering the Future"

"This day shall be a day of remembrance for you," the LORD instructed Moses and Aaron while the Hebrews were still slaves in Egypt. "You shall celebrate it as a festival to the LORD; throughout your generations you shall observe it as a perpetual ordinance" (Exod 12:14 NRSV). The festival would be a *commemoration* of something that had not yet *happened*—the passing over of the Hebrews' houses when the LORD brought destruction upon Egypt, and a journey in freedom and reliance on God's gracious promise.

We may be so used to hearing about the Passover that we haven't noticed the unusual sequence of events—in the twelfth chapter of Exodus, God instructs the people to celebrate a salvation that hasn't occurred yet. "Tell the whole congregation of Israel that on the tenth of this month they are to take a lamb for each family, a lamb for each household" (Exod 12:3 NRSV). And already, before the meal has happened even *once*, God declares it is to be an *annual* event, something every *subsequent* generation will take part in. It's almost as if, by enacting the ritual of consuming the roasted lamb with unleavened bread and bitter herbs, and then taking some of the blood of the lamb and smearing the doorposts and lintels, all with loins girded and sandals on their feet and staff in hand, they were living as if their *release* from suffering and cruelty and oppression that God had promised had *already* come to *pass*. It's almost as if, by *preparing* for their *escape* from slavery, *they* were *participating* in bringing it *about*.

The major national holidays associated with *our* nation's freedom were all organized *after* the events they commemorate had occurred.

There *was* no Independence Day until sometime *after* July 4th, 1776. No one set off fireworks or had picnics to celebrate the Declaration of Independence *before* it was signed. Memorial Day and Veterans' Day came *after* battles raged and lives were lost and the dead had been buried and the surviving soldiers came home from the fields of combat. But the Bible specifies that the plans for the celebration of *Passover* were laid before the exodus *happened*. God told Moses and Aaron to instruct the people to *remember* something that lay in the *future*. And God commanded their children and their children's children to celebrate it in the same manner, as if to join their ancestors in preparing for a freedom march that happened a long time ago, before they were born. Somehow, by doing so, they would learn afresh who they still were—God's people, ready always to march out of empire and into the land of Gods promised fruitfulness and peace, trusting always in God's promised preservation from danger, hoping always that God's promised future would conform to the ritual enactment of liberation and salvation for even the *least* of the community. And, so, those who participate in the liturgy of Passover *today* are taking part in God's saving deed every bit as much as their *ancestors* did who stood on the shore of the Red Sea, poised to pass through the waters rolled up on either side of their miraculous pathway out of Egypt. God's promise to their *ancestors* is a promise God makes to *them* as *well*. God's graciousness to their *ancestors* is graciousness to *them* as *well*. God's gift of salvation to their *ancestors* is a gift of salvation to *them* as *well*, who remember how to prepare for a future of creation's goodness restored, a future of justice and freedom.

"This is my body that is for you" (1 Cor 11:24b NRSV), Jesus said to his disciples gathered together for the Passover meal the night before the crucifixion. "This cup is the new covenant in my blood" (1 Cor 11:25b NRSV). He blessed the bread and broke it and gave it to them. He poured the wine and passed the cup, inviting them to feed on him, to ingest him, to receive life from him. He had not yet been put to death by the authorities who wanted him silenced and out of the way. But already, the disciples were asked to engage in an act of *remembrance* of what was *yet to happen*, to enact ritually the death they did not understand was going to occur the next day, and to participate in the communion that the spirit of the risen Christ would establish *after* the resurrection among his followers in Jerusalem, in all Judea and Samaria, and to the ends of the earth, not just in the *first* generation of believers, but in all *subsequent* generations to the end of time. Coming to the table, feeding on the bread broken, drinking the wine poured, remembering the humble and obedient death of the Son of God in the very act of graciously sharing a meal generously offered at a table from which no one is turned away hungry, no race or nationality is excluded, no man, woman, or child is considered too sinful to find a seat, no one is too poor to afford, no person is so friendless as to feel unwelcome. And there, in the very words of thanksgiving and the very deed of breaking and sharing the bread and pouring and sharing the cup, the Lord Jesus Christ is known to be risen from the tomb and present among his followers, offering a foretaste of the kingdom of heaven.

Sometimes, people understand Jesus' command to "[d]o this in remembrance of me" (1 Cor 11:24c NRSV) as making of the eucharist a *memorial* service for a Jesus who died a long, long time ago. But the apostle Paul recorded Jesus' words from the Last Supper in his first letter to the Corinthians because the Christians in Corinth had made of the *Lord's* Supper a meal that was anything *but* generous and gracious and inclusive. It was Paul's concern that they remember, and remember rightly, who Jesus *was* and who the risen Christ *is*. They had turned the feast based on Christ's humble obedience for the salvation of all humankind into a smorgasbord of gluttony and selfishness, the indolent rich taking the best seats in the house church and grabbing more than a fair share of the eats while the poorer, less prestigious members of the church community who showed up after a hard day's work had to settle for leftovers out in the kitchen. The Lord's Supper, as it was being conducted at Corinth, was hardly a foretaste of the kingdom of heaven that Jesus had promised. To be greedy about the food and dismissive of the underprivileged was hardly to be eating in *remembrance* of *Jesus*, much *less* living in remembrance of his teaching and his deeds of compassion. It was certainly not taking to heart the new covenant that Jesus died on the cross to establish, certainly not showing forth the salvation that Jesus died on the cross to achieve. "When you come together," Paul rebuked the Corinthians,

> it is not really to eat the Lord's supper. For when the time comes to eat, each of you goes ahead with your own supper, and one goes hungry and another becomes drunk. What! Do you not have homes to eat and drink in? Or do you show contempt for the church of God and humiliate those who have nothing? . . .
>
> For I received from the Lord what I also handed on to you, that the Lord Jesus on the night when he was betrayed took a loaf of bread, and when he had given thanks, he broke it and said, "This is my body that is for you. Do this in remembrance of

me." In the same way he took the cup also, after supper, saying, "This cup is the new covenant in my blood. Do this, as often as you drink it, in remembrance of me." For as often as you eat this bread and drink the cup, you proclaim the Lord's death until he comes (1 Cor 11:20–22b, 23–26 NRSV)—

you show to the world and to your neighbor who is most in need the value that God places upon every single human being, and the hope that God has for every single human being, and the love that God expects each of us to show for every single human being, that will one day be revealed in the fullness of the heavenly banquet where the feasting will never end and the praise of God will never be exhausted and the fellowship of Jesus with his disciples will never cease.

What we do when we gather at this table to eat and drink in remembrance of Jesus Christ is to give a *present* witness to the *future* that God has made possible *through* Jesus Christ for all creation. And to participate in that future *today* is to take part in bringing it about. "For as often as you eat this bread and drink the cup, you proclaim the Lord's death until he comes" (1 Cor 11:26 NRSV); you deny all of the world's vain promises and false hopes; you rebuke all of those who scoff at the weak and the poor and the humble and the hopeful; you reject all the claims and vanities of despots and demagogues; you confound all the calculations and platitudes of the manipulators and the pundits; you defy all mortal wisdom and cultural dictates; you leave behind all the hardscrabble effort to put yourself at the center of the universe and, instead, embrace the call to live for others; you break all the chains of history's past and breathe in the air of freedom on the far shore opposite the land of slavery to oppression and sin and death. And maybe, just maybe, if *more* people spent *more* time proclaiming Jesus' death until he comes, the whole world would find itself living in God's future.

Remember how Jesus got up from the table, took off his outer robe, and tied a towel around himself and poured water into a basin and began to wash the disciples' feet and to wipe them with the towel and said, "I have set you an example, that you also should do as I have done to you" (John 13:15 NRSV)? One day, all shackles will be loosed. One day, all stomachs will be full. One day, all people will be respected and accorded dignity. One day, all injuries will be healed. One day, all wrongs will be forgiven. One day, all creation will be at peace. One day, all the world will sing praise to God, who sacrificed his Son on the cross for its salvation. In a few minutes, at Christ's own invitation, we will have the opportunity to engage again in eating the bread and drinking of the cup, his body broken and his blood shed, in remembrance of him. In a few minutes, at Christ's own invitation, we will take part in remembering the future God has in store.

Good Friday
Spanish Springs Presbyterian Church, Sparks, Nevada
April 10, 2009

Isaiah 52:13—53:12
Hebrews 10:16-25
Mark 15:1-47 (read in sections, as noted below)

Mark 15:1-5

For the *first* readers of Mark—the persecuted church in the time of Nero—the arrest and trial of Jesus were not something far away in memory or exotic in experience. They knew of such terror happening among believers of their *own* day—trumped-up charges, whispered slanders, half-truths and out-and-out lies used to justify hauling believers before magistrates. Like Jesus, they too were accused of "many things" (Mark 15:3 NRSV), none very specific. It was the perfect opportunity for settling scores rooted in jealousy and pride and fear.

Believers could at least take comfort in the knowledge that their Lord, now risen and powerful, had faced the same disgrace and hatred, had triumphed, in fact, even at the cost of his own death. But on Good Friday, there was as yet no resurrection. In the middle of the night, deserted by his friends, beset by fear and perhaps even harboring some doubt, Jesus was hauled before the council and then before the high priest and accused of blasphemy. The Sanhedrin voted that Jesus must die—there was never really any question about what their decision would be—but they did not have the power to put one of their own to death. Only the Roman governor could do that. So the chief priests and elders and scribes and the whole council bound Jesus, and took him to Pilate.

Pilate did not read any charges against Jesus, just asked him the question, "Are you the King of the Jews" (Mark 15:2a NRSV)? In fact,

Rome had eliminated the kingly title in Israel by this time. *Pilate* cannot have considered Jesus any sort of *threat* to Roman rule. Jesus did not answer Pilate directly; perhaps Jesus knew Pilate could not possibly understand what sort of king he was. Historians tell us that silence in the face of an accusation was considered an admission of guilt in Roman courts. Was Mark advising the persecuted Christians of *his* time to stand before the magistrates in quiet dignity and calm confidence? "Jesus made no further reply, so that Pilate was amazed" (Mark 15:5 NRSV).

Mark 15:6-15

Pilate didn't care one way or the other about the guilt or innocence of Jesus. Fairness and justice were not large in Pilate's sense of duty—only acting in the best interests of Rome, keeping public order, guaranteeing the uninterrupted flow of tribute into the imperial coffers. He knew what was behind Jesus' arrest—simply the jealousy of the chief priests. To call this pitiful man standing before him a revolutionist was a joke. But the cooperation of the chief priests had been useful to Pilate in the past to keep the mobs in check, and the Jerusalem rabble *did* have a reputation for being riotous. What was an innocent person's life, if it meant preserving order in this wretched outpost of Caesar's empire? And so we have the legacy of Pilate's smallness as a human being, a moral dwarf if ever there was one, weighing an innocent person's life against the concerns of what was easy, and finding justice not worth the trouble.

Not that we should feel superior—how many times have we, even standing at the checkout line in the supermarket, not bothered to concern ourselves with the working conditions of the people who make the products we buy, for instance, or the cost to *future* generations of our desire to live comfortably and conveniently *today*? In truth, Jesus' conviction was a foregone conclusion as soon as the council decided they would take him to Pilate, not because Pilate the governor was powerful, but because Pilate the man had no spine. He had the authority to sentence any person who was not a Roman citizen to die, or to grant amnesty to any criminal, if he so chose. Stirred up by the chief priests, the crowd called for the release of a petty insurrectionist named Barabbas. Pilate asked the crowd what he should then do with *Jesus*, if he were to release *Barabbas*. "Crucify him!" (Mark 15:13 NRSV) they shouted back. "Why, what evil has he done?" (Mark 15:14a NRSV) Pilate asked, as if it made any difference to him. Perhaps he was just curious to know how effective the chief priests had been in orchestrating their plan. But that only made them shout all the louder, "Crucify him" (Mark 15:14b NRSV)! "So Pilate, wishing to satisfy the crowd, released Barabbas for them; and after flogging Jesus, he handed him over to be crucified" (Mark 15:15 NRSV).

Mark 15:16–20

Some people in our time and place voice dismay that prisoners, even murderers, have rights of dignity and due process that must be guaranteed. But it is one mark of a *civilized* people that *we*, as a society, refuse to stoop down to the same level as those who stab at the very heart of human dignity by committing the most heinous crimes, so that justice for us is not a matter of private vengeance. Rome was not so civilized. Once condemned to death, a prisoner had no rights.

So the soldiers were able to do with Jesus as they liked, with impunity. As the council had mocked him at trial, so now the soldiers mocked him in his punishment. And to the sarcasm of a purple cloak, they added the torture of a crown of thorns. They thought it was preposterous that anyone should presume to think the Jews could have a king so long as the Roman military occupied Israel, much less *this* defenseless man, already bruised and bloody from his beatings of the night before while in the custody of the temple guards. But when our chosen victims do not answer our taunts and our jabs, the fun is quickly spoiled. The soldiers finally wearied of their amusement. They reclaimed the purple cloak they had draped on his shoulders and gave him back his own now-ragged clothing. "Then they led him out to crucify him" (Mark 15:20b NRSV).

Mark 15:21–24

He had not been a part of the crowd that called for Jesus' death, Simon of Cyrene. He had only just come into the city from the countryside and found himself engulfed in a boiling mob. Perhaps he had known Jesus; at least, his sons Alexander and Rufus seem to have been known to some of Jesus' friends. The soldiers seconded the hapless man to carry the crosspiece for Jesus. Weakened by the beatings the night before and the beatings of the morning, Jesus must have been unable, as was customary, to bear the timber himself, perhaps, as artists have pictured it, had stumbled and fallen under its weight. At a place ominously named "The Skull," they stripped Jesus totally of his clothes, nailed his hands to the ends of the crossbar, and hoisted it up and fastened it to the upright post. Then they nailed his feet to the post.

Death normally came to crucifixion victims in a day or two, usually from exposure or suffocation. Jesus refused to die in a stupor, would not take the narcotic concoction of wine and myrrh. He sweated to dehydration under the Middle Eastern sun, and was jeered at in his nakedness, unable even to brush the flies off of his bloody wounds, while his executioners made sport of his plight, dividing the spoil among themselves, the very last worldly things that he could claim as his own. "And they crucified him, and divided his clothes among them, casting lots to decide what each should take" (Mark 15:24 NRSV).

Mark 15:25–32

It may be that the criminals alongside Jesus were also accused of insurrection, as was Barabbas, who had been released. The inscription "King of the Jews" suspended above him was a joke by the soldiers, but also a warning to anyone who might dare to challenge Roman rule. As at the *beginning* of Jesus' ministry, so now at its *end*, the temptation to take the easy way out was put before him. They mocked him. Even the chief priests and scribes, who considered themselves so dignified, guardians of the faith, charged with being the protectors of Israelite society's helpless, came out to ridicule. Defenders of the faith? Vipers and white-washed sepulchres! And the prophecies of the Psalms and the prophets were fulfilled: "All who see me mock at me; they make mouths at me, they shake their heads; 'Commit your cause to the LORD; let him deliver—let him rescue the one in whom he delights'" (Ps 22:7–8 NRSV)! "I am an object of scorn to my accusers; when they see me, they shake their heads" (Ps 109:25 NRSV). "He was despised and rejected by others; a man of suffering and acquainted with infirmity; and as one from whom others hide their faces he was despised, and we held him of no account" (Isa 53:3 NRSV). "Those who were crucified with him also taunted him" (Mark 15:32b NRSV).

Mark 15:33–39

It was like the terrible day of judgment, or like the astronomical testimony to the death of a great leader—darkness covered the land, for three hours. Were there loud wails of doom and despair, or the quiet murmurings of awe and wonder? The scripture is silent. But confirmed by the sun being blotted out or not, it was surely an afternoon of absolute darkness, the most dismal event in human history, the most despicable injustice of human imagining.

How blind people were! The sun might as *well* have been blotted out. And then, a loud voice from the cross, echoing the Psalms, misunderstood by those who had gathered to mock and jeer. But the power they thought they held over Jesus was almost at an end. He had given them a rather poor show, actually. Their gruesome amusement at the expense of a human life was relatively brief, by the average length of executions.

Jesus died only about six hours after he had been raised to the cross. Whatever perverse pleasure they took in watching a person die an excruciating death was abbreviated at about three in the afternoon when Jesus gave a loud cry and breathed his last. He had been in terrible pain—the pain of his wounds, the pain of his abandonment. Was his cry one of anguish, one of surrender, one of dismay, or one of triumph?

One officer felt disgust at his soldier's duty and at the system that so little valued righteousness and that so poorly cared for human life. Of all those present, he, ironically, was the only person who had any inkling of what was really taking place. And Mark used his words to write his Gospel's epitaph on the identity of Jesus Christ. "Now when the centurion, who stood facing him, saw that in this way he breathed his last, he said, 'Truly this man was God's Son'" (Mark 15:39 NRSV)!

Mark 15:40–47

Resurrection of the Lord (Sunrise)
First Presbyterian Church, Ponca City, Oklahoma
April 5, 2015

Isaiah 25:6–9
Acts 10:34–43
Mark 16:1–8

"Where We Know the Resurrection"

You and I are participating in what has long been a popular tradition of coming together to celebrate the resurrection of Jesus Christ at an Easter sunrise service. From the National Mall to the Hollywood Bowl and thousands of places in between, and in many other places around the world, there is something that Christians find special about greeting the sunrise on this first Sunday after the first full moon after the beginning of spring in commemoration of the women discovering the empty tomb early on that first Easter morning. We know the tomb was empty because Jesus had been raised by the power of God, vindicating everything Jesus had said and done, defeating the powers of hatred and envy that had brought about his execution, defeating the powers of death that had seemed to bring an end to the Son of God who did only good and spoke only truth. Of course, those women who first discovered the empty tomb *didn't know* it signaled a *triumph*—only more *heartbreak*, only more *disappointment*, only more *dismay*. Not only had Jesus' enemies *killed* him, but now, perhaps, someone had been so indecent as to remove his body from where it had been laid.

"When the sabbath was over, Mary Magdalene, and Mary the mother of James, and Salome bought spices, so that they might go and anoint him. And very early on the first day of the week, when the sun had risen, they went to the tomb" (Mark 16:1–2 NRSV). Remarkably, they hadn't thought about how they were going to get *into* the tomb, didn't discuss that practical detail until they were almost *there*. But, as it turned out, the stone that sealed the entrance had *already* been rolled away. They

"Where We Know the Resurrection" 151

were fearful when they saw a young man dressed in a white robe sitting in the tomb. "'Do not be alarmed,'" he said; "'you are looking for Jesus of Nazareth, who was crucified. He has been raised; he is not here. Look, there is the place they laid him. But go, tell his disciples and Peter that he is going ahead of you to Galilee; there you will see him, just as he told you'" (Mark 16:6–7 NRSV).

But, Mark says in his account of that first Easter, the women fled in terror, and they were too afraid to tell anyone. The young man dressed in a white robe told them that Jesus had been raised, but they seem to have had no idea what that meant, and we don't know that the women had ever heard Jesus explain beforehand about resurrection. It was all too strange, and it appeared as if the tragedy of Good Friday had only been compounded. The empty tomb communicated *nothing* about what had actually *happened* to Jesus. According to the original ending of Mark's Gospel, that *first* Easter sunrise was a time more of *perplexity* than *joy*, a time more even of *fear* than of *celebration*. For the *first* people who gathered for sunrise on the third day after the crucifixion, something *more* was needed.

Like a lot of visitors to Jerusalem, I visited, a few years ago, the Church of the Holy Sepulchre, which encompasses within its walls the place that most evidence points to as Calvary, or Golgotha, the rocky hill on which Jesus was put to death, and, in another part of the church, the tomb commonly accepted as the place where Jesus' body lay for three days. Only, the tomb is now located within a shrine; the cliff into which the tomb would originally have been cut is no longer there, so it is rather difficult to imagine what it all must have looked like two thousand years ago. I wasn't really prepared for that. It was rather like when, as a child (and a native Texan at that), I first visited the Alamo. Based on television shows and movies, I had expected it to be located impressively on a hill surrounded by fields of bluebonnets as far as you could see. But instead, of course, the Alamo is hemmed in on every side by modern downtown San Antonio and dwarfed by office buildings, permitting not a *hint* of what it was like in the days of Davy Crockett and Jim Bowie. About a mile away from the Church of the Holy Sepulchre, north of the old city of Jerusalem, is the so-called Garden Tomb, discovered in 1867 and now preserved in a park-like setting that is much more in keeping with what I had always pictured. Most scholars think the Church of the Holy Sepulchre is more probably the site of Jesus' tomb, but the Garden Tomb helps us envision better what Mary Magdalene and Mary the mother of James and Salome saw when they came to where Jesus had been laid before the sabbath had begun.

As I have grown older and have progressed in my faith, I have come to consider that the resurrection is really less about the discovery of the *empty tomb*, but more about what happened *afterward*. In Matthew's account, sometime after the disciples had left Jerusalem and assembled in Galilee, the risen Christ appeared to them there and gave them the Great Commission. In Luke and in John, and in a later ending to Mark, the risen Christ appeared to the disciples in the house in Jerusalem where they were staying—confirmation not only that the tomb had been *emptied*, but, like his appearance to the disciples in *Matthew*, that Jesus was *alive again*. Tradition suggests that the room where, in Mark and Luke and John, Jesus appeared to his disciples after the resurrection, was the *same* place where he had shared his last supper with them. Pilgrims coming to Jerusalem to celebrate the Passover needed someplace to *do* it; it is likely that several houses had large rooms that were rented out for the purpose, sort of like banquet rooms or event centers today, and it is not unreasonable to think that the disciples, having no other place to stay in a crowded Jerusalem filled with Passover pilgrims, had continued to stay there over the sabbath. Today, visitors to Jerusalem can see an upper room in a building on Mount Zion thought by many to be the location of the Last Supper and, perhaps, where Jesus, risen from the dead, appeared to the disciples later on Easter day. The walls are not original—the current building dates from perhaps the 1200s—but they are said to enclose the same space occupied by the original Upper Room.

It is in such a place as this, I think, that the meaning of Easter is better understood, even, than at the empty tomb. It was not the place where Jesus' dead body had last been seen and was now missing from their sight that inspired the disciples to faith in the resurrection, but the experience of Jesus alive again among them as they shared a meal just like on so many prior occasions, heard his gracious words, received his blessing, felt his love.

What leads people to believe in the resurrection is *experiencing* the risen Lord. Our best proof of the resurrection is not that the first visitors to the tomb early on the third day after the crucifixion found the tomb empty, and now we have gathered out here on the church lawn as the sun has arisen on Easter Sunday to imitate that. Our best proof of the resurrection is that, in a few minutes, we will gather in the Fellowship Hall to share a companionship we would not *have* if Jesus were not alive today, and that, a couple of hours from now, many of us will gather in the sanctuary around the Lord's table in Jesus' name and find him there, too, as he promised, among those who have gathered in his name and are taking and eating the bread, taking and drinking the cup, in remembrance of him as he has told his followers to do. The tomb was a temporary scene in the transition from the cross back to the dining room, the transition from the Jesus bound by the limitations of time and space to the Christ who is Lord of all, *un*bounded by calendar and geography. The words of the young man dressed in a white robe have a new and important meaning for us believers in the risen Christ *today*. Jesus is no longer *there*, lying *dead* in a tomb outside of Jerusalem. Christ is *here*, and Christ is *alive*.

Resurrection of the Lord
First Presbyterian Church, Dodge City, Kansas
April 3, 1994

Acts 10:34–43
1 Corinthians 15:1–11
John 20:1–18

"The World Turned Upside Down"

Easter. In the gray twilight of the dawn, Mary Magdalene stood weeping in front of a tomb in a garden not far from where, two days before, she had watched in disbelief as her hopes had died. According to the usual characterization of Mary, she had had a knock-about sort of existence until she met Jesus, making her way in life by the only means that seemed open to her in a fashion that she was not proud of, but trying to maintain *some* dignity in spite of circumstances. Probably no one had ever really cared for her or about her. If she was a prostitute, as tradition has it, she could not have *aspired* to such a role; it just *happened*, somehow, and she paid daily for surrendering to it—never knowing the happiness and security of real love, of a home and family, of the respect of others, of feelings of self-worth—and could see no way out of it. Strange that her neighbors cursed and condemned *her*, when the *men* who *came* to her suffered no shame, endured no loss of respect, and apparently felt no remorse! She was a woman, and women were always considered to be the ones at fault in such things—that was the way of the world. But then she had met Jesus, and he had turned her insensitive and hostile world upside down with his respect for her and his forgiveness and acceptance of her. And as his disciple, she had discovered respect for, and forgiveness and acceptance of, herself.

In a few brief weeks or months, Mary's world had changed entirely. Her days had become brighter, her nights had become more serene, she had found a sense of belonging that had given her hope. She was learning to trust. She was developing faith. She could not explain it, could scarcely believe it, but so it had been, until just two days before, when he to whom she had become so devoted was arrested as a blasphemer and a usurper, and was executed like a criminal just a few yards from where she stood but beyond the reach of her trembling hands. Her world had been turned upside down again. Had the weeks or months with Jesus just been a fanciful dream? A mirage upon her life's desertscape? A giddy vacation from which she now must return to her old life's sordid reality of meaningless liaisons and vain gossip? As a last act of devotion born of the love Jesus had shown her and the hope Jesus had given her, Mary had arisen while it was still dark to come to the tomb, just to be near him again, perhaps, drawn by affectionate memories of the happiest days she had ever known.

And then, the final, unbearable cruelty upon her broken heart—even Jesus' corpse had been snatched from her. The stone was rolled away—someone must have robbed the grave!—and she had run to tell some of the others, who must have raced on ahead of her back to the garden, and then left the place before Mary returned. Now, she was *alone* with her *double* grief—or so she thought. A voice spoke to her gently. "Woman, why are you weeping? Whom are you looking for" (John 20:15a NRSV)? She supposed the man standing near her to be the gardener, and said to him, "Sir, if you have carried him away, tell me where you have laid him, and I will take him away" (John 20:15c NRSV). And when the one whom she had thought was the gardener said to her "Mary!," she turned and recognized that it was Jesus—Jesus raised from the dead! And Mary's world was finally righted again, once and for all. It was no whimsy or imagination, but the truest reality.

We are so familiar with the story—most of us have grown up with it—that we may not realize the total revolution Easter worked for those early Christians, and therefore the total revolution it *should* work for *us* and *could* work for the *whole world*. Any sort of salvation by God, it had long been taught, depended upon righteousness, and righteousness depended upon the law of God, but the law was so intricate, and God seemed so far away! What hope was there? Only the hope that someone would make life more bearable on *earth*, that someone would stop the foreign soldiers from stomping through the crops, that someone would stop the tax collectors from bleeding the public, that someone would stop the pagans from desecrating the holy places. A few had thought *Jesus* might be that someone. But the system had chewed him up, good though he was, devout though he was, wonder-worker though he was, and on Good Friday it looked to most people like the world would go on pretty much the same as it had *before* Jesus, and it looked to his followers like their lives would return to pretty much the same as they had been *before* Jesus. For a brief while, not only Mary Magdalene, but so many others had experienced a new zest for living, new meaning, new hope. But then Jesus was crucified. He must not have been God's promised one after all.

But then came the resurrection! The empty tomb, and the appearances of the risen Jesus to his disciples. And all of the hopes and dreams returned—more than returned!—for God had stamped his mighty "Yes" on forgiveness and healing and compassion by raising Jesus the forgiver and healer and compassionate one from the dead. "'Rabbouni!'" said Mary, "(which means Teacher)" (John 20:16b NRSV). "Mary Magdalene went and announced to the disciples, 'I have seen the Lord'" (John 20:18a NRSV). And the disciples, possessed by the joy of the resurrection and filled with the power of the Spirit of the risen Christ, went out and started turning the world upside down by declaring forgiveness and working miracles and demonstrating compassionate love in every corner of the known world. And as they did so, they discovered just how radically their *own* little worlds had been turned upside down by the joy of the resurrection and the power of the Spirit of the risen Christ.

Too often, we who are familiar with the story come devoutly to worship on Easter to celebrate the resurrection of Christ as sign and seal of our salvation from sin and death, but then never really explore the *significance* of the resurrection, never really let the good news of God's raising Jesus Christ, his Son, from the dead become for us the good news of God's enthronement of Jesus Christ as risen Lord. Too many of us utter a prayer for God's forgiveness and file away a hope that our death will not be final, but then never really allow the resurrection to transform our *lives*—transform the way we *think*, transform the way we *act*, transform the way we *hope*, transform the way we *love*. Too many of us never really let Easter work the revolution upon us and our world that God intended. Too many of us never become resurrection people, but continue to look at ourselves as we did before, and to regard other people as we did before. Why can we not let go of our desire for scientific proof? Why can we not let go of our need to control? Why can we not look with loving hearts and compassionate eyes on every person, no matter who they are? Why can we not live lives of profound joy and boundless gratitude? Those *first* believers did.

The book of Acts gives us a startling example of how profoundly the conviction of the resurrection faith can, should, and does turn the world upside down. In these days of suspicion and anxiety, we hear a fresh crop of slurs against people whose skin is not like ours, whose speech is not like ours, whose names are not like ours. Intolerance and disrespect of others is increasing, even and especially, it seems, among people who otherwise regard themselves as believers. And we dismiss much injustice and justify much prejudice. The ancient Jews had always considered their nation and their race to be superior to other peoples; God had chosen *them*, after all. There was a special prejudice against the Romans—pagans who had conquered the promised land.

Peter, disciple of Jesus, certainly shared the common notions of his day. For all the times Jesus healed Romans or befriended Samaritans—another people hated by the Jews—or dined with tax collectors and harlots—abominable people according to the Old Testament—or ministered to lepers—unclean sinners under the judgment of the law,—Peter had never understood that following Jesus must mean a change in his attitude and action toward these and others. Like many otherwise good people, Peter had permitted his hatreds and his judgments and his prejudices and his grudges to define his world. And when Jesus was arrested and executed, those hatreds and judgments and prejudices and grudges may even have been reinforced, at least insofar as his feelings about the Romans were concerned, for it had been a Roman governor who had pronounced sentence on Jesus, a Roman cross upon which Jesus had died, a Roman spear which had pierced Jesus' side, a Roman soldier who had stood guard at Jesus' tomb. When Peter learned the truth of the resurrection—not only the puzzlement of the empty sepulchre, but his actual conversations with the risen Jesus,—he was joyful beyond belief, certainly beyond his old belief that life ends with death. God had worked a mighty act which turned upside down Peter's thinking about the way things are. And in so doing, Peter perceived that God had put his stamp of truth upon everything Jesus had said and done. Peter and the other disciples, too, could go forth confidently to do mighty acts, convinced of the truth of Christ.

And while Peter was doing so, preaching in Joppa, three men came, sent by a Roman centurion to ask him to come and preach at his house—under a Roman roof and at a Roman dinner table. Can you imagine what Peter would have said to that invitation back before the resurrection? But Peter had indeed become the rock upon which the universal church of Jesus Christ would be built! The Spirit of the risen Lord seized hold of him, and the old hatreds and judgments and prejudices and grudges crumbled beneath the truth of God in Jesus Christ. Easter had put joy into Peter's life. Now Easter turned Peter's world upside down. "'I truly understand that God shows no partiality,'" he told Cornelius the centurion and his household,

> "but in every nation anyone who fears him and does what is right is acceptable to him. You know the message he sent to the people of Israel, preaching peace by Jesus Christ—he is Lord of all. That message spread throughout Judea . . . : how God anointed Jesus of Nazareth with the Holy Spirit and with power; how he went about doing good and healing all who were oppressed by the devil, for God was with him. . . . They put him to death by hanging him on a tree; but God raised him on the third day . . . . He commanded us to preach to the people and to testify that he is the one ordained by God as judge of the living and the dead. All the prophets testify about him that everyone who believes in him receives forgiveness of sins through his name." (Acts 10:34b–37a, 38, 39b, 40a, 42–43 NRSV)

Cornelius the Roman centurion was converted to faith in Jesus Christ, but notice how Peter the apostle was converted anew by the power of the Spirit and the truth of the resurrection.

Dear people, each of us comes to Easter with some hurt, some regret, some ill feeling, some intolerance we have allowed to shape our personal world and to distort God's purpose of redeeming *his* world. In its own way, our past may be as wretched as Mary's, our attitude may be as prejudiced as Peter's. But this Easter, as we commune with each other and with the risen Christ at his table, whether you are new to the faith or have been a Christian as long as you can remember, let the good news of the resurrection really take *hold* of you! Let it command your full attention and transform your whole perspective. Let the truth of the risen Christ turn your world upside down. And then watch it turn this whole world of war and hunger and lust and pride upside down until, at last, it is right side up.

Second Sunday of Easter
Spanish Springs Presbyterian Church, Sparks, Nevada
April 19, 2009

Acts 4:32–35
1 John 1:1—2:2
John 20:19-31

"Beyond Charity"

We live in a society that has traditionally claimed private ownership as one of its guiding principles. The strength of the nation, some would maintain, is the free reign that capitalism gives to the natural desire to acquire, to possess, to own. The American Dream is frequently defined in terms of home ownership—a place to live that is uniquely and exclusively yours and no one else's. The laws of the land have been constructed largely on the notion of protecting private property rights so that illegality is commonly thought of as a trespass of some sort—an incursion on the privilege of ownership and exclusive use.

At the same time, a lot of us consider the United States to be a Christian nation, perhaps more so than any other. Certainly, it has the highest rate of weekly church attendance of any nation, even though that number is declining and the lead story in a recent issue of *Newsweek* proclaimed that the percentage of Americans identifying themselves as Christians has fallen by 10 percent in the past twenty years, from 86 to 76 percent. Indeed, when the person who eventually became the forty-fourth president spoke of the need to spread the wealth, roughly the equivalent of a call to share the blessings, he was denounced by some as a socialist. "What's *mine* is *mine*," people seemed to be saying in response to the notion. "And I'm not going to let *any* of it become *yours*." And yet one of the chief characteristics of the young Christian church as described in the book of Acts was that "the whole group of those who believed were of one heart and soul, and no one claimed private ownership of any possessions, but everything they owned was held in common" (Acts 4:32 NRSV). Moreover, just a few verses later, when a man in the church named Ananias sold a piece of property he owned and kept some of the proceeds for himself, not turning the whole amount over to the apostles to spread the wealth, to ensure no one was in need, but giving only *some* of it, as if to charity, the man was struck dead, and then his wife Sapphira, too.

The behavior Luke describes in Acts may be a rather idealized picture of how the early church operated, but there was certainly an expectation among the early followers of Jesus that Christians would not claim *anything* as their own to use exclusively or to use up entirely. An early Christian writing—and one that very nearly made it into the Bible—called *The Didache*, or "The Teaching," says,

> Do not be like those who reach out to take, but draw back when the time comes for giving. If the labor of your hands has been productive, make an offering as a ransom for your sins. Give without hesitating and without grumbling, and you will see Whose generosity will requite you. Never turn away the needy; share all your possessions with your brother, and *do not claim that anything is your own*. If you and he are joint participators in things *immortal*, how much more so in things that are *mortal*? (Did. 1:4)[1]

What Luke was describing in Acts, and what *The Didache* was instructing the early church to do, looks an awful lot like the exact *opposite* of the American dream, would have earned the saintly evangelist and the godly teacher the title "communist" or "socialist" in our label-happy political culture. But the *result*, as Luke describes it, was a situation that *also* looks the opposite of what America has *become*—"There was not a needy person among them" (Acts 4:34a NRSV). In fact, there is not a *bit* of evidence in the Bible that God is interested in labels, and a whole *lot* of evidence that God wants people to be well-fed, properly housed, and healthy, and that the early Christians *understood* that, even if, within a few years, they failed to *practice* it. The resurrection of Jesus had unleashed a powerful sense of responsibility for one another and freed his followers from concern about trying to secure their own future by acquiring and possessing. Perhaps they understood that the very notion of security as something that can be brought about by buying or arming or storing up is *idolatry*, as Martin Luther once observed, and a sign of failure to trust God, whose own Son gained his Father's approval not by *keeping* what was his, but by giving it *away*, including even his *life*. Even the clothes he

---

1. Staniforth, *Early Christian Writings*, 229 (emphasis added).

was wearing were taken away when he was crucified, and were turned to someone's profit.

Some of us may have gotten the impression somewhere along the way that the Christian faith isn't at all concerned with things like money and possessions, and perhaps we were very happy to think that's true. But in *Luke's* view, as in the rather insistent view of the prophets long before Jesus and in the teaching of Jesus himself, all these seemingly mundane matters are integrally connected to faith. And through the resurrection of Jesus, by which he came to be understood as Lord, all these seemingly mundane matters became urgently connected to his followers' testimony in speech and in act that Christ had been raised from the dead. Any people who believe that God vindicated the ways and words of Jesus by emptying the tomb and filling the hearts and minds and souls of his followers with his Spirit *must*, the apostles insisted and the writers of scripture proclaimed, live in a radically *different* way from people who *don't* believe it, starting with their conviction that life is to be lived *in community* and *for one another*. The resurrection had changed history, had dramatically altered the world's course, had turned its values upside down. The same wonder-working power of the Spirit, Luke tells us in Acts, gave tongues to timid disciples to become bold apostles, made it possible for a lame man to walk and a dead woman to come back to life, *and* loosened people's tight grip on their personal property and enabled them to sell what they had and give to people who had nothing.

The point of selling possessions and giving up claims of ownership and offering everything for the use of all is not just a recommendation to charity. And any Christian who hears people speak of giving to the church or giving to the hungry or giving to the homeless as "charity" should correct the person who said it. We ought, indeed, to banish the word from our vocabulary, at least in terms of what most people think of when they hear it. For one thing, the word "charity," as we normally use it, implies an *option*—we can *choose* to *give* or *not* to give. The Bible teaches that, for the *Christian*—for someone who has eternal life through the resurrection of the Lord Jesus Christ—there *is* no option. Eternal life is not a *private privilege* but a *communal joy*. Life in Christ must inevitably lead to fellowship, if it is genuine—community, and not just a quick "How are you?" to accompany a brief handshake on Sunday morning, but a heart's embrace of each other and a complete commitment to the well-being of one another. To have genuine and everlasting communion with *God* through *Jesus Christ* requires having genuine and everlasting communion with *each other*, for, as John taught, if we do not love our *neighbor*, whom we *see*, then we cannot *possibly* love *God*, whom we do *not* see. Self-reliance and rugged individualism and the "what's mine is mine" attitude they foster are 180 degrees opposite the way life *ought* to be lived, in fact, what *eternal* life—life with God in Jesus Christ, life as Jesus Christ lived it in dedication to God—*is*. To live with and for *Christ* is to live with and for *others*, just like *he* did. *Failure* to do so, failure to regard everything we have—time, talent, treasure—as really something entrusted to us for the good of *all*, and therefore to be *shared* with the entire *community*, is to *deny* the *resurrection*. Jesus' sacrificial death and resurrection to eternal life make *genuine* fellowship with each other, *real* community, not only *possible*, but *inevitable*, if we truly have *faith*.

The *ultimate* material blessing we have been given to be shared with others is the earth itself. This week, we observe Earth Day. It is not a special day on the Christian calendar, but Christians should recognize it as a reminder of our daily and constant call to be stewards of everything we have been given. The earth and its resources are not a commodity to be carved up and possessed, certainly not something to be used up and spoiled. When I pollute God's good earth, foul its soil and its water and its air, I injure *others* who are every bit as entitled to the earth's goodness as *I* am. When I poison God's good earth, make deadly its soil and its water and its air, I deny the *next* generation the fullness of God's gift that was handed down to *me* by the *previous* generation. When I litter God's good earth, toss my wasteful discard into its soils and its water and its air, I show a disregard for God the giver and the property rights of all my *fellow* beings who have an *equal* claim to ownership of the earth with *mine*.

Fortunately, the almost militant disregard of the earth that has been shown by some church groups in recent decades, and which has supported the stubborn political resistance to environmentalism, is breaking down. Whether the dire damage done to the environment can be remedied, and whether the escalating deterioration can be arrested, is unknown. But, however much damage has already been done, however difficult it will be to remedy, the fact is that people who truly believe in the resurrection of Christ will subordinate their claims of personal privilege to the well-being of the community, will share what they have freely and gladly in order that all may have enough, will commit themselves to the vision of a green earth, a blue sky, and clear water. God gave the earth, every square inch of it, as a gift for the benefit of all. We are all neighbors, for we all live in the same neighborhood—Earth. Will we *acknowledge* that we form one community?

Jesus was not born, did not die, was not raised, to inspire a business, but to establish the church. And Jesus was not born, did not die, was not raised, to organize a charity, but to make possible eternal life. Christ was raised up on the cross to draw all people to himself. He died for the sake of all. Looking down from the cross *with* him, how can *any* of us exclude *anyone* from the circle of our fellowship? Christ was raised up from the tomb to lift all people to eternal life, that is, unending life, life as Christ lived it. Looking in at the empty chamber and seeing the folded graveclothes, how can any of us think we can keep going about our days and weeks and months and years in the same old habits of self and pride and greed and fear? Indeed, the habits of sin? Surely, Easter should convince us that our *real* security is not in what *we* possess, but in the one who possesses *us*. And when our hands are set free from the habits of grasping and holding on so they can let go and share, we will already, with great power, be giving our testimony to the resurrection of the Lord Jesus, and great grace will be upon us all. And there will not be a needy person among us, for we will no longer be thumping our chest, pointing to ourselves, promoting our interests, claiming our privilege, but living and serving and loving like Christ—not a dead memory but a living Savior,—giving all we once claimed as our own *beyond* charity in the light of fellowship with God and with each other.

Third Sunday of Easter
Spanish Springs Presbyterian Church, Sparks, Nevada
May 4, 2003

Acts 3:12–19
1 John 3:1–7
Luke 24:36b–48

"The Resurrection Body"

It created quite a stir in some Protestant circles in my hometown of Denver when a new Roman Catholic church opened on South Monaco Parkway, a couple of blocks south of Yale and a few blocks north of Hampden. The architecture was striking—a dramatic sweeping roof line that peaked over the altar, and that was visible for many blocks. But what was more interesting than *that* was the *name* of the church—the Church of the Risen Christ—and the fact that, lone among Catholic churches in Denver at that time, the cross at the front of the sanctuary was just that—a *cross*, not a *crucifix*, that is, a cross with a crucified Jesus on it, the usual depiction of Jesus dying or dead.

The cross, of course, is one of the very earliest symbols for the Christian faith. We have seen in recent sermons that it is a paradox; the sign by which we identify our faith and hope in the living Lord Jesus Christ was actually the Roman instrument of cruel torture and shameful execution. I don't know exactly when artistic convention among the early Christians routinely began depicting Jesus hanging on the cross—some graffiti from very early in the Christian era seems to show the crucifixion of Jesus, though it is impossible to know whether it was drawn by the *faithful* or by someone who sought to *ridicule* the faith. I don't know exactly when, in Protestant churches, the crucifix was abandoned, and the simple, bare cross appeared in sanctuaries. Probably it was when the Catholic Mass—interpreted as a repetition of Christ's sacrifice—was abandoned by Protestants in favor of the Lord's Supper, interpreted as a meal at which we understand the *living* Christ to be *spiritually* present.

At any rate, the crucifix, the cross bearing the body of the suffering and dying Jesus, has long been a standard feature of Roman Catholic worship places and many Roman Catholic homes, whereas the cross in *Protestant* churches and *Protestant* homes is one from which the body of Christ is *absent*. What intrigued so many Protestants in Denver about the Roman Catholic Church of the Risen Christ was the obvious emphasis on the *resurrection* rather than the *passion*, which they understood to be an interest in the *present* power and activity of Christ rather than the suffering *death* which, in theological understanding, worked our atonement. To put it another way, it seemed to many Protestants that the Catholic church, or at least one Catholic congregation, was coming out of the shadow of Lent and into the full daylight of Easter.

Well, in fact, Easter is just as joyous an occasion in Catholic churches as in Protestant ones, and perhaps Catholics have traditionally given even more attention to the Easter event over a period of weeks. Martin Luther observed that *every* Sunday *ought* to be and *is* a little Easter—a celebration of God's raising Jesus from the dead on the first day of the week. But only comparatively recently, and owing largely to the broader use of the lectionary, have *Protestants* recognized that Easter is a *season* as well as a *day*—that, with the first disciples, we note the resurrection appearances of Jesus all the way from Easter morning to the time, forty days later, when the appearances ceased (in the book of Acts, Luke tells us it was forty days after the resurrection that Jesus was taken up into heaven and, we believe, enthroned at the right hand of God, that is, endowed with all divine power and authority), and then we celebrate ten days later the endowment of the followers of Jesus with a *share* of his power and authority by the Holy Spirit at Pentecost.

The season of Eastertide makes us mindful that Easter Day was not a flash in the pan, so to speak, but the wondrous beginning of something that continues *today*. And the Gospel record of that first Eastertide makes us mindful that the resurrection was not an event that radically *divorced* believers from life in the world, rendering daily activities irrelevant and insignificant. The resurrection was the event that compels our radical *commitment* to God's purpose of redemption *in* the world, impressing each moment with miraculous potential and making each relationship vitally important. Eastertide—the period during which Jesus *continued* to appear to his followers in his resurrection body—is an insistent acknowledgment that the resurrection is not something that is purely spiritual, but emphatically physical. And the *doctrine* of the *resurrection* is not about the immortality of the soul—the Greek hope of leaving the body behind as a moral nuisance, nasty and despicable. The *doctrine* of the *resurrection* is about God's powerful and enduring commitment to life in fellowship with him, life eternal, life free from the limitations of sin and death even here, even now.

"Jesus himself stood among them and said to them, 'Peace be with you.' They were startled and terrified, and thought that they were seeing a ghost" (Luke 24:36b–37 NRSV). Now, a ghost is something that is without substance, thought to be an apparition or a mere shadow of the person who has died, something to fear, something to avoid. In fact, there are no such things as ghosts. But the Gospels are very clear that the early believers were not experiencing a hallucination. They were not just imagining Jesus' *shadow* present with them. They weren't seeing a *ghost*. And they weren't being visited by some nomadic spirit that had no interest in or sympathy for the human condition or the real physical world.

> [Jesus] said to them, "Why are you frightened, and why do doubts arise in your hearts? Look at my hands and my feet; see that it is I myself. Touch me and see; for a *ghost* does not have flesh and bones as you see that *I* have." And when he had said this, he showed them his hands and his feet. . . . [H]e said to them, "Have you anything here to eat?" They gave him a piece of broiled fish, and he took it and ate in their presence. . . .
>
> Then he opened their minds to understand the scriptures, and he said to them, "Thus it is written, that the Messiah is to suffer and rise from the dead." (Luke 24:38–40, 41b–43, 45–46 NRSV)

Notice two things that Luke apparently thought were very important: the resurrected Christ had flesh and bones and was even able to eat, and the resurrected Christ was the same Jesus who had been crucified, drawing special attention to his hands and his feet, where the nails had been driven that fixed him to the cross on Good Friday. Easter does *not* mean that God despises the earth and all that God created. Easter does not mean that *we* may therefore disregard the physical needs of physical people in this physical world. Easter is the season of Jesus' *physical* appearances to his followers that demonstrated God's mighty vindication of the most genuinely human person who ever walked this earth—the very one who was rejected and abandoned and tortured and put to death because of his gritty mercy and his bodily healing and his earthy hospitality and his truth about real-life situations. Easter is the season of the empty cross, but the hands and feet of the resurrected one will have the scars of the nails that human hands drove into his flesh and that affixed him to the cross. The *risen Christ* is the *same Jesus* who *died*. And those who *believe* in the risen Christ must understand that faith in *Jesus* is faith that God *loves* the *world* and *esteems* the *truth* and *saves sinners*, and *vindicates* suffering for the sake of the world, suffering for the sake of the truth, suffering for the sake even of sinners. We can't follow the *risen* Christ if we are *disengaged* from the *world* or from the needs of *suffering humankind* or *injured creation*. Easter is forever joined to Good Friday. The bare cross must always remind us of the crucifixion as well as the resurrection. To follow the *risen Christ* is to follow the one who bore the *cross* and then *died* on it.

Paul testifies repeatedly that the *church* is now the body of Christ. The resurrection body is still in the world, even after the ascension of Christ, and *we* are *it*. And if that is *so*, then we have to remember Jesus' emphasis on the scars, the evidence of the suffering, and death, even, that was required to work salvation, the testimony that the victory of eternal life comes only by way of obedient surrender to the purpose of God—the trust in God that makes possible forgiveness, healing, feeding, welcoming, and embracing the world's outcasts—the same sort of faithful servanthood that led to Jesus being rejected and denied and abandoned, led to Jesus being condemned, tortured, and killed. We frequently and rather easily acknowledge ourselves, the church, to *be* the body of Christ. We must testify, in this era of cheap grace and the "McDonaldization" of the Christian faith, that the body of Christ risen from the tomb and present with the disciples had flesh and bones—it was physical, interacting with the world into which Jesus was born and for which Jesus died—and they were able to identify the resurrected body of Christ by its *wounds*—the marks of faithful servanthood in the world and unquestioning trust in God's will of life in fellowship with him for the purpose of the redemption of all creation.

Jesus Christ is the model for the church's life and ministry. But the church is genuinely the body of Christ only if it, too, bears the marks of obedient ministry *to* and for the sake *of* a sinful and suffering world. Being a part of the resurrection body is no *escape* from the troubles of human life. Being a part of the resurrection body is redemptive engagement with the world's hurts and injuries and fears and sorrows. We have been promised eternal life with Christ in the resurrection. Jesus will recognize the church as truly his own body by the marks of the nails in *our* hands and *our* feet—by the selfless and redemptive love the church has shown the world in the name of the risen Christ, even though it lead to rejection and ridicule and persecution.

"'Have you anything here to eat?'" (Luke 24:41b NRSV) Jesus asked them. Now, certainly, that would be a queer thing for a ghost to ask—or for a disembodied spirit that thought that attending to physical welfare and earthly needs was not the proper business of disciples. "They gave him a piece of broiled fish, and he took it"—with his nail-scarred hands—"and ate in their presence" (Luke 24:42–43 NRSV). The resurrected body is flesh and bone, and still needs to be fed. The resurrected body is still concerned with the physical needs of the world, like hunger and disease and homelessness and abuse and oppression and joblessness and injustice and war, even though the cross is now bare. Christ does not invite us to an imaginary table, with imaginary food and drink. Christ invites us to be nurtured for the resurrection life by eating from a real loaf and drinking from a real cup.

Easter is always preceded by Good Friday. The resurrection only comes after the crucifixion. The hands that broke the bread and handed it to the disciples the night *before* the *crucifixion* are the same hands that broke the bread and handed it to the disciples on the evening *after* the *resurrection*. The empty cross proclaims our *vindication*, but we also need to acknowledge Christ's body on the cross as a reminder of our *vocation*—to serve as Christ served, to obey as Christ obeyed, to love as Christ loved, to trust as Christ trusted, and, therefore, to offer *ourselves* for the sake of *others* as Christ offered *himself* for *our* sake. The church is the resurrected body of Christ in the world today, with flesh and bones, ministering to the real needs of the world. "Look at our hands and our feet; see that the church is truly the body of Christ himself."

Fourth Sunday of Easter
Spanish Springs Presbyterian Church, Sparks, Nevada
May 3, 2009

Acts 4:5–12
1 John 3:16–24
John 10:11–18

"We Know Love by This"

People who decide to read through the entire New Testament, starting with the Gospels, naturally find a lot of similarities between Matthew, Mark, Luke, and John. Many of the stories about Jesus, many of the sayings of Jesus, are very much alike from one Gospel to the next, although there are also some very notable differences. But beyond the details of the various signs and miracles, and beyond the specifics of the various sermons and teachings, there is the repeated theme of Jesus preaching about the kingdom of God and announcing forgiveness and healing people and feeding them and befriending them, and the resentment it all caused among the authorities who eventually put Jesus under arrest and put Jesus on trial and put Jesus to death, and then the discovery of the empty tomb on the third day after the crucifixion.

When, in the course of reading through the New Testament, people reach the book that we call The Acts of the Apostles, it may seem to them that they've read *before* about some of the incidents and episodes recounted there. In a way, they *have*. But *now*, it's not *Jesus* who is preaching and healing and being persecuted and arrested; it's his *followers*, especially those of the disciples whom the Bible begins to refer to as "apostles." After Pentecost, after the Holy Spirit came upon them when they were gathered together following the ascension of Jesus, the apostles were able to do many wonders and signs that remind us of the sorts of things *Jesus* had done, and the response of the people who witnessed and heard about what the *apostles* were doing was much the same as the response of the people who witnessed and heard about what *Jesus* had done—including the anger and hostility of the establishment.

Fairly early on in the book of Acts, for instance, Peter and John were on their way into the temple to pray, and they encountered a lame man who had been carried in to where he could beg for alms. As we heard last week, Peter told the man he didn't have any *money* to give him, but that he would give him something *else*, and he said to him, "'in the name of Jesus Christ of Nazareth, stand up and walk,'" (Acts 3:6b NRSV) and the man *did* so—in fact, was able to enter the temple with the apostles, "walking and leaping and praising God" (Acts 3:8b NRSV)—and the people who saw him walking and praising God were filled with wonder and amazement at what had happened to him, much like what often happened in the *Gospels* when *Jesus* restored people to health and soundness. Peter took the opportunity to tell the crowd about Jesus, whom they had handed over to the authorities and rejected, and how *he* was the one about whom the prophets had spoken:

> While Peter and John were speaking to the people, the priests, the captain of the temple, and the Sadducees came to them, much annoyed because they were teaching the people and proclaiming that in Jesus there is the resurrection of the dead. So they arrested them and put them in custody until the next day, for it was already evening. . . .
> The next day their rulers, elders, and scribes assembled in Jerusalem, with Annas the high priest, Caiaphas . . . (Acts 4:1–3, 5a NRSV)

and others. "When they had made the prisoners stand in their midst, they inquired, 'By what power or by what name did you do this?'" (Acts 4:7 NRSV)—the question that those who think *they're* in charge *always* ask.

It is no coincidence, these similarities between what *Jesus* said and did and what the *apostles* said and did, and the reaction of the different people who saw and heard about it, and the arrest and detention and trial. Hadn't Jesus himself told the disciples that they would have power to do the same sorts of things *he* had done, and would even be given words to say, and also that they should expect to be persecuted and rejected and arrested and put on trial and even put to death for being his followers? It was all coming to pass—including, in some cases, being put to death for healing people and showing them mercy and treating them as friends. Yes, of *course* it was—the *world* had not changed because of Jesus' crucifixion and resurrection. It was the same place it *had* been. People were *still* sick and infirm and hungry and sin-ridden. People were *still* proud and jealous and hateful and vengeful. There *was* something *new* in the world—the power of the Holy Spirit unleashed and emboldening and empowering apostles whom the world would otherwise never have even noticed. Probably they hardly even recognized *themselves*, so transformed had they become by the Spirit from timid homebodies with narrow dreams to fearless proclaimers of the resurrection. Were these the same fisherfolk from Galilee?—Peter and John, who were now standing before a tribunal in Jerusalem and declaring,

> "Rulers of the people and elders, if we are questioned today because of a good deed done to someone who was sick and are asked how this man has been healed, let it be known to all of you, and to all the people of Israel, that this man is standing before you in good health by the name of Jesus Christ of Nazareth, whom you crucified, whom God raised from the dead. This Jesus is
>
> > 'the stone that was rejected by you, the builders;
> > it has become the cornerstone.'
>
> There is salvation in no one else, for there is no other name under heaven given among mortals by which we must be saved." (Acts 4:8b-12 NRSV)

The chief priests and elders were so taken aback by such boldness from two men so uneducated and ordinary that they were thrown into confusion. "They said, 'what will we do with them'" (Acts 4:16a)? And they ordered them not to speak or teach in Jesus' name. That wouldn't be possible, the apostles responded. So the chief priests and elders threatened them, but then they let them go—*this* time. The apostles knew they were in danger, but something inside them would not allow them to remain sedentary or silent. Something was compelling them to be willing to lay down their *lives*, even, for the sake of others—for the sake, even, of restoring to dignity and wholeness a man lame from birth who had had to endure a lifetime of insults and pity and grunts of disgust while holding out his hand for coins from passersby.

"We know love by this," wrote an early pastor and theologian, "that he laid down his life for us—and," he added, "we ought to lay down our lives for one another" (1 John 3:16 NRSV). We know love—love is defined for us—by what Jesus did: he laid down his life for us. His life was not *taken* from him without his *consent*. He *knew* what would happen if he kept up his ministry of forgiving and healing, of feeding and befriending, of teaching the ways of the kingdom of God by word and demonstrating them by example. He knew what would happen if he went to Jerusalem, the very headquarters of all those who controlled and condemned, who enjoyed prestige and asserted privilege, who could not bear the thought that *they* weren't in charge of salvation, who didn't understand the first thing about loving *God* and thus who couldn't *begin* to love *neighbor*. "How does God's love abide in anyone who has the world's goods and sees a brother or sister in need and yet refuses to help" (1 John 3:17 NRSV)? That question is as poignantly urgent today and in contemporary congregations as it was in the time of the apostles and among the very first generation of Christians.

"Little children, let us love, not in word or speech, but in truth and action" (1 John 3:18 NRSV). Talk is cheap, and sentimentalism scarcely less so. Love is the motive that translates words *about* Jesus into Christ-like *deeds*. Love is not a sentimental feeling or an emotional satisfaction. It is not just religious talk or praise music sung over and over and over. It is not even just self-denial, which can result in a pridefulness which is ultimately all about *self*. Love is an active willingness to surrender what we value as having *worth* in our lives in order that the life of *another* may be enriched, made whole, healed, saved. Jesus was *willing to* and *did* give up what was of the greatest worth—his own self, fully aware of the cost but fully obedient in the face of the need. And by giving up *his* life, he worked the gift of *eternal* life for you and for me. We know love by this. So, when Peter and John came upon the man who, because of his lameness, daily had to beg, they could not refuse to help, though it might draw the same penalty *Jesus* paid for healing. "So they arrested them and put them in custody" (Acts 4:3a NRSV). It wasn't just Peter and John who were proclaiming the good news by preaching and healing, but others too were being arrested for doing what Jesus had commanded them to do. And when they were let go, they *continued* to preach the resurrection and to heal in Jesus' name. And some of them were arrested again. And some of them were put to death.

In Germany in the 1930s, when Jewish families were disappearing from their homes and Jewish businesses were being torched, the German state church and the majority of German Christians remained silent, decided it was safer not to ask questions, not to risk their own security by standing up *for* their *neighbors* and taking a stand *against* the *officials*. In America in the seventeenth and eighteenth and nineteenth centuries, when an entire race was being sold into slavery, whole denominations declared it was not the business of the church to question what was an economic system, not a moral issue. In the 1950s and 1960s, when African-Americans were being lynched, the vast majority of white Christians thought it wasn't *their* business to become involved. In the 1990s and into the first decade of the twenty-first century, some church leaders are saying certain civil rights issues should not be championed by their denomination because it might mean some people might leave the church, and therefore the church's income would be diminished. Ought not the church of Jesus Christ to be willing to imitate the *ways* of Jesus Christ, even laying down its life for others? Eternal life is not about future survival beyond the grave (or even the future survival of the institutional church). Eternal life is what people already have within the community whose love for one another demonstrates a quality of living that is real and indestructible, regardless of threat to fortune or to reputation or to body. Eternal life is what Jesus offered *all through* his life. Eternal life is what Peter and John had and what prompted them to restore soundness of limbs to the crippled beggar, and to explain to the guardians of the status quo who sought to *silence* their witness that it was *impossible* to keep silent the truth of God in Jesus Christ, the good shepherd who lays down his life for his sheep. We don't *have* to devote our lives to trying to save *ourselves*—we *have* a Savior. And only by giving our life up for *others* can we hope to have any life real enough to endure hatred, real enough to endure persecution, real enough to endure beyond the grave.

There is no real life apart from obedience to God's command to love. But love is not just a matter of saying the word—in fact, that isn't really love at all. Genuine love is something that must be *done*, and the person in whom it becomes habit, the person in whom it becomes a joy, the person in whom it becomes the goal of life because it was the way Christ lived, has the eternal life Jesus promised. "We know love by this, that he laid down his life for us—and we ought to lay down our lives for one another" (1 John 3:16 NRSV). Isn't that what it means to be the church?

Fifth Sunday of Easter
Spanish Springs Presbyterian Church, Sparks, Nevada
May 21, 2000

Acts 8:26–40
1 John 4:7–12
John 15:1–8

"From Believers to Disciples"

As we read the New Testament, it is always important to remember that, although its words are very significant for us as *individual* Christians, they were written in the first instance for the *church*—for Christians gathered together in selfless commitment to their Lord. The authors of the various books of the New Testament had specific audiences in mind. They wrote from the perspective of their experience within particular congregations. They wrote, in other words, not about *theoretical* Christianity, not about Christianity in the *abstract*, but on the basis of *their* experience of the faith within real human communities. Certainly, they hoped to encourage their *readers* toward an ideal of loyalty to Christ not yet fully achieved. Their congregations were far from perfect in their devotion. Perhaps *none* of them had matured to the fullness of the stature of Jesus Christ. But they had a vision of what the risen Christ had begun to do in their *own* lives and in the lives of the people *around them*.

Their interest was to see faith move people beyond *intellectual* assent to commitment of the *heart*; beyond the *outward* forms of religion to true *dependence* upon *Jesus Christ*; beyond the *vocabulary* of spirituality to genuine Christ-like *living*; beyond *sentiment* to *action*, all within the community of faith. They were aware that the mystery religions of the Near East stressed identifying with savior gods in dramatic rituals, but that such religions made no ethical demands upon the believer, did not even require exclusive allegiance to the particular god. They knew about the Gnostics, who taught that we can only be saved through special knowledge which Christ disclosed only to the worthy. They were familiar with the temptation to claim Christianity as an individual possession or to shroud it in secret rites known only to the select few. But none of that, they were convinced, was the gospel of Jesus Christ. None of that was the faith Christ had entrusted to the church. The gospel is free. The good news is accessible to all. Faith bears fruit by finding strong root in Jesus Christ and by giving witness to the resurrection and by channeling lives into service and, above all, into deeds of love. "My Father is glorified by this," said Jesus, "that you bear much fruit and become my disciples" (John 15:8 NRSV).

In the closing words of the Gospel of Matthew, Jesus said to the eleven gathered on a mountain in Galilee, "Go therefore and make disciples" (Matt 28:19a NRSV). *Not* just *converts. Not* just *believers*, but *disciples*. The words are not interchangeable. There is more involved than just semantics. A person can change from spouting non-Christian ideas to professing Christian teachings without ever becoming a *disciple* of Jesus Christ. It happened frequently in Africa and Asia and even Northern Europe when, in mass conversions, entire tribes would become nominally Christian upon the command of their tribal chief or their king. For some people in our own society, Christianity is merely a matter of terminology, adopting a new set of catchwords like a person would change from one brand of detergent to another. Many of us in the church viewed the Jesus Movement of the early 1970s with less than full enthusiasm because it seemed that so many young people were being turned on to Jesus without understanding that Christ requires life-long and absolute and sacrificial loyalty. It was good, of course, that a lot of people were at least *introduced* to Christ's teachings, but many of these folks regarded him as simply another *guru*; they never gave the living Lord their *sole allegiance*, and they soon moved on to their next fad.

A person can become a *believer* without ever committing to *discipleship*. The rolls of many churches include a lot of such people—folks who affirm belief in Christ, but believe in a lot of other things, too. Nearly 90 percent of Americans say they believe in God, and an impressive majority identify themselves as Christians. But is belief in Christ as strong as the call of a Sunday morning tee time? Or the profit motive? Or sexual indulgence? Or national supremacy? Discipleship begins where we start to *commit* ourselves *exclusively* on the basis of our Christian belief. It takes *substance* as faith moves us *beyond* national borders and racial prejudice and economic theories and self-interest. It takes hold when we step radically beyond all *lesser* allegiances and live *in* and *for* Christ. Discipleship involves so much more than sentiment, so much more than nice thoughts, ever so much more than saying, "Yes, I'm a Christian. But no, I don't worship regularly. No, I'm not interested in studying about the faith. No, I don't feel any obligation to serve the needy. No, I don't love my enemies. No, I don't really make Jesus Christ the highest priority in my life."

Discipleship requires fruitfulness. And fruitfulness depends upon being strongly attached to Jesus Christ. In what has come to be known as his farewell discourse in the Gospel of John, just before he was arrested, Jesus likened himself to a vine and his followers to branches of the vine. "'Abide in me,'" he said,

> "as I abide in you. Just as the branch cannot bear fruit by itself unless it abides in the vine, neither can *you* unless you abide in *me*. I am the vine, you are the branches. Those who abide in me and I in them bear much fruit, because apart from me you can do nothing. Whoever does not abide in me is thrown away like a branch and withers; such branches are gathered, thrown into the fire, and burned. If you abide in me, and my words abide in you, ask for whatever you wish, and it will be done for you. My Father is glorified by this, that you bear much fruit and become my disciples." (John 15:4–8 NRSV)

The central verb throughout the passage is "abide." The word means to "stand fast," to "remain," to "continue being." The word connotes *permanence*. It speaks of *commitment*. It provides the key to understanding the distinction between *believers* and *disciples*. And by including these words of Jesus to the eleven gathered with him, John's Gospel does *more* than simply report what was said on the night of our Lord's arrest. These words are *also* meant to speak clearly to the Christians of John's *own congregation* and to the whole church in every *subsequent generation*.

The early Christian congregations were puzzled that some of their number were not steadfast in their faith, but that they instead failed to match their actions to their words, or even fell away from the faith community altogether. Many, we can imagine, were attracted to the church by the beautiful sentiments of the teachings of the gospel and by the appealing closeness of the faith community at its best, but perhaps they did not understand or were not prepared to change their ways of living so that *each* of their *actions* and *all* of their *thoughts* would reflect Jesus Christ. There seemed to the evangelist to be no more suitable and effective way of strengthening the faith of his community, or of helping its members to become more conscious of their moral commitments as Christians, than to remind them of their ultimate dependence upon unity *with Christ* and the obligations which that entailed. They must root their lives and their ambitions in *no one* and *no thing* other than Jesus Christ. They must find their motive from no reward other than serving the one with whom they shared the dearest fellowship. They must seek their life's agenda in no other authority than God's own purpose into which Christ had initiated them with his own death and resurrection.

"Bearing fruit" clearly refers to winning over believers. But it goes far beyond the common conception of evangelism to encompass *all* the fruits of a life which is lived in close union with Christ. It includes a fruitful life in community which bears witness to itself in faith and especially in love. We abide in *Christ*—the *branches* abide in the *vine*—when we draw not only our *nourishment*, but our very *identity*, from *him*. It is not just saying, "Yes, I think his teachings were wise." Not even, "Yes, I think his teachings were *true*." *His* death and resurrection to *new life* must become *our* death and resurrection to *new life*. *His* way of thinking must become *our* way of thinking. *His* way of caring for people must become *our* way of caring for people. *His* way of looking at situations must become *our* way of looking at situations. *His* priorities must become *our* priorities. *His* love must become *our* love. Well-intentioned *believers* become genuine and effective *disciples* by *bearing fruit*, and, *above all*, by *love for neighbor*, for brother and sister, whether in our own home or in our own church or in our own town or half a world away. Only by bearing *fruit*, and *especially* the *fruit* of *love*, does Jesus accept *believers* to become *disciples* who are dear to him and who serve him.

Living by love's guide is absolutely necessary to Christian discipleship. A sermon perhaps intended for the very same congregation that John's Gospel reminded of the need to abide in Christ like a branch abides in the vine, reaches its climax with these words:

> Beloved, let us love one another, because love is from God; everyone who loves is born of God and knows God. Whoever does *not* love does *not* know God, for *God is love*. God's love was revealed among us in this way: God sent his only Son into the world so that *we* might *live* through *him*. In this is love, not that *we* loved *God* but that *he* loved *us* and sent his Son to be the atoning sacrifice for our sins. Beloved, since God loves *us* so much, *we* also ought to love *one another*. No one has ever seen God; if we love one another, God lives in us, and his love is perfected in us. (1 John 4:7–12 NRSV)

Listen to that last sentence again: "[I]f we love one another, God lives in us, and his love is perfected in us" (1 John 4:12b NRSV). Our love for *each other* is the way *God's* love is *fulfilled*, the *manner* in which *God's* love is brought to actuality in the world. It is through our relations with our fellow human beings, through our acts of love toward them, that *God's* love makes its way into the world *today*. We cannot live in love toward *God* while we are bearing ill-will toward *one another*, or even being *indifferent* to one another. Christ Jesus loved exactly as God loves. And *we* abide in Christ, *we* stand fast in him, *we* remain in him, *we* continue being in him, when everything we *do*, when everything we *say*, when everything we *think*, is patterned on and motivated by Jesus Christ. *That* is how we will bear fruit as Christ *wants us* to bear fruit; *that* is how *we* will be Christ's true disciples as he *wants us* to be his disciples, and not by way of our *own* doing, but by the gracious gift of the Holy Spirit that is bestowed upon anyone who is committed to moving from *belief* to *discipleship*.

That requires *all* of us to *prepare* for being disciples. And so, our session has organized itself to encourage us and enable us to participate in a church school program intended to prepare people, young and old alike, for discipleship; to encourage and enable us to give of ourselves in every way out of loving gratitude to God; to encourage and enable us to take advantage of opportunities to act out God's love in avenues of mission, and to tell people of the good news, not only within the walls of the church but in the work place and at leisure and in school and wherever we may be; and to plan for times of refreshment and encouragement with each other as a true community. Making disciples—that is our business as the church. Abiding in Christ—that is the way we *become* disciples *ourselves*. Speaking and acting always in love—that is how they will know we not only *believe* in Jesus Christ, but are his *disciples*.

Sixth Sunday of Easter
Spanish Springs Presbyterian Church, Sparks, Nevada
May 28, 2000

Acts 10:44–48
1 John 5:1–6
John 15:9–17

"From Servants to Friends"

Friendship was a favorite topic among Greek and Roman writers. It is a human relationship that was highly valued in the Mediterranean world. In fact, it still defines many privileges and taboos in modern Near Eastern society. Many of the great philosophers of the ancient past have contributed to our perception of the mystery of love's bond between friends. "[I]n its essence," wrote Aristotle, "friendship seems to consist more in *giving* than in *receiving* affection."[1] Friendship is founded upon the desire to give of oneself for the benefit of another. So *genuine* friendship is radically *contrary* to the ethic of self-gratification and the habits of self-assertion. Although scripture does not speak a great deal about the characteristics of friendship, the Old Testament gives prominent place to the extraordinary relationship between Jonathan and David, and between Ruth and Naomi. More extraordinary still is the Bible's description of Abraham as the "friend of God" (Jas 2:23 NRSV). And it tells us that God used to speak to Moses "face to face, as one speaks to a friend" (Exod 33:11a NRSV).

It was perhaps reflecting upon this particular quality of friendship, this ability to address each other "face to face," that the Jewish philosopher and biblical scholar Philo wrote at about the time of Christ: "[T]o whom should [a person] speak with frankness but to [a] friend?"[2] Our ability to talk openly, our ability to speak from the heart, depends upon the trust that marks true friendship—trust that the other person cares enough

---

1. Aristotle, 483 (emphasis added).
2. Philo, *Quis Rerum Divinarum Heres*, 295.

about what we think, what we feel, what we dream, what we fear, that we will be taken seriously and will not be belittled, rejected, or ignored. It presupposes the other person's *good will* toward us and *honesty* toward us and *compassion* toward us. It presumes a genuine *mutuality* of caring and consideration, and a true *reciprocity* of forbearing and forgiving. It requires a conviction that the other person is disposed to be interested in our opinions and willing to be inconvenienced by our needs, is ready even to defend us from threat of harm because that other person values *our* life in the same measure as his or her *own*. Complete *openness* with one another in fact rests upon *love*. And *genuine* love is costly, involving sacrifices that not everyone is willing to make. How often have we been disappointed in our friendships? Each of us has had some experience of confidences being broken, of our deepest yearnings being ridiculed, of our requests being neglected, by a person whom we had *thought* was a *friend. Then* it was we discovered that we had misplaced our trust, had been unwise in our candor, and had been profligate in our love.

Last Sunday's Gospel reading from John was the first several verses of Jesus' discourse on the vine and the branches. We saw how abiding in Jesus as the *branch* abides in the *vine* results in *discipleship*, how *apart* from the vine the branch withers and produces no fruit, and how God desires that *we* abide in *Christ* and so bear fruitfully, especially in deeds of love. This morning's Gospel reading continues the subject of our abiding in Christ, but it takes us beyond our *tasks* of discipleship into a more *intimate* discussion of our relationship with Christ. Jesus says here that, in his choice and acceptance of disciples, he is handing *on* the love which the Father has for him and which surrounds him and which gives effect to his ministry. We become *disciples* by abiding in him and bearing fruit of loving deeds, but Jesus says that the very act of bearing fruit as disciples is itself, at the deepest level, *love—love begetting love*, our love for him and for each other. Being a disciple of Jesus is a gift, an indication of his trust and confidence; it is a fruitfulness which grows in the soil of Jesus' love. And being a *disciple*, doing the deeds of *love*, is love in its very *essence*, as Jesus himself demonstrated in his earthly ministry—love which is *true*, love which is not conditioned upon the other person's loveliness or lovability. "As the Father has loved *me*, so I have loved *you*," said Jesus; "abide in my love" (John 15:9 NRSV). The love *we* show to *others* is the evidence that we have openly received the love which *Jesus* has bestowed upon *us*. "If *you* keep *my* commandments, you will abide in *my* love, just as *I* have kept my *Father's* commandments and abide in *his* love" (John

15:10 NRSV). And what is Christ's commandment? "[T]hat *you* love one *another* as *I* have loved *you*" (John 15:12 NRSV).

The disciples frequently referred to Jesus as "Master," a term that is used not only by students of their teacher, but also by slaves when speaking of their owner. Indeed, the very words "commandment" and "obey" bring to mind the relationship between servants and those they must serve. The disciples seem to have regarded themselves as being not only in the role of *pupils*, but as *servants* following the wishes of Jesus and of God himself. In the ancient world, a *slave* was in a far different class from those who were *served*. Slaves were subordinate in all things, and had few rights, for they were regarded as property, essentially the same as a piece of furniture. They could be sold, they could be put to death. Their sole reason for *being* was to obey every command of their owner. To *refuse* to obey or to *fail* in their task meant *punishment*, sometimes severe. They might be highly skilled, and in some respects even more learned than the people they served, they might be entrusted with great responsibilities, but slaves they were and slaves they remained, and the social structure was dedicated to maintaining that distinction. Even those who served faithfully for many years remained essentially chattel. If their owner died, they could be inherited by the owner's descendants; but they certainly were in no position themselves to inherit any of the wealth they had helped to create and preserve and perhaps augment.

The Gospels show there was a clear distinction between Jesus and his disciples. We never read that the disciples challenged Jesus' authority over them. They never suggested that Jesus should organize his ministry in democratic fashion, or that together with Jesus they were in any sense a committee of equals, in which no one's opinion carried any more or less importance than any other. The disciples might argue among themselves which one was the most worthy, but they seemed convinced it was right that Jesus should have authority over them all. They considered themselves his subordinates. And the very fact that Jesus spoke to the disciples of commandments and obedience must have established a certain distance between him and them, the teacher from the pupils, the master from the servants, and suggested that there were prescribed orders whose detailed and unquestioning observance was the duty of every follower. Indeed, Israel sometimes conceived of its historical relationship with God in these *same* terms—a servant obliged to satisfy his or her master.

Most of us are inclined to look upon *our* relationship to Christ in much the same way the *disciples* did. In our legalistic frame of mind, in our fondness of lists and our mechanical approach to faith, Jesus' words in John, "[K]eep my commandments" (John 15:10a NRSV), set many of us sailing into the rest of scripture to compile a neat compendium of the do's and don'ts that Jesus pronounced in the Gospels. Our purpose is not only to regulate our *own* behavior, but the behavior of *others* as well. We are, most of us, every bit as eager as the *Pharisees* were to catalogue all the specific acts or failures to act which define whether or not a person is living correctly. But that is very much to miss the point of what Jesus is saying here, and what *John* was saying *about* Jesus in his Gospel. John did not regard the Christian faith as a bunch of rules to obey. He certainly did not think the motive for Christian behavior was simply to avoid punishment. He was calling his *own* faith community to a *higher* motivation for discipleship and to a more magnanimous standard of behavior.

For John, the *proper* consideration was that we should guide ourselves by the model of Jesus' own obedience, which led him to give up his life because of his *love*. According to *John's* account, the *single clearly stated* commandment in Jesus' final words to his disciples is that they *love* one another—love one another even to the degree Jesus loved *them*. And with the crucifixion looming before him, Jesus says of his love for the disciples, "No one has greater love than this, to lay down one's life for one's friends" (John 15:13 NRSV). And then, in one of the most astonishing statements in the scriptures, Jesus says, "You are *my* friends if you do what I command you" (John 15:14 NRSV). The relationship between Jesus and his disciples was no longer to be characterized by the gulf of inequality that exists between teacher and student or master and slave, but by the openness and mutuality and truth and love that binds friend to friend.

A commandment there *still* is—the commandment to *love*. But in the *simplicity* of that commandment and the very *nature* of that commandment, the *distance* between Jesus and his disciples is eliminated. "I do not call you *servants* any longer, because the servant does not know what the master is doing; but I have called *you friends*, because I have made known to you everything that I have heard from my Father" (John 15:15 NRSV). Openness and honesty and truth and love—the stuff of friendship! "You did not choose me but I chose you. And I appointed you to go and bear fruit, fruit that will last, so that the Father will give *you* whatever you ask him in my name. I am giving you these commands so that you may love one another" (John 15:16–17). Master and servants, the relationship between Christ and his disciples had been, but *now* it is transformed into that submission which is perfect *freedom*, for the disciples are taken into their master's confidence as *friends* to share all he has received from the Father. They are about to look right in and know Jesus as he *really* is, without any secretiveness, and to share the *essence* of who Jesus is—the very love of God which made Jesus the *servant* of all people. They are about to learn the trust and the absolute dependence upon him that not only produces *belief* in him but moves them to *risk* on him and which convinces them never to doubt his *loyalty* to them.

And through Jesus' words to his disciples, John speaks directly to you and me about the intimate and wholehearted relationship to which Christ calls us. What he asks of us is *more* than mere *obedience*—simple *obedience* is the response of a *slave*. We are invited into a relationship in which Jesus gives *himself* to *us totally*, hiding nothing, holding back nothing, in which we inherit the kingdom he has prepared. Philo observed, "It would be simple-minded to believe that *servants* rather than God's *friends* inherit the land of virtue."[3] "It is yours," Jesus says to us, "because it is mine. Everything I have I am giving to you. Everything that is mine belongs to you. The command is simple: trust my promises, and pour your life out in love for *others* as *I* have poured out *my* life for *you*."

That's what he means by friendship. If we are no longer *slaves*, then we have become *free*, and we live *now* as his disciples in the openness and mutuality that are the privilege of a friend. The commandment is not merely to obey a set of *orders*, but to cement a *friendship*—taking seriously what Jesus takes seriously, giving up our pride and self-concern as Jesus abandoned pride and self-concern, being open and honest as *Jesus* was open and honest, dealing with *each other* in truth and trust in the way *Jesus* deals with *us* in truth and trust. And what is it that is so important to Jesus that he summons us to share with him in it completely? That we love one another as he loved, accepting and forgiving and serving not only those whom *we* judge to be *worthy* of our love, but *all those whom Jesus loves*, whether the *world* considers them lovable or not, whether the *world* judges them *acceptable* or not, whether the *world* dares to condemn *us* for loving them or not. That is the will of God that his own Son has shared openly with his disciples. That is the loving commandment of Jesus our friend.

---

3. Philo, *De Migratione Abrahami*, 157.

Ascension of the Lord
Spanish Springs Presbyterian Church, Sparks, Nevada
June 1, 2000

Acts 1:1–11
Ephesians 1:15–23
Luke 24:44–53

"'Up, Up, Up,' Not 'Away'"

Last Sunday morning, the focus of the sermon was the fact that Jesus, on the night of his arrest, spoke to his disciples and called them friends. No longer servants of the Master, no longer just students, even, of a wise rabbi, but friends. That must have had an extraordinary impact upon Peter and James and John and Andrew and the others. They loved Jesus. They admired Jesus. They had come to trust Jesus—even to the point of leaving their homes and their families and their jobs, and following him as he traveled here and there preaching, healing, even as far as Jerusalem. Some had *stumbled* in their trust *later* that night when Jesus was seized by the police, and the next day when he was crucified. Only one of the Twelve came to the cross. None of the men even came to see where he was buried, it seems, until the women reported that the tomb was empty. But they were all joyful, if at first unbelieving, when he appeared to them in his resurrected body, and ate with them in his customary way, taught them as he had always done, showed his usual sensitivity to their innermost thoughts and desires and fears.

The disciples were *close* to Jesus before the crucifixion. But their relationship seems to have *deepened* by way of these appearances of the *resurrected* Jesus. So, when the time came for Jesus to be carried into heaven, we might expect that the disciples would have been profoundly sad, distressed that their friendship was being terminated in a cloud—almost like Jesus dying *again*. And yet, Christ's followers today celebrate the ascension with a special day on the calendar. And the Gospel of Luke itself tells us that when Jesus disappeared from their sight at Bethany, it was not an occasion for weeping and distress, but for adoration and gladness. "And they *worshiped* him, and returned to Jerusalem with great *joy*, and they were continually in the temple blessing God" (Luke 24:52–53 NRSV). The appearances of their good friend came to an *end*, and they gave praise with good cheer.

Now, if that were the *end* of the scriptures, it would be an extraordinarily odd thing to *rejoice* at the *disappearance* of their *friend*! Luke, though, knew what had happened *after* that event at Bethany. He wrote about it—in the book we know as The Acts of the Apostles. And, since Luke wasn't personally present at Bethany that day, I suspect he read some of the *subsequent* story back into the end of his Gospel. For Luke knew that what, to all outward appearance, *should* have been a time of *sorrow* and *anguish*, was *in fact* the necessary precondition to a timeless *delight*—an eternal friendship with the living Son of God.

As much as we can know *about* Aristotle and Galileo and Browning, none of us can actually say that we *know* them. Their thoughts and their insights, as far as we can glean them from the words they wrote or the words that were written *about* them, can be woven into *our* thinking and *our* worldview. We may even find comfort and inspiration in having their books on our shelf or their busts on our mantel. With a little effort, we may become experts on the various facts of their lives. But it is only in an *idiomatic* sense that we could ever say we *know* them, or that they are our *friends*. They are long dead. We can't have a conversation with them. *They have no knowledge of us*, or any *interest* in *us*, can't really calm our specific fears or give us courage for our particular challenges. They can't love us, can't even *like* us, however much we think we would love or like *them* if they were still alive. But it was very different for the disciples of Jesus, and for countless others who had never even *met* Jesus before the crucifixion and resurrection—they had an overwhelming sense that Jesus was still with them, still bringing new understandings to their minds, still the host at their meals, still loving them, still praying for them, still counseling them, still forgiving them. And it wasn't just a sentiment, it wasn't an hallucination, it wasn't a dream. They were experiencing a peace, a confidence, a power to say and do things that they simply didn't *have* before Christ's resurrection—miracles of healing and persuading and forgiving that were like the miracles *Jesus* had worked. It was as if Jesus were still with them. In fact, that was the only possible explanation—Jesus had not only been raised from the dead, but Jesus had been given the authority to rule their hearts and direct their actions from on high. Jesus may have withdrawn from their view, but Jesus had not gone away, and he was as powerfully present with them as he had been when they could see him and touch him and hear him speak. They could *still know* him. He was *still* their *friend*.

The first few verses of the book of Acts indicate four times that Jesus had gone "up" from the disciples—five times, if you count the summary of his Gospel that Luke provides in the first couple verses of Acts. "[H]e was lifted up" (Acts 1:9 NRSV). The disciples "were gazing up toward heaven" (Acts 1:10 NRSV). Two men in white robes suddenly appeared and said to the crowd gathered there, "[W]hy do you stand looking up toward heaven? This Jesus, who has been taken up from you into heaven, will come in the same way as you saw him go into heaven" (Acts 1:11 NRSV). Jesus was physically taken up into the place where God dwells. But nowhere does Acts say Jesus had gone "away" from the disciples. Indeed, the entire rest of the book of Acts demonstrates rather emphatically that Jesus had *not* gone *away* from the disciples *at all*, but was still very much *with* them. He was no longer a rabbi. He was no longer a victim on a cross. He was no longer a babe in a manger. But he was still with his followers, and even more fundamentally so, as Lord of their lives, Lord of all creation in fact, and head of the church.

The best way they could find to express the *truth* of Christ's lordship and living presence with them was the language of royalty—Jesus had been exalted and enthroned at God's right hand—a place of honor and authority and approval. Far from being dejected and downcast by the departure of Jesus, the disciples rejoiced and praised God. Rather than looking back longingly on the old days in Galilee and the simple, predictable, secure life they had known before he ever came along and summoned them to follow him, they looked expectantly for power from on high and then confidently went forth to spread the gospel far and wide, preaching the good news and establishing the church in the face of innumerable dangers and against improbable odds. Something *marvelous* was about to happen, they felt that day at Bethany, just like something marvelous *always* happened when Jesus was with them. And the *reason* for their eager expectancy was that Jesus was *still* with them, because although he had gone up, up, up, he had not gone away. He was still working powerful miracles, only *now* he was doing it through *them*. And every single one of them knew that the miracles they were accomplishing were not their *own* doing; it was the risen and living Lord Jesus Christ who was accomplishing the miracles *through* them.

It seems to me that one of the evidences of the truth of scripture is that it doesn't glorify, at all, the people who wrote it. Not one of the Gospels focuses attention on its author. And Luke barely mentions himself in the book of Acts. There would be no purpose, I think, in *making up* stories about the continuing power of a dead hero. The apostles were convinced that Jesus, once executed and buried, had been raised to life again, and was still alive and exercising power to heal and comfort and encourage and forgive and bring to faith. And their belief was *validated* in the daily experience of believers who had never *seen* Jesus. He was in *heaven*, they concluded, but he was not remote. They could no longer *touch* him, but he was every bit as real *after* the *resurrection appearances* as he had been *before* the *crucifixion*. He had gone up, but had not gone away. His physical hands and feet were no longer present on earth, but the ministry of the hands and feet of countless saints in deeds great and modest bore witness to his living presence. The things they did, they didn't do simply in his *memory*. They did them by his *power*.

The teachings and miracles of Jesus didn't expand as rapidly as they did beyond Jerusalem and Galilee in the ordinary haphazard course of human communication. They didn't evoke the response of love and devotion over the generations just because they were pleasant to think about. They didn't draw people into the counter-cultural foretaste of the kingdom of God that is the church because they appealed to human vanity or greed or lust—the motives that seem to account for *most* human activity. They didn't conquer the most powerful empire in the world through the ingenuity of any *human* battle plan or through the deadly effectiveness of any weapon fashioned by *human* hands. Relying on their own abilities, seeking only to honor a dead teacher, no Peter, no James, no John, no Andrew could have *begun* to accomplish what history tells us about the spread of the gospel and the growth of the church. It could only be the power of God that Peter, James, John, and Andrew had come to know in the person of Jesus, their teacher, their friend, now their Lord. And the Christ who was still *with* them propelled *them*—and countless *others* of their *own* generation and every generation *since*—into the daring and adventurous life of working miracles even greater than Jesus himself had accomplished during his earthly existence.

No one can know a dead hero. Someone who stopped living long ago cannot be truly our friend. What do *you* make of the Bible's account of the ascension of Jesus to the right hand of God? Is it a fairy tale? Is it ancient history? Is it pure speculation, and rather pointless at that? Or is it the only possible explanation of your own experience of Christ in your life, and in the life of your church? I have to tell you that, as an historian, I can only explain the gutsy persistence and daily practical sacrifices of the church over the centuries in terms of Christ's living presence with the faithful. And, as a pastor, I can only explain your presence here on a pleasant Thursday evening taking part in the radically counter-cultural activity of worship, as on Sunday mornings, and in service like picking up other people's garbage alongside the highway, and in your own separate ministries beyond the church—clothes closet, caring for sick friends and relatives, tutoring, and the rest—and your remarkably patient, very stubborn conviction that, despite all the obstacles we have encountered, Spanish Springs needs a Presbyterian church and God intends for it to be—I can only explain these things as your response to knowing Jesus Christ as your friend and your Lord—the knowledge that Jesus Christ is not only alive, but living inside you, giving strength and purpose to your arms and legs, courage and wisdom to your thoughts and words. Jesus is no mere memory, nice but distant. Jesus is alive. And he is present here [inside me], here [among the people], and here [at the table].

Seventh Sunday of Easter
First Presbyterian Church, Ponca City, Oklahoma
May 17, 2015

Acts 1:15–17, 21–26
1 John 5:9–13
John 17:6–19

"Lord, Make Us Apostles"

It is sometimes disconcerting to a person who has been elected for the first time to the governing board of a church—in the case of Presbyterians, to the session—to discover how much of their time and effort goes to matters seemingly far removed from Christ's great commission. The daily routine of spiritual office is filled with secular details, many of them trivial in comparison with the Great Ends of the Church. Not a few church officers have become disillusioned with the earthly tedium of repairing sidewalks and replacing water heaters and ordering candles and finding substitute church school teachers. When we are enthused to get on with spreading the good news of Jesus Christ, such issues can appear to be the distractions of the devil.

Imagine the case of the eleven remaining original disciples of Jesus who, having witnessed his glorious ascension on the clouds to a position at the right hand of God, took up as their *first* item of business selecting a replacement for Judas the betrayer. They felt the need to restore the number of the inner circle of church leaders to twelve, the same number as the tribes of ancient Israel. What a transition that must have seemed, to be at one moment mesmerized by the sublime sight of Jesus' glorification, and the next moment mulling over the mundane and even distasteful business of a church election to replace a traitor. But even, or especially, for such an administrative matter, the disciples first prayed for God's guidance. Then they cast lots—the usual procedure was to put into a bowl some stones with a name written on each, and then shake the bowl until one of the stones fell out; the person whose name was on *that* stone was thought then to be *God's* choice. And the choice fell to Matthias, about whom scripture then has nothing else to say.

For some reason, however, the process and the choice were important. Perhaps it was because this was the first decision the disciples had had to make about their life together and about the life of the church in the absence of Jesus. The disciples had to realize that it was for some great and history-changing purpose that they had been privileged to witness what Jesus had said and what Jesus had done and what *God* had said and done *through* Jesus. Jesus had been raised to heaven; he was no longer among them to set their agenda and to establish their itinerary. The disciples now had to accept responsibility for their *own* decisions for the future of the church, for their *own* conduct in continuing Christ's ministry. From *our* perspective as people who have never otherwise *heard* of Matthias, that *first* decision they made together was not a *lofty* one. The purpose of filling the twelfth position on the board may seem unimportant in itself.

But look at the requirement that Peter specified for leadership in the church—the thing that was considered most important for an apostle: "So one of the men who have accompanied us during all the time the Lord Jesus went in and out among us, beginning from the baptism of John until the day when he was taken up from us—one of *these* must become a *witness* with us *to his resurrection*" (Acts 1:21–22 NRSV).

For all their human foibles and their occasional doubt and their frequent short-sightedness, being designated and recognized as an *apostle* was of fundamental significance. The twelve apostles were the vital *link* between the risen Lord and the church. They were the authoritative transmitters of the traditions of the earthly ministry of Jesus "from the baptism of John until the day when he was taken up," (Acts 1:22a NRSV) and they were especially the guarantee of the truth of the resurrection.

That twelfth position on the board was not simply one to be filled by a warm body. It was, as the *other* eleven positions were, a place for someone who would be a *witness* to Christ's *resurrection*, a *testifier* to Christ's *resurrection*, a *proclaimer* of Christ's *resurrection*, someone whose whole *life* was a demonstration of the truth of the gospel and the present power and authority of the risen Christ as living Lord. Such people the church would send out in Christ's name to publish the good news in their very being. They, too, would have to deal with the *mundane* business of church life; even the more glamorous and adventurous task of traveling to distant lands and preaching before foreign dignitaries would rest upon such practical details as arranging transportation and finding lodging and funding it all. But the very mission of the church, whether the world would ever know of Jesus Christ the Son of God and acknowledge him as Lord and Savior, or whether he would vanish from memory and be forgotten by history, depended upon *them* as *witnesses* to the *resurrection*.

Many generations later, there is *still* a need for apostles if the good news of Jesus Christ is to be made *known* in the world and if the ministry of Jesus Christ is to *continue* in the world. *Contemporary* apostles can no longer be chosen from among those who were in the company of the first disciples. Obviously, no one alive today was there with Peter and the rest beginning from the time when John was still baptizing until the day of Christ's ascension. But the cause of Jesus Christ *still* requires people who will go out into the world and proclaim the gospel in word and deed. And the essence of their testimony must be a *witness* to the *resurrection*—that Jesus Christ, who ministered to the lowly and the sick and the sin-ridden, who *defied* those who would turn the *law* of God into a tool of *oppression* and who would turn the *house* of God into a *business*, who finally was arrested and executed for doing *good* and speaking the *truth*, this same Jesus Christ, God raised from the dead and appointed to the seat of honor and power and glory at his own right hand in the heavenly places, and his power and his authority are still real and at work in the world today through his church.

For many years before there *was* a written New Testament, and for several centuries before the written New Testament as we know it was adopted as a closed authoritative collection—"scripture," if you will—the knowledge of what God had done in Jesus Christ depended upon the faithful oral transmission of the tradition of faith from one person to another, from one generation to the next. There were no video cameras at the crucifixion or the resurrection or the ascension. We have no notarized affidavits from the officials. What *we* know rests upon the witness of the first apostles—individuals who had nothing to gain from fabricating fantastic stories but in fact suffered greatly, many of them, because of their testimony; individuals who were limited in their understanding of just what was happening and why, but who perceived God's purposeful and providential hand in the life, death, and resurrection of Jesus; individuals who had an overwhelming sense of Christ's abiding and powerful presence with them to continue his ministry of forgiving and healing and comforting and bringing to faith.

No wonder the church has, throughout history, been so concerned to maintain the authentic tradition of the apostles, and to make certain it was being handed down correctly and completely and without distortion. And when, in the long period of the Dark Ages, the witness became *perverted*, and the church grew wealthy by its landholding and by hanging *on* to its riches rather than spending them in ministry to those in need, and the grace of God was lost again in ecclesiastical legalisms of human invention, and Christ became the possession of the elite rather than the compassionate friend of the orphan and the widow and the prisoner and the outcast, there came a need for a great Reformation to recover the pure witness of the apostles once *again*, and to send out a *new* company of witnesses to Christ's resurrection and to make it, once more, good news.

The need for apostles—for people who will give witness to the resurrection—is once again great. The need for apostles—for men and women who put their faith in God's promises of providential care as Jesus taught, rather than keeping to themselves what God intended for *all* to share—is particularly critical in our age of consumerism and materialism and individualism. The need for apostles—for old and young who believe strongly that the power of the risen Christ is real and is more real even than the truisms of politicians and the theories of economists and the wisdom of talk show philosophers—is especially important with so many voices threatening doom on the one hand and preaching self-indulgence on the other. The need for apostles—for people of every race and nationality who recognize that raising Jesus from the tomb was God's own testimony to the authority of Christ and Christ's example of peace and justice and humility and forgiveness—is increasingly vital in a time of growing hatred and intolerance and mean-spiritedness in public debate and private behavior. The need for apostles—for Christians who are truly thankful for God's love and mercy in their own lives and who know the power of the risen Christ at work in their homes, in their communities, in their churches—is absolutely necessary to stem the wave of cynicism and meaninglessness and rootlessness that are pulling our world apart. *We* need *apostles*—not just names on church rolls, not just people who *talk about* God, but *apostles—witnesses* to the *resurrection*—who live out their faith in the risen Christ and his present power and authority even when they are attending to the most mundane business of life, the least glamorous ministries, the grittiest jobs in the kingdom. By such, the kingdom grows, the church becomes more nearly the reality to which it points, and the fame and honor and glory of Jesus Christ are spread abroad. We need apostles.

Matthias might have looked very much like you or I look, might have been raised in a family very much like yours or mine, might have come from a background very much like any of us has had. But Matthias was called to a task vital in the cause of making Jesus Christ known and bringing people to acknowledge him and to trust him and to stake their lives upon him as Lord and Savior. Matthias was chosen to be an apostle. He was chosen to be a witness to Christ's resurrection, to proclaim the faith in all circumstances, to live in faith at all times, believing in Christ's promises and acting upon them constantly, ever thankful for God's abundant goodness and generous mercy, and *demonstrating* that thankfulness in goodness and mercy toward others, all through confidence in the *present* power and authority of the risen Christ.

Are *we* so full of faith that *we* are living witnesses to the resurrection? Are people looking at *us* and seeing the *truth* of Jesus Christ living and breathing through *our* words and actions? Are we acting confidently and thankfully in our family life, in our church life, in our vocations, in our citizenship, as people who believe in the power and authority of the risen Christ? Or are we living with and acting upon the *same* assumptions that the *rest* of the world does—the rest of the world that *rejects* the wisdom of spending oneself for others, the world that *ridicules* the blessedness of a forgiving heart, the world that *ignores* the truth that everything we have is a gift from God given to us as stewards, the world that *denies* the possibility that *anyone* could rise from the dead?

O Lord, make us apostles—witnesses to Christ's resurrection in all that we think, do, and say, at home, at work, at school, at leisure, at church, at civic gatherings, with family, with friends, with co-workers, with fellow church members, with the stranger we meet in the street. And may our witness to the resurrection transform every task into a sign of the kingdom and a testimony to the promised return of Christ Jesus our Lord. Amen.

Appendix

The Week of Prayer for Christian Unity, January 18-25, is an annual ecumenical observance of Christ's prayer that his church should be one. Using scripture passages chosen by an international ecumenical committee, worship materials are provided through the Graymoor Ecumenical & Interreligious Institute.

Week of Prayer for Christian Unity
Holy Cross Catholic Community, Sparks, Nevada
January 19, 2009

Ezekiel 37:15-19, 22-24a
Romans 8:18-25
John 17:8-11

"Bound Together"

They had been divided from each other for three and a half centuries, the Northern Kingdom of Israel, or Samaria, and the Southern Kingdom, Judah. They had had their differences since long *before* the nation had fallen apart into two *separate* countries, but the differences had grown over the generations since. Their political institutions developed along separate lines. Their religious practices diverged, as well. Over time, each thought the other was heretical. Eventually, the Northern Kingdom was absorbed into the Assyrian Empire, and many of its citizens were exiled into other lands while foreigners were settled in Israel in their place, so that the nation's sense of destiny was confused and its identity was lost. The ten tribes that had made up the Northern Kingdom of Israel essentially vanished from history. By the time the Southern Kingdom of Judah was invaded by the Babylonians, it was unable to defend itself. A *united* kingdom, as in the days of *David*, might well have been strong enough to fend off its enemies. But, once divided, North and South proved to be vulnerable, and the neighboring empires exploited their weakness.

By the time Ezekiel came along, it was hard enough for his audience, the exiles in Babylon, to imagine a day when they would be back in their own homes in Jerusalem, much less a return to the halcyon era of David's rule over a single nation, strong and prosperous and free. They might have yearned for the good old days that not even their grandparents had known, but they hardly dared believe those days could return. Where were their Northern cousins to reunite *with*? They were scattered over the face of the known globe by then. To think of God bringing Israel and Judah back together was as foolish as . . . expecting dry bones to be covered with flesh and stand up and walk again!

Estrangement has a way of growing deep and bitter. Injuries and insults, real and imagined, have a way of festering over time. And while estranged, two parties, which perhaps once cared deeply for each other and which were intricately intertwined in each other's lives, rather naturally grow apart, so that every year of estrangement, every *day* even, makes reconciliation that much more difficult. Think how difficult it was for the Union and the Confederacy to come back together to form one United States, not only in name but also in outlook, after the Civil War. Presbyterians north and south were only able to accomplish it finally in 1983, and by then it was a task much more complicated than it would have been in 1883, had the churches set aside their pride and embraced the vision of the gospel. By all accounts, it has not been easy for West and East Germany to reunite, despite many ties of family and friendship and culture and history. But there was a hunch that division was wrong and a conviction that unity was right—the same sort of hunch and conviction that led Korean Christians, joint heirs of a divided land, to offer this text as the scriptural theme for the Week of Prayer for Christian Unity in 2009—the belief that God wills community wherever there is estrangement, healing wherever there is wound, reconciliation wherever there is division.

I suspect it is the same sort of hunch and conviction that bring us together here tonight—and perhaps even embarrassment before the eyes of God and before the eyes of a disbelieving world—to give witness that God purposes and Christ commands and the Holy Spirit can make possible a unity of *all* God's people, a thousand years even after the breach between Catholic and Orthodox, hundreds of years even after the breach between Catholic and Protestant, and between Lutheran and Presbyterian and Episcopalian and Methodist and Baptist and all the rest.

And it is not enough simply to be *intellectually aware* that God *desires* unity among the divided segments of Christendom, any more than it was enough simply to be *intellectually aware* in *Ezekiel's* time that the centuries-old division between North and South was contrary to God's will. Action needed to be taken—visible, physical—to do something about it, though it might immediately be of little more than symbolic effect; an act to show that the prophet had been listening, a sign to communicate the purposefulness of God to the people:

> Mortal, take a stick and write on it, "For Judah, and the Israelites associated with it"; then take another stick and write on it, "For Joseph (the stick of Ephraim) and all the house of Israel associated with it"; and join them together into one stick, so that they may become one in your hand. And when your people say to you, "Will you not show us what you mean by these?" say to them, Thus says the Lord GOD: I am about to take the stick of Joseph (which is in the hand of Ephraim) and the tribes of Israel associated with it; and I will put the stick of Judah upon it, and make them one stick, in order that they may be one in my hand. . . . I will make them one nation in the land, on the mountains of Israel; and one king shall be king over them all. Never again shall they be divided into two kingdoms." (Ezek 37:16–19, 22, NRSV)

God would again be present in the sanctuary, where all of God's people would come together to worship him, and all the other nations of the world would come to know of the truth that there is a God in Israel, and Israel's God is the one true God beside whom there is no other—a God eager to bless, a God eager to forgive, a God eager to reconcile.

Perhaps the sticks were bundled one alongside the other, making a sturdier pole than either of the two sticks would have been alone. That would have been a particularly strong and poignant sign for people who had experienced the tragedy of a kingdom, weakened by division, having fallen to Assyria and Babylon. Or perhaps the sticks were held by Ezekiel end to end, so that together they were greater in length, visibly more impressive. Either way, the point was to make the two into one, a symbol of what God promised to do with the two halves of his chosen people so they would be bound in covenant not only with God but with each other for the sake of constituting a blessing to the entire world.

But notice that it was not just that they would be *joined* again. They would be made *pure* again; all the ways in which they had each been *unfaithful* would be set *right*—almost as if it was impossible for *either* of them to be *faithful* while *separated* from the *other*, almost as if it was necessary that there be *unity* if there was to be not only *peace* but *purity*. Each had considered the other to be apostate, flawed in belief, wanting in practice. In fact, the two kingdoms were *both* right about the other—in the process of falling away from each *other*, each had fallen away from *God*. Separately, but in a concert of disobedience, they had slandered God by renouncing God's purpose of community. It was only in their *reunion* that they would "never again defile themselves with their idols and their detestable things, or with any of their transgressions" (Ezek 37:23a NRSV). Their very act of *separation* and *estrangement* was a *defilement*, an *idolatry*, a *detestable act* that, no matter how improbable a reconciliation seemed, God would not allow to continue, but would take bold measures to remedy. God's plan was clear: God would bring back his disparate people under a single king, one shepherd, like David, perhaps even someone in David's line. If the peoples of Israel and Judah obeyed him, if they accepted his rule, the divisions would end, and they would not only be reunited as a nation, but would once again be poised to be the blessing to all creation that God promised Abraham.

Could it be that what we are doing symbolically tonight—peoples who have been separated by divisions of long-standing, all of which should move us to repentance, worshiping together—is a step in making us, against all human improbability, truly one people ruled by a descendant of David the king, one shepherd of a single great flock? Could it be that, dissolved as we have become over time into the intermixture of the world's ideas and influences, there is nevertheless a possibility—no, a *certainty*—of finding our true selves by asserting our unity? Could it be that, in part because of what we are doing in this service of worship, one day *none* of us will be known by any name other than that of Christ?

We have come from different houses of worship and different traditions of faith in Jesus Christ, like so many individual sticks, each deeply etched with decades and centuries of traditions of belief and practice, but also weathered by brokenness and separation, sometimes seemingly more committed to the identity we have branded upon *ourselves* than to the identity given to us through baptism in the name of the Father, Son, and Holy Spirit, sometimes seemingly more impressed by the wounds our *forebears* suffered at the hands of *each other* than the wounds *Christ* suffered on the *cross*—the Christ who prayed on the night before he was put to death by those who rejected his ministry of reconciliation, "Holy

Father, protect them in your name that you have given me, so that they may be one" (John 17:11b, NRSV).

> The word of the LORD came to me: Mortal, take a stick and write on it . . . ; then take another stick and write on it . . . ; and join them together into one stick, so that they may become one in your hand. And when your people say to you, "Will you not show us what you mean by these?" say to them, Thus says the Lord GOD: I am about to take the stick of Joseph . . . ; and I will put the stick of Judah upon it, and make them one stick, in order that they may be one in my hand. . . . Then they shall be my people, and I will be their God. (Ezek 37:15–19, 23c, NRSV)

List of Sources Cited

Aristotle. *The Nicomachean Ethics*. Translated by Harris Rackham. The Loeb Classical Library. Cambridge, MA: Harvard University Press, 1982.
Gossip, Arthur John. "The Gospel According to St. John, Exposition." In *The Interpreter's Bible*, Vol. VIII, edited by George Arthur Buttrick, 437–811. 12 vols. Nashville: Abingdon, 1980.
Hillerman, Tony. *Coyote Waits*. New York: Harper & Row, 1990.
Lenker, John Nicholas, trans. *Luther's Large Catechism: God's Call to Repentance, Faith, and Prayer*. Minneapolis: Lutheran, 1908.
Long, Thomas G. *Hebrews* Louisville: John Knox, 1997.
Niebuhr, H. Richard. "Faith in Gods and in One God." In *Radical Monotheism and Western Culture*, edited by Robin W. Lovin et al., 114–26. Louisville: Westminster/John Knox, 1993.
Philo. *De Migratione Abrahami*. In *Philo IV*, translated by Francis H. Colson and George H. Whitaker, 123–269. 10 vols. The Loeb Classical Library. Cambridge, MA: Harvard University Press, 1968.
———. *Quis Rerum Divinarum Heres*. In *Philo IV*, translated by Francis H. Colson and George H. Whitaker, 270–451. 10 vols. The Loeb Classical Library. Cambridge, MA: Harvard University Press, 1968.
Staniforth, Maxwell, trans. *Early Christian Writings*. London: Penguin, 1968.
Steinke, Peter L. *Healthy Congregations: A Systems Approach*. Bethesda, MD: The Alban Institute, 1995.

www.ingramcontent.com/pod-product-compliance
Lightning Source LLC
Chambersburg PA
CBHW071441150426
43191CB00008B/1197